Fire In My Heart

Edited By

Mike Willis

ISBN 1-58427-025-X

Guardian of Truth Foundation
P.O. Box 9670
Bowling Green, Kentucky 42102

Table of Contents

Introduction

On January 16-17, 2003 the Guardian of Truth Foundation sponsored the staff writers meeting for *Truth Magazine*. The sessions were held in Bowling Green, Kentucky. In previous years, we have invited different speakers (both staff writers and others) to address our staff writers meeting and the various participants have appreciated the period of time for study and discussion.

For the 2003 staff writers meeting, staff writers were encouraged to bring at least one preacher with them to attend the meeting. As the number of attendees grew, we began to see how much interest was generated by the lectures that were planned. In trying to raise the quality of presentation at these lectures, we asked the various speakers to prepare a manuscript for publication. This book is the product of these lectures.

The speakers at the staff writers meeting discussed various relevant issues of our day, referring specifically to the men and lessons that are under review. The documentation is provided to aid anyone who wishes to follow up to check to see if what is said is true. The various speakers had no intention of misrepresenting anyone, although they cited and reviewed specific materials circulating among us.

In addition to the lessons that were presented, we have reproduced my material previously published in *Truth Magazine* on "The Chronology of the Bible" and Ron Halbrook's "Gospel Preaching, Gospel Preachers, Gospel Papers: The Heritage of *Guardian of Truth*" from the July 20, 1995 *Guardian of Truth*.

We are happy to present this series of lessons for the profit of our readers, just as we who attended benefitted from our study of these subjects and, of course, from our association with each another. The series is appropriately titled "Fire in My Heart" because the various speakers' hearts burn with spiritual fervency in addressing the different issues and challenges that threaten God's people. This is not a time for men to quench the Spirit, but the time to speak out and speak up so that souls may be warned about the various things which threaten God's people in the early twenty-first century. Some have said that we have no issues threatening brethren today; if that is the case, this is a unique time in church history because there never has been a time when Satan relented in his attack against God's children.

Some brethren who tire of controversy have taken a "bury one's head in the sand" approach to the various issues affecting brethren. Many of those churches which have taken that approach have already allowed dangerous influences to gain a foothold among them without even recognizing it. The kind of preaching being done in many such pulpits is preparing the soil for further inroads of loose teaching. About the only thing that is categorically condemned is anyone who exposes a false doctrine and false teacher by name. Brethren who have exposed such false teaching and teachers are viewed as outdated, if not judged as factious brethren who are a threat to the Lord's people. This attitude toward the truth prepares the soil for every kind of apostasy because the kind of exposure necessary to resist false teaching and to stop the mouths of those who spread it is not tolerated (Tit. 1:10-11). As a result, about anything can be taught among brethren, except the teaching which exposes their false doctrine. Like denominational people about us, many have become tolerant of many aberrant teachings but they will not tolerate those who reply to such errors.

The editor and staff writers of *Truth Magazine* do not share that philosophy. We think that the best way to offset the influence of false teaching is to alert brethren to the teaching and who is teaching it, examine the arguments being presented, and prepare replies to those doctrines to help brethren withstand the assaults of Satan. Publishing the material in this book is one among many efforts to do this work. The Board of the Guardian of Truth Foundation hopes that others may benefit from the material presented in this book, just as we who heard the material presented were helped.

Mike Willis
September 2, 2003

Fire In My Heart:
Saga of a Spirit Stirred

Larry Ray Hafley

Then I said, I will not make mention of him, nor speak any more in his name. But his word was in mine heart as a burning fire shut up in my bones, and I was weary with forbearing, and I could not stay (Jer. 20:9).

Those were the words of Jeremiah as he wrestled against spiritual wickedness and political powers in high places. They are the words of a man, yet spoken with the voice of God. They throb with indignation and frustration. They thunder with determination.

Truth — ceaseless, relentless truth — may be despised and rejected of men, but it will not go away. Present principalities and powers may disdain the man of God, but they cannot chain the word of God. "I suffer trouble, as an evil doer, even unto bonds; but the word of God is not bound" (2 Tim. 2:9). While the messenger may be imprisoned, his message, though withstood, cannot be withheld. David felt the same divine compunction. "My heart was hot within me; While I was musing, the fire burned. Then I spoke with my tongue" (Ps. 39:3). So did the apostles. "We cannot but speak the things which we have seen and heard" (Acts 4:20).

Opposition Is Certain

Jeremiah had been told to expect opposition, "They shall fight against thee" (Jer. 1:19). So testify the prophets. There are those "who cause a person to be indicted by a word, And ensnare him who adjudicates at the gate, And defraud the one in the right with meaningless arguments" (Isa. 29:21). "They hate him that rebuketh in the gate, and they abhor him that speaketh uprightly" (Amos 5:10). From Abel to Amos, from Jonah to John, sacred history's pages are blotted and dotted with the tears and fears of those who suffered at the hands of "unreasonable and wicked men."

It is no less true today. We see the victims of those who hide daggers of death and harm beneath smiling cloaks of grace and charm. They speak great swelling words, "having men's persons in admiration because of advantage" (Jude 16). They gush "good words and fair speeches" and splash them over unsuspecting souls. Yet, their tart tongues, poisoned pens, and carnal keyboards are piercing spears and pointed swords against those whom they cannot answer in fair and open discussion.

We must be wary, brethren, lest we become weary in well doing and faint in our minds. As the experiences of Elijah and Paul prove, it may happen to the best among us (1 Kings 19; 2 Cor. 1:8-11).

Ways to Dampen the Heart Aflame
Looking diligently lest any man fail of the grace of God; lest any root of bitterness springing up trouble you, and thereby many be defiled (Heb. 12:15).

1. David, Fleshly Lusts: As Psalms 32 and 51 indicate, David was long troubled by his private, personal sin, his adultery with Bathsheba (2 Sam. 11). It wore him down. It tortured his mind, heart, and conscience with tears, fears, and silent screams of guilt and despair. His response was repentance, confession, and prayer. So it must be with all who are overtaken in sin. There can be no rest to the heart that seeks to harbor the word of God while providing haven for sin. When some depart from the faith, seemingly without a cause, it may well be that secret sin is the termite that has eaten and consumed the vitality of their faith and undermined their hope.

2. Demas, Worldly Spirit: "For Demas hath forsaken me, having loved this present world" (2 Tim. 4:10). Many have quenched the spirit's flame by dousing their souls with the water of this world's wealth. No, it is not wrong for a Christian to be rich in this world's goods. Barnabas and Philemon may have been men of means, monied men. However, the admonition of 1 Timothy 6:8-12 applies to all who would not have the fire of zeal extinguished by the gold, goods, glitter, and glamor of this world.

And having food and raiment let us be therewith content. But they that will be rich fall into temptation and a snare, and into many foolish and hurtful lusts, which drown men in destruction and perdition. For the love of money is the root of all evil: which while some coveted after, they have erred from the faith, and pierced themselves through with many sorrows. But thou, O man of God, flee these things; and follow after righteousness, godliness, faith, love, patience, meekness. Fight the good fight of faith, lay hold on eternal life, whereunto thou art also called, and hast professed a good profession before many witnesses (1 Tim. 6:8-12).

3. Diotrephes, Dominating Defiance: Perhaps Diotrephes had a number of outstanding character traits which endeared him to many and blinded them to his pursuit of power and preeminence. Whether that be true or not, this we do know: "I wrote unto the church: but Diotrephes, who loveth to have the preeminence among them, receiveth us not. Wherefore, if I come, I will remember his deeds which he doeth, prating against us with malicious words: and not content therewith, neither doth he himself receive the brethren, and forbiddeth them that would, and casteth them out of the church" (3 John 9, 10).

Obviously, such an attitude will hinder and destroy the ability and influence of any man. However, it is often the case that such intractable, selfish, ego-centered men are the cause of the loss of those who see no way to deal with them and, so, they give up. The fire in their bosom flickers and dies. We are speaking here of those who were cast "out of the church" by Diotrephes. What became of them? Were they recalled and reclaimed by the apostle John when he came and confronted Diotrephes? Or, were they disconsolate and bitter and made reprobate to the faith? Eternity alone will reveal the damage done by the spirit of Diotrephes in quelling the flame of salvation in the hearts of those whom they cast out.

4. Demetrius, Weapons of His Warfare: Though the weapons "of our warfare are not carnal," the weapons used against us often are (Acts 19:23-29; 2 Cor. 10:3-5). The carnal weapons of the wicked can hurt the righteous deeply. We cannot respond in kind "with malicious words." We cannot use the allurements and enticements of this world to appeal to lost souls, but Demetrius can do so! He is not bound by the strictures of the Scriptures. Thus, he can offer security while we present sacrifice. He extends moral compromise and complacency while we demand courage and conviction. He can offer excuses for the pleasures of sin and justify it to the fleshly mind. We, on the other hand, can offer, not acceptance of sin, but repudiation of it, or else eternal condemnation for it (Gal. 5:19-21; 6:7, 8). With the odds stacked against us, the hearts of many grow cold. Unable to resist carnal weapons, they surrender their own, and the flame of their heart is put out.

Jeremiah felt all these pressures and more. He lamented his lot. "For each time I speak, I cry aloud; I proclaim violence and destruction, Because for me the word of the Lord has resulted in reproach and derision all day long" (Jer. 20:8). False prophets spoke of "peace," while he spoke of "violence and destruction." Which message would you rather hear? So, they mocked him for his constant "gloom and doom," "the sky is falling" message (Jer. 20:10).

Still, he could not relent. Jeremiah could not keep silence. He could not, yea, he would not allow the burning fire in his heart to be stifled and smothered! Like Paul, his spirit was stirred within him when he saw the city and the nation "wholly given to idolatry" (Acts 17:16, 17). Likewise, today, we must "keep not silence." "I have set watchmen upon thy walls, O Jerusalem, which shall never hold their peace day nor night: ye that make mention of the Lord, keep not silence" (Isa. 62:6).

Kindling For a Spirit Stirred
1. In the World. Can one look about in today's society, in our homes, schools, and neighborhoods, and not have his heart and soul set ablaze for the righteousness of God?

Isaiah 5:20 is as appropriate for our generation as it was for the one in which it was spoken. "Woe to those who call evil good, and good evil; who put darkness for light, and light for darkness; who put bitter for sweet, and sweet for bitter!" If one is opposed to homosexual behavior, he is a "homophobe." If he campaigns for that lifestyle, though he partakes not of it, he is "good." It is morally and politically correct to say, "Let us kill the unborn child, but let us never execute a murderer." We can slay the child, but we must save the murderer of his mother! We may not teach children in schools that fornication is wrong, but we may tell them that drugs are. We cannot pass out Bibles to students, but we can pass out religious material about Islam. We cannot pray in schools, but the school nurse can provide condoms for students who request them. The life of Christ cannot be mentioned in a high school graduation speech as a pattern for our behavior, but the latest hedonistic, immoral, reprobate, rock star can be praised in the same forum. High schools may not be allowed to have a prayer before a high school football game, but they will be sued by the American Civil Liberties Union if they do not allow homosexuals to establish their own independent club to promote their sexual agenda (Pikeville, Kentucky; Houston, Texas, 2003). What is wrong with this picture?!

The social-political nature of false religion, with its rituals and holidays borrowed by Catholicism from pagan feasts, and adopted by mainstream Protestantism, continues unabated. Such institutions are wrought with unbelief and ungodliness. They are carnal to the core in philosophy and offer no true spiritual hope for souls lost in sin. The churches that still claim to be led by faith in the blood of Christ, who say they still believe in his actual death, burial, and resurrection from the dead, have been so caught up with the emotional frenzy of Pentecostalism that they view their feelings and emotional ecstasy as the only real truth. If they have "felt" it or "experienced" it, it is the truth, no matter what the Bible teaches. They profess that they know God, but their illusions and delusions of spiritual fantasy have blinded them to objective study and understanding.

As a result, moral relativism guides a society with laws which have no anchor or base in established truth. Thus, they are laws which may be changed by the lusts of their makers. For example, physicians once took an oath which, in essence, forbad abortion. Psychologists once saw homosexual behavior as being perverse. Now, because the lusts of men rule, and because a law is what men desire, and not what objective truth demands, long established laws, such as those regarding abortion and homosexuality, are rendered null and void.

The same pattern has been followed in religious life. There is no certain, absolute truth. Jesus is who you want (rather, "feel") him to be. Faith is a blind leap in the dark. If you say you believe it, and if you act enthusiastically enough, then whatever it is that you believe, it is "truth" for you. Preachers, pastors, and priests used to know what it meant when we said to them, "You don't have 'Bible' for that." No longer. Today, the Bible is an archaic relic, full of mythological stories and legends that have no real basis in fact. The creation, Noah, Jonah? Such men never lived and the events associated with them are ancient lore and idle tales. If, though, as noted earlier above, some are found who believe the Bible, they generally are so bound and blinded by their mysticism, a mixture of Pentecostalism and subjective superstition, that they cannot see, hear, or learn.

It was to such a world of confusion, idolatry, and superstition that the Savior came. It was into such a world, blind and having no light, the Lord sent the apostles. Before them, it was Noah who preached to a world gone mad with evil. "Every imagination of the thought of (their) hearts was only evil and that continually" (Gen. 6:5). "The earth also was corrupt before God, and the earth was filled with violence" (Gen. 6:11). If God expected Noah to preach to such a generation, surely he demands no less of us.

Brethren, do these things not blow the flickering coals of your heart into flame? Some may say that such considerations are defeating and discouraging. No! Rather, they are like the shoe salesman who went to a far country to sell shoes. When he saw that no one in the country wore shoes, he immediately came back home dejected. Another shoe salesman went to the same land and quickly ordered a ship load of shoes because, as he excitedly explained, "No one over here has any shoes to wear!"

2. In the Church. Obviously, one must have a love for the lost and for the Lord in order to be properly motivated. "Horror hath taken hold upon me because of the wicked that forsake thy law. . . . Rivers of waters run down mine eyes, because they keep not thy law. . . . I beheld the transgressors, and was grieved; because they kept not thy word" (Ps. 119:53, 136, 158).

Some say that this only applies to a love for the alien sinner. They say, "We need to quit trying to resolve 'brotherhood issues' and get back to teaching the lost." (1) Perhaps someone should have given that advice to the author of 1 and 2 Corinthians, Galatians, and Hebrews! Who would charge that Paul was too busy "trying to save the church that he had no time to teach the lost"? (2) Paul sent Timothy to Ephesus for the express purpose of commanding some that "they teach no other doctrine" (1 Tim. 1:3). "Paul, you should have sent Timothy to teach the lost and not to dictate to the brethren concerning what is to be taught. You're causing Timothy to violate 'church autonomy.'" Again, who would say such a thing to Paul? Not me! *Yet, we often hear such reprimands.* (3) The apostle Peter wrote two letters to brethren and churches scattered over a large geographical expanse. He warned them about false teachers, commanded them to cling to the words of the apostles and prophets, and sounded like he thought that even the elders of the churches needed to be exhorted to do their work (1 Pet. 5:1-3; 2 Pet. 2:1, 2; 3:1, 2). If this is not part of the work we are to do, why did Paul say for us to follow his ways and for Timothy to encourage other faithful men to do likewise (1 Cor. 4:16, 17; 2 Tim. 2:2)?

The reason that some would deny us the right to do such work is because their liberal agendas are being deposed and disposed of. Rather than attempting to defend their errors, they shriek, "If you were busy teaching the lost, you wouldn't have time to trouble and divide churches." When that cry is heard, you know two things. First, that you have "gigged" what needs to be "gigged," and, second, you know that it is time to increase the pressure of truth with even stronger preaching (Isa. 58:1)!

What factors have revived the spirits of many among us today? (One might say that the items cited below have been a bane, a discouragement to the people of God, and so they have been. However, as the persecutions of the saints, designed to smother the gospel, served rather to spread it, so the spirit of softness and compromise has hardened the resolve of many.)

First, languid hearts were kindled anew when the full import and impact of brother Ed Harrell's version of "unity-in-diversity" was proposed in a series of articles in *Christianity Magazine,* 1988-1990. Though fellowship with brother Hailey's error was later disavowed by some, the principles were not.

Second, our hearts did burn within us when those same principles, however unwittingly, were applied by brother Ferrell Jenkins to the error taught with respect to creation and the days of Genesis 1. As brother Harrell had advocated fellowship with brother Hailey, so brother Jenkins did not find the error of Shane Scott on the days of Genesis a sufficient cause for a lack of unity and fellowship (Florida College, 2000). (**Author's Note:** *See the Addendum to this article for further details regarding brother Jenkins' comments alluded to above.*)

Third, the late brother Homer Hailey, in a book published posthumously, says, according to F. Lagard Smith in his introduction, that *"Hailey reaches the interesting conclusion that for the wicked the soul ceases to exist, as it is destroyed in hell"* (emphasis mine, LRH).

Does the knowledge of these facts not stir and stimulate the fire in your bosom unto greater zeal? Neither the "everlasting fire" of hell nor the singeing, scorching flames of the everlasting gospel shall be extinguished. That "word like as a fire, saith the Lord," shall burn the chaff of error with unquenchable fire, so help us God (Jer. 23:29).

Note, brother Hailey's advertised error is called an "interesting conclusion." Earlier, as brother Harrell did not consider brother Hailey a "false teacher," and as brother Jenkins cannot say that the days of Genesis 1, when considered as epochs of time, represents false doctrine, we are made to wonder if brother Hailey's posthumous proclamation concerning the annihilation of the wicked in hell will be regarded as simply an "interesting conclusion," rather than a false doctrine. Brother Harrell later said he could not call brother Hailey a "false teacher" because, in his words, "I am persuaded by his conduct and his arguments that he honestly believes that he is faithful to God's teaching on the subject" (*Divorce & Fellowship*, FC Open Forum, Feb., 1991). Will the same be said concerning brother Hailey's views regarding eternal punishment? You may count on it!

What next? Is Jonah just another fish tale, and will heaven last as long as we thought it would (Matt. 25:46)? If a prominent brother were to teach such concepts, would he be given a wink and an understanding shrug of acceptance, while those who expose and oppose him are treated as malicious, pernicious outcasts?

We are told that the controversy over the days of Genesis 1 "is not a salvation issue." Again, what of Jonah? Is the virgin birth a "salvation issue"? Is brother Hailey's false teaching on hell a "salvation issue"? May one teach that the days of Genesis 1 are epochs of time, that Jonah was not swallowed by a great fish and put back upon earth in three literal days, that the virgin birth of Jesus is not true, and that hell is the annihilation of the wicked, and still be received as a faithful preacher of the gospel?

If so, brethren, expect that the next generation among us will accept and
tolerate instrumental music in worship for the same reason. Namely, it is not
a "salvation issue." The "how and what of Bible baptism" will no longer be
a concern. For them and to them, the "mode and method" of baptism will
not be a "salvation issue." The taking of the Lord's supper and a contribution into a church's treasury upon the first day of the week will cease to be
areas of concern (Acts 20:7; 1 Cor. 16:2). The importance of the nature
and character of Christ and his kingdom will be denied on the very
same basis; that is, that those are not "salvation issues." If you doubt
these fatal forebodings, look at the history and evolution of the Christian Church, Disciples of Christ. Look, too, at Rubel Shelly and Max
Lucado. One does not have to be a prophet to see what will occur when
men begin to apologize, sympathize, and compromise with error. On such
matters, we must learn from history, both sacred and secular (1 Cor. 10:1-
13; Heb. 3:7-4:11; 2 Pet. 3:5-7).

Will those who take their pen and tongues against the error taught by
brother Hailey on the doctrine of eternal punishment be castigated for slan-
dering a great man who has gone to his grave? If the future is anything like
the past, here is what will transpire. With a sad countenance, some will
express their "sorrow" that brother Hailey's "peculiar" or "disputed" view
has come to light after his passing. (They will not classify it as "false doctrine." Instead, it will be referred to as a "peculiar" or "controversial view.")
They will disavow agreement with brother Hailey and then proceed to blast
those who are "using the bones of a great man to further their standing as
defenders of the faith." Audible "amens" will resound. There will be ap-
plause in some circles. Meanwhile, the distinguished one will have pad-
ded his own dossier as a sophisticated "defender of the faith" among
those who believe that a real defense of the gospel is beneath their
dignity. The truth will be an after thought and those who stand for it and
contend for it will be made to appear as "little men" with "contentious
hearts" who pick over the dead bones of honored men in order to gain
"brotherhood notoriety." Brethren, the very thought of such snide, disin-
genuous condescension ought to kindle Jeremiah's fire in our bosoms as the
idolatry of Athens stirred Paul's.

Fourth, one of the most blatant statements, showing that there are, indeed, as brother Connie W. Adams has said, "two mind sets" among us,
was printed in *Christianity Magazine* in November 1986, in a letter to the
editors (Ed Harrell, Dee Bowman, Paul Earnhart, Sewell Hall, Brent Lewis).
The letter was published without comment. Though its author did not mean
it to be so, I believe it represents one of the most dangerous, destructive
views regarding the nature of preaching that I have ever seen.

Below is the letter to which I have referred. It is in italics. My comments are interspersed in brackets within the letter.

"I Got'em Told"

One of the different attitudes portrayed by Christians today is that of "getting them told." This attitude of "Sin is black, hell is hot, and that's where you are going," is making people think that members of Christ's church are soul haters.

[First, can someone document this charge? Assuming the negative twist to the words, "getting them told," can someone cite a specific example? Surely, with all the recording of sermons today, if there is such an attitude being "portrayed by Christians today," there ought to be evidence of such an attitude on display. Where is it?

Second, is the author's letter a case of trying to "get'em told"? Since he is striving to expose a bad attitude among brethren, is he guilty of trying to "get'em told"? Do his efforts to "get'em told" make people think he is a soul hater, too?

Third (without presuming a negative connotation of telling someone the truth), yes, it is the object of faithful preachers and teachers of the gospel to "get'em told" (Isa. 58:1; Ezek. 3:17-21). Paul was pure from the blood of all men because he "got'em told" (Acts 20:26, 27). In effect, 2 Timothy 4:2 says, "get'em told." "Preach the word; be instant in season, out of season; reprove, rebuke, exhort with all longsuffering and doctrine." In essence, if that text does not say, "get' em told," what does it say?

Fourth, note, "This attitude of 'Sin is black, hell is hot, and that's where you're going. . . .'" *Isn't it?* Is sin black (darkness)? Is hell hot? Is hell where the unrighteous are going, or have I missed something (1 Cor. 6:9-11; Gal. 5:19-21; 6:7, 8; Rev. 21:8)? Evidently, words along that line — "Sin is black, hell is hot, and that's where you are going" — were used by the apostle Paul. Why else would Felix have trembled (Acts 24:25; Heb. 10:29)? "Knowing therefore the terror of the Lord, we persuade men" (2 Cor. 5:11).

Fifth, the fact that some may erroneously conclude that faithful preachers are "soul haters" does not necessarily impact what is preached. Some say that Christians believe in "water salvation." Does their charge prove there is a flaw in our preaching? They say we do not believe in the Old Testament, nor "in the power of the Holy Ghost." Do their charges prove the fault lies with us? While we must examine ourselves, let it be understood that the scurrilous taunts of unbelievers are not proof that Christians are "soul haters" (Acts 24:5; 1 Cor. 4:9-14; 2 Cor. 10:10-18; 13:5; 1 Pet. 3:15). Likewise, the misguided charges of our own brethren to the same effect do not prove that we are "soul haters."

Sixth, would the words of Jesus in Matthew 23:33 be like unto one who would say that "Sin is black, hell is hot, and that's where you're going"? Jesus said, "Ye serpents, ye generation of vipers, how can ye escape the damnation of hell?" If not, please distinguish between the two statements and show why one is proper, but the other is not.]

Do we truly know the value of a soul? The gospel of Christ is positive and exciting.

[Yes, "The gospel is positive and exciting." I suppose this is why the Jews in Acts 7 were cut to the heart and stoned Stephen. It also explains why Felix "trembled" (Acts 24:25). It is why Paul was chased from town to town and faced with death nearly everywhere he preached. It must have been that "positive and exciting" gospel that he preached that caused him to be in such physical jeopardy (2 Cor. 11:24-28)!

Did the Lord "truly know the value of a soul" when his words caused some to turn away (Mark 10:17-22; John 6:60-66)? Did Paul "truly know the value of a soul" when he preached "the gospel of God with much contention," so much so that he had to flee town under cover of darkness (Acts 17:10; 1 Thess. 2:2)? Worse, did some think him to be a soul hater because of his arguments against evil men and their errors (Acts 22:22, 23; 24:5, 6)?]

When we go out in to the world we are to be lights in the darkness. What we so often find is that many are just a thick fog to add to the gloom. We should be showing the world that we are a very blessed people by our actions and that God shows mercy and goodness to those who serve Him.

[While it is certainly true that "we are to be lights in the darkness," and that we should show ourselves as the children of light, I wonder if the author is following his own advice. Is he a light to those whom he criticizes or is he "just a thick fog to add to the gloom"? He says that "many," not a few, but "many are just a thick fog to add to the gloom." How pervasive is this "thick fog" and "gloom"? Since "many" are involved, it must be fairly extensive. When he speaks of it in this fashion, is he trying to "get'em told" again? Is he but "just (another layer of) thick fog to add to the gloom"?

Observe how "nice" they are who speak against those with whom they disagree. It is alright for them to speak of "many" people as being "a thick fog to add to the gloom," but if we dare to say that "Sin is black, and hell is hot, and that's where you're going," we are "soul haters." When they speak of the bad attitude of "many," they are "good guys," but if we challenge their assessments and judgments, we are the "bad guys." When folks invent a game, I suppose they may play by their own rules.

Yes, we should show the world "that God shows mercy and goodness to those who serve Him." It is also true that we should show the world the other side of the coin, that God shows his wrath to those who fail to serve him. "Behold therefore the goodness and severity of God: on them which fell, severity; but toward thee, goodness, if thou continue in his goodness: otherwise thou also shalt be cut off" (Rom. 11:22). I wonder if Paul was "just a thick fog to add to the gloom" when he dared to show the "severity" of God as well as his "goodness"?]

It is so discouraging to go to a worship service where Christians are singing as though their next breath may be their last. Then one of the men who calls himself an evangelist (a bearer of the good news?) proceeds to blast denominations for using mechanical instruments and for unscriptural baptism.

[The next time you go to a worship service and sing songs of praise and listen to a man who "proceeds to blast denominations for using mechanical instruments and for unscriptural baptism," remember that you should find that experience "so discouraging." Again, it would be good if someone could document such a "discouraging" experience. Where is the proof that such a "discouraging" event has occurred? Where is the example of it? At which congregation did it occur, and who was the preacher when brethren sang heartily and then the preacher ruined it all by "blast(ing) the denominations for using mechanical instruments and for unscriptural baptism."

Preacher friends, after a great song service, if any of you have ever dared to get up and "blast denominations for using mechanical instruments and for unscriptural baptism," remember that there is some doubt about your credentials as an "evangelist." You may not truly be an evangelist if you do such a thing. No, you may be one who just "calls himself an evangelist (a bearer of the good news?)." *Note the question mark.* If you, preacher, have ever spoken against denominational error with respect to mechanical instruments and unscriptural baptism, you are not a real "evangelist." No, according to the question mark, when you preach in that manner, you just "call" yourself one. You are not a true "bearer of the good news."

Was Jesus a "bearer of the good news" when, after being asked a question, he proceeded to "blast" the Pharisees for their vain worship and human traditions (Mark 7:1-13)?

Were the apostles "bearers of the good news" when they proceeded to "blast" the Jews for their misunderstanding of the nature of Christ and their unscriptural use of circumcision? Was Paul a "bearer of the good news" when he began his letters to the Corinthian and Galatian churches with kind words and then proceeded to "blast" them for their evils and errors? He even blasted the apostle Peter "before them all." Should we call him, "Thick Fog Paul"?

Occasionally, we are reproached for the use of sarcasm (1 Kings 18:27). However, notice the use of it above — *"one of the men who calls himself an evangelist (a bearer of the good news?)."* See how subtle is the implication that those who preach the truth against denominational error are not true "evangelists" and bearers of the good news?

Once again, it appears that the author was trying to "get'em told." When he uses such verbal barbs is he showing that he is a light in the darkness, or is he "just a thick fog to add to the gloom"?]

> *The world is full of hungry people, and the gospel is the recipe that will fill them up. Jesus Christ had a very powerful and positive ministry. He knew there was a time to be tough, but if we are sensitive to people's feelings, we will notice that they hardly ever respond positively to something put negatively. What we Christians need to do is put to practice what is generally known as "The Golden Rule" and treat people the way we would like to be treated!*

[Yes, "Jesus Christ had a very powerful and positive ministry," but remember it was that "powerful and positive ministry" that caused him to be put to death!

So, though the author says there is "a time to be tough," we know that he does not mean that in being "tough" one should "blast the denominations" for their vain worship and false doctrines. Nor does he mean that by being "tough" we should warn people that "Sin is black, hell is hot, and that's where (they're) going" if they do not repent. Seeing that one must "be tough" at times, we should like to know his definition of being "tough." What, exactly, would one do in order to be "tough"? We know what he cannot do. He cannot rebuke error and specific false doctrines, or plainly tell the lost the nature of sin and its eternal consequences. Therefore, we should like an example of how one could "be tough" without being "just a thick fog to add to the gloom."

Note this rule, *"If we are sensitive to people's feelings, we will notice that they hardly ever respond positively to something put negatively."*

Was Stephen insensitive to the feelings of his audience? Is that why he was stoned to death (Acts 7:51-60)? Was Paul equally insensitive? Is that why he was constantly fleeing town by night, being let down over a wall in a basket, and being conveyed under armed guard from one court room to another? How sensitive was Jesus "to people's feelings" as indicated by their reactions to his preaching? He "offended," "shamed," "insulted," and "angered" his audiences (Matt. 15:12; Luke 4:28; 6:11; 11:45; 13:17).

Since insensitive people do not notice that people "hardly ever respond positively to something put negatively," is this why Jesus said:

Except ye believe that I am he ye shall die in your sins (John 8:24)?

Except ye repent, ye shall die in your sins (Luke 13:3)?

Except a man be born again, he cannot see the kingdom of God (John 3:3)?

Not every one that saith unto me, Lord, Lord, shall enter into the kingdom of heaven; but he that doeth the will of my Father which is in heaven (Matt. 7:21)?

How sensitive was Paul to the feelings of his shipmates when he said, "*Except* these abide in the ship, ye cannot be saved" (Acts 27:31)? Did he expect them to "respond positively to something put negatively"?

No one would argue that we ought to violate "The Golden Rule." No one believes that preaching always must hurt and harm before it can help and heal (Acts 2:37; 7:54) . The situation must be considered. "And have mercy on some, who are doubting; save others, snatching them out of the fire; and on some have mercy with fear, hating even the garment polluted by the flesh" (Jude 22, 23). "And we urge you, brethren, admonish the unruly, encourage the fainthearted, help the weak, be patient with all men" (1 Thess. 5:14). At times, "sharpness" must be used (2 Cor. 13:10). When it is called for, "The Golden Rule" is not being ignored.

For we are to God the fragrance of Christ among those who are being saved and among those who are perishing. To the one we are the aroma of death to death, and to the other the aroma of life to life. And who is sufficient for these things? For we are not, as so many, peddling the word of God; but as of sincerity, but as from God, we speak in the sight of God in Christ (2 Cor. 2:15-17).

The message we preach is the fragrance of Christ. To the saved, it is the aroma of "life to life." That is, it is the aroma of spiritual life in Christ here, and eternal life in heaven after awhile (Mark 10:30). To the lost, it is the aroma, the odor, of "death to death"; that is, the gospel tells them that they now are dead in their sins and that, ultimately, they will be cast into hell, "which is the second death" (Rev. 21:8). "Of how much worse punishment, do you suppose, will he be thought worthy who has trampled the Son of God underfoot, counted the blood of the covenant by which he was sanctified a common thing, and insulted the Spirit of grace? For we know Him who said, 'Vengeance is Mine; I will repay, says the Lord.' And again, 'The Lord will judge His people.' It is a fearful thing to fall into the hands of the living God" (Heb. 10:29-31). "For our God is a consuming fire" (Heb. 12:29). That may not sound "positive and exciting." It may be seen by the lost as "a thick fog to add to the gloom," but it has one advantage; namely, it is the word of the truth of the gospel.]

Conclusion

Jeremiah is well known as "the weeping prophet." Every faithful Christian can identify with his tears. Only a burning bosom can shed tears of sorrow and consternation. Only the heart burdened with love and concern for the wayward and the wandering can weep for them.

Despite his love and faithfulness, Jeremiah was unpopular. He would not join the false prophets in their predictions of peace. He spoke of "violence and destruction." Therefore, "Now it happened, when Jeremiah had made an end of speaking all that the Lord had commanded him to speak to all the people, that the priests and the prophets and all the people seized him, saying, 'You will surely die'!" (Jer. 26:8). Jeremiah did not flinch or flee. Rather, said he, "As for me, here I am, in your hand; do with me as seems good and proper to you" (Jer. 26:14). Thus, it was that unto the end the word of God burned with triumphant zeal in the heart of Jeremiah. May the same flame of faith and torch of truth burn in the hearts of many today.

Addendum

Days of Genesis One — Does It Matter?

The following questions may be of interest to some:

> Could you explain why it is important not to believe that it took eons of time for God to create the earth? How do I answer someone who says, *"Why does it matter what one believes about creation? It is not a matter of salvation."*

It matters because: (1) Twice, Moses argued that since the Lord created the heavens and the earth in six days and rested on the seventh day, so

Israel was to work six days and rest on the seventh day (Exod. 20:8-11; 31:12-17). If the days of Genesis 1 were not six days, in the same sense that the days of Exodus 20 and 31 are six days, the basis of the argument for the Sabbath rest is eroded. *Does that matter?* If the days of Genesis 1 were "eons of time," does it matter that the props are knocked out from under the argument of Exodus?

(2) Jesus said that Adam and Eve were created "in the beginning" (Gen. 2:21-24; Matt. 19:4, 8). "But from the beginning of the creation God made them male and female" (Mark 10:6). However, if the days of Genesis 1 were multi-millions of years, and since God created them on the sixth day, they could not have been created "in the beginning of the creation," but, rather, toward "the end of the creation." *Does that matter?* Does it matter if the Lord was wrong about it? Does it matter that male and female were not created until "eons of time" *after* the beginning of the creation, if it be so that the days were hundreds of millions of years in duration?

(3) Jesus spoke of "the blood of all the prophets, which was shed *from the foundation of the world*" (Luke 11:50, 51). Then, he named Abel as the first — "from the blood of Abel unto the blood of Zacharias." If, though, the creations days were "eons of time," and if Abel was not born until after those "eons," how could it be said that the blood of prophets had been "shed from the foundation of the world"? Hence, the Lord was wrong about their blood being shed "from the foundation of the world." *Does that matter?*

Do Other Items Matter?

Does it matter whether or not the flood was universal or local? Scripture declares it to be universal (Gen. 6:17; 7:17, 19, 21; 2 Pet. 3:5-7, 10-13). Many of the same modernists who deny the days of Genesis 1 also deny the universal flood of Noah. Shall we say, "What does it matter what one believes about the flood? It is not a matter of salvation"? If we may set aside and dismiss the days of Genesis 1, upon the same basis we may disavow the flood.

Jesus spoke of Naaman's healing of leprosy (2 Kings 5; Luke 4:27). If a brother were to question the reality of Naaman's cleansing, or if he were to declare that the seven dips Naaman allegedly took were actually seven days of "praying through" for his healing, would it matter since it has "nothing to do with our salvation"?

Jesus spoke of the "three days and three nights" Jonah was in the belly of the great fish (Matt. 12:40). Suppose a brother begins teaching that the story of Jonah is another "fish story." Should we give the brother a pass and shrug it off, saying, "What does it matter what one believes about the flood and a literal Jonah? It is not a matter of salvation."

Too, if the days of Genesis 1 are not real days, or it does not matter if they are or not, does it matter if Jonah was three days and three nights in the belly of the great fish? Could he have been there (if he was ever truly there at all), for three years, rather than three days, or must those three days be literal? If a brother teaches that Jonah was there for three years, and not three literal days, shall we refuse to correct him and charge that those who disagree are full of hate and only want to divide brethren, and make a name for themselves?

Jesus endorsed the serpent of brass lifted up by Moses and compared it to his own lifting up on the cross (John 3:14-16; cf. 12:32, 33). Now, if Jesus could be wrong about the first couple being created "in the beginning," and if he could endorse a mythical fish story, could he also give credence to a snake healing that never occurred? "What does it matter what one believes about the serpent of brass and the healing of many in Numbers 21? It is not a matter of salvation."

Jesus expressed belief in the events regarding the destruction of Tyre, Sidon, and Sodom (Matt. 11:20-24). He endorsed the prophetic description of their doom. Indeed, he based the reality of judgment against the cities of his day on the judgment those towns had received. Suppose a devout and talented brother should deny those cities were doomed by divine fiat. Should we accept him and his error and criticize those who try to correct him? "What does it matter what one believes about those cities? It is not a matter of salvation."

May one deny the days of Genesis 1, Noah, and Naaman, question the certainty of the brass serpent, jumble Jonah, and impugn the reality of Sodom's judgment and justify it because those facts do not pertain "to salvation"?

If So, Where Does It End?

In order to help us see where such things may lead, let me cite the words of an esteemed brother in the Lord which typify and unwittingly help to justify the position reviewed above. At the Florida College lectures in February 2000, brother Ferrell Jenkins addressed the days of Genesis 1 controversy and made these comments:

> Now, I think we run into a problem when we say "must," one of these views must be correct. And I've got a good brother friend who said one place that these must be long ages, and I can't say that. But on the other

hand, I can't say they must be 24 hour ages. There were some arguments made for that like Exodus 20 and some arguments I didn't have time to deal with that I did have them in my notes here. And you can argue, you know, you can make a good case either way for that, all of those things like that. . . . And there is nobody in our brotherhood who can say, "This is it, and you've all got to agree with my view."

Now brethren, that's the history that we come from. And I'm sad to say that those who are younger and who may only be 10 years old or 15 or 20 years old, because it's been always a certain way in your life doesn't mean its always been that way. And it's time people who were older spoke up and said, "Look, what goes around comes around." Not to be wishy-washy, not to compromise on any biblical truth, but to say there are just some things so difficult that I may not be able to draw the same conclusion you've drawn on those and then to give that opportunity for people (Ferrell Jenkins, *Making Sense of the Days of Creation,*" Florida College, February 8, 2000).

Below are some parallels to brother Jenkins' comments. *I do not attribute them to him*, but they are comparable to his preceding statement. Suppose one were to speak of the Genesis flood as brother Jenkins spoke of the days of Genesis one.

First Parallel: Now, I think we run into a problem when we say "must," (that) one of these views must be correct. And I've got a good friend who said that the Genesis flood was a local, not a world-wide event, and I can't say that. But, on the other hand, I can't say it must be a total flood. There are some arguments made for a world-wide flood like Genesis 6-8, and some arguments I don't have time to deal with. And you can make a good case either way for that, for all of those things like that. . . . And there is no body in our brotherhood who can say, "This is it, and you've all got to agree with my view."

Now, brethren, that's the history that we come from. . . . Not to be wishy-washy, not to compromise any biblical truth, but to say there are just some things so difficult that I may not be able to draw the same conclusion you've drawn on those and then to give that opportunity for other people, too.

Second Parallel: Now, I think we run into a problem when we say "must," (that) one of these views on marriage, divorce, and remarriage must be correct. I've got a good friend who said that one may divorce for any reason before he becomes a Christian and keep his second wife after he obeys the gospel, and I can't say that. But, on the other hand, I can't say divorce must be for fornication. There were some arguments made for that like Matthew 5:32; 19:9 and some arguments I don't have time to deal with.

And you can make a good case either way for that, and there is no body in our brotherhood who can say, "This is it, and you've all got to agree with my view."

Now, brethren, that the history we come from. . . . Not to be wishy-washy, not to compromise on any biblical truth, but to say there are just some things so difficult that I may not be able to draw the same conclusion you've drawn on those and then to give that opportunity for other people, too.

Third Parallel: Now, I think we run into a problem when we say "must," (that) one of these views on polygamous marriages must be correct. I've got a good friend who said that one may marry multiple partners, and I can't say that. But, on the other hand, I can't say they must not marry multiple partners. There were some arguments made for one marriage partner like 1 Corinthians 7:2 and some arguments I don't have time to deal with. And you can make a good case either way. . . . And there is nobody in our brotherhood who can say, "This is it, and you've all got to agree with my view."

Now, brethren, that's the history that we come from. . . . Not to be wishy-washy, not to compromise on any biblical truth, but to say there are just some things so difficult that I may not be able to draw the same conclusion you've drawn on those and then to give that opportunity for other people, too.

Fourth Parallel: Now, I think we run into a problem when we say "must," (that) one of these views on baptism, music in worship, the organization and work of the church, must be correct. And I've got a good friend who said one time that these things are not essential, and I can't say that. But, on the other hand, I can't say they must be essential. There are some arguments made for baptism, and singing, like Acts 2:38 and Ephesians 5:19, and some arguments I don't have time to deal with. And you can make a good case either way for baptism, music in worship, all of those things like that. . . . And there is nobody in our brotherhood who can say, "This is it, and you've all got to agree with my view."

Now, brethren, that's the history that we come from. . . . Not to be wishy-washy, not to compromise any biblical truth, but to say there are just some things so difficult that I may not be able to draw the same conclusion you've drawn on those and then to give that opportunity for other people, too.

Where does it stop? Or, does it even matter? "*Is it nothing to all ye that pass by?*"

Changing Attitudes

Connie W. Adams

The movement to restore New Testament Christianity grew out of a merging of attitudes toward the Scriptures. The conviction that the word of God is all-sufficient and that the silence of the Scriptures should be respected put the leaders of this movement on a collision course with the religionists of their day. Catholicism offered three sources of authority: (1) the Scriptures, (2) tradition, (3) the living voice of the living church expressed through popes and councils. Protestants held the view that whatever the Scripture does not forbid is allowable. This attitude opened the way for the proliferation of denominations and sects we see now. But the plea of the restoration leaders was different. They appealed to a "thus saith the Lord" expressed either in direct statement, approved apostolic example, or necessary implication.

They perceived the Scriptures to be inspired of God (2 Tim. 3:16-17), the word of God as opposed to the word of man (1 Thess. 2:13). They regarded the Old Testament writers as men "moved by the Holy Spirit" (2 Pet. 1:20-21). The New Testament authors wrote "in words which the Holy Spirit teacheth" (1 Cor. 2:13). The motto, "We speak where the Scriptures speak and are silent where the Scriptures are silent," was another way of saying what Peter said long ago. "If any man speak, let him speak as the oracles of God" (1 Pet. 4:11). On that basis, restorers were able to replicate the New Testament pattern in name, worship, work, and organization.

As men grew weary with what they considered obstacles imposed by adherence to a strict pattern, they began to sound out a different message and even to question the reality of a pattern at all. The spirit of Noah had become a burden to them. "Thus did Noah; according to all that God commanded him, so did he" (Gen. 6:22). The development of the missionary society in 1849 was preceded by a changed attitude toward the all-sufficiency of the local church to do all that God required. The pattern on organization had become too burdensome. The addition of instrumental music in worship in 1859 and years following, grew out of a changed attitude toward the authority of the Scriptures. They decided they could "speak" where the Scripture did not speak. Neither the Missionary Society nor the use of instruments in worship would ever have been accepted among congregations unless there had first been a change in attitude toward the authority of the Scriptures. This looseness in attitude manifested itself in other ways, even to the introduction of modernism among the disciples. People do not change their practices until they first change their attitudes. Two mind-sets became evident: one took a loose (liberal) attitude toward divine authority while the other assumed a strict (conservative) stance. Those two attitudes could not coexist for long. Of course, there was a period of discussion and debates, but division came town by town and congregation by congregation. In some places the process was short while in others it was longer in coming, but it did come, whether sooner or later.

The controversy of the 1950s and 1960s over church support of private organizations (such as orphan homes, colleges) and over sponsoring churches in evangelism brought to the fore symptoms of the deeper problem. First of all, there was a lessening of respect for the divine pattern on the nature, work, and organization of the church. There were sermons, articles, and debate speeches which made light of a pattern. But none of that could have occurred without a change in attitude toward divine authority. Those who opposed these innovations were blacklisted, quarantined, ridiculed, and called ugly names. But behind all of that was the shifting of attitudes. There were some who claimed to be "middle-of-roaders" but their sympathies were clearly with the innovators and their sharpest words of censure were reserved for those who took a more conservative stance on these issues.

And now, sadly, there are ominous clouds on the horizon and some places have already felt the brunt of the storm. Questions having to do with marriage, divorce, and remarriage, the identity of false teachers among us, the limits of fellowship with them, whether or not Romans 14 provides a safe haven for these and other errors, whether the days of creation were literal days of 24 hours or long ages of time, and now the first clouds of a devastating controversy over eternal punishment, are appearing in the west. We have been well into this controversy for the last fifteen years. But these, and whatever other issues may arise, did not happen all at once. Behind them there was a shifting and changing of attitudes reflected in several ways. I direct your attention to at least some of them.

Attitudes Toward Truth and Error
"Ye shall know the truth, and the truth shall set you free" (John 8:32). "Sanctify them through thy truth: thy word is truth" (John 17:17). "I am the

way, the truth and the life" (John 14:6). To Pilate Jesus said, "For this cause came I into the world, that I should bear witness unto the truth. Every one that is of the truth heareth my voice" (John 18:37). The revelation of God through Jesus Christ assumes man's ability to understand and act upon truth. If this is not so, then all of our preaching and writing is empty. The demand that we "earnestly contend for the faith once delivered to the saints" (Jude 4) presupposes that we can first identify that faith. If we cannot, then it is impossible to contend for it.

But in the controversy over marriage, divorce, and remarriage and the issue of fellowship, we have been told again and again that the issue "lacks clarity." In the sixteen articles written by Ed Harrell in *Christianity Magazine* (February 1989-May 1990), he raised the issue of "clarity" numerous times. In articles 5, 6, and 7 there are special headings devoted to "clarity." If the Scriptures are clear on the subject then we can all speak with one voice. If they are not, then we have to go slow in drawing lines of fellowship. The statements made in Matthew 5:31-32, 19:3-12, Mark 10:11-12, Luke 16:18, and Romans 7:1-4 are clearly given. Unless someone has an axe to grind or a relative or friend to justify, or unless he has a great deal of expert "help," there is no reason to wonder what the truth of God is on this subject. What Paul wrote about fellowship with those in sin and error does not lack clarity. "And have no fellowship with the unfruitful works of darkness, but rather reprove them" (Eph. 5:11-12). What John wrote is equally clear: "If there come any unto you and bring not this doctrine, receive him not into your house, neither bid him God speed: For he that biddeth him God speed is partaker in his evil deeds" (2 John 9-11). What Paul wrote about our relationship with those who teach error is plain. "Mark them which cause divisions and offenses contrary to the doctrine which ye have learned; and avoid them" (Rom. 16:17).

Some have argued that the controversy over the creation days is not a "salvation issue." I suppose by that they mean it lacks "clarity." We are faced now with the looming controversy over eternal punishment. Is that, too, to be relegated to the realm of Romans 14 and excused because it "lacks clarity"? When Jesus described hell as a place "where their worm dieth not and the fire is not quenched" (Mark 9:44, 46, 48), did his words "lack clarity"? Ben Franklin, well known gospel preacher who averaged preaching 340 times a year for forty years, has a sermon in his two-volume set *The Gospel Preacher* entitled "The Adaptation of the Bible to Man" in which he contended, I believe correctly, that "the Bible as it is, is adapted to man as he is." The fact that "God hath spoken" implies man's ability to understand what he said. If that is not so, then none of us can entertain the hope of heaven.

So then, when we hear brethren who find larger and larger gray areas and fewer and fewer areas where absolute truth abounds, then you have located an attitude shift and the branches of that tree will bear bitter fruit.

Attitudes Toward False Teachers

"But there were false prophets also among the people, even as there shall be false teachers among you, who privily shall bring in damnable heresies . . . and many shall follow their pernicious ways; by reason of whom the way of truth shall be evil spoken of" (2 Pet. 2:1-2). Note the expression "damnable heresies." Heresy involves a chosen opinion which leads to the crystallizing of a party of followers. This chosen view is opposed to revealed truth. It is "damnable" because it results in eternal punishment for those caught up in it and who die clinging to the false hope it creates. The teaching of error is no light matter. The consequences are eternal. In the context of 2 Peter 2, men of evil intent are described. But this is not the only passage that deals with those who teach error and lead brethren astray. Paul warned of Hymenaeus and Philetus who taught that the resurrection is past already, said they overthrew the faith of some and that their words were cancerous (2 Tim. 2:16-18).

Ed Harrell and many others since have insisted that it is not proper to refer to a brother who teaches error as a false teacher unless his character is flawed. If it is clear that he has sinister motives in teaching his error, then we may properly call him a false teacher. But if not, we must regard him as simply mistaken. To call him a false teacher reflects upon his character. It is upon this ground that some have charged that attacks were made on the character of Homer Hailey and other brethren when he, and others, were identified as false teachers. Ed Harrell referred to these as "unheroic attacks" on an aged warrior. No, a thousand times no! Brethren opposed the content of his teaching which was false. Most of those who reviewed his teaching went out of their way to express goodwill toward him personally. It is this approach which leads some to judge every issue on which brethren write in disagreement as an attack on the character of another. They want to relegate all such discussions to the realm of unbrotherly wrangling. Is it possible for brethren to wrangle? Of course. But all discussion of differences in teaching do not fall into that category. To argue that it does is further evidence of a huge change in attitude toward error and those who promote it. Gospel preachers used to be set for the defense of the gospel. They were ready, willing, and able to defend the truth when error raised its head. Now, they are regarded as war mongers, Pharisees, wranglers, and legalists. The attitude has changed from regarding men skilled and fearless in upholding the truth as heroes to looking upon them as uncouth at best, and villains at worst.

Attitudes Toward Preaching

"Preach the word; be instant in season, out of season; reprove, rebuke, exhort with all long-suffering and doctrine. For the time will come when they will not endure sound doctrine; but after their own lusts shall they heap to themselves teachers, having itching ears; and they shall turn away their ears from the truth, and shall be turned unto fables. But watch thou in all things, endure afflictions, do the work of an evangelist, make full proof of thy ministry" (2 Tim. 4:2-5). This solemn charge is clear, concise, and challenging. It tells us what to preach, when to do it, what to include, and why it must be done repeatedly in order to fulfill the measure of our duty.

Expository preaching sparked the restoration movement. Better yet, Jesus and his apostles called their hearers to the text of Scripture and expounded upon them. At the synagogue in Nazareth, Jesus read from the prophet Isaiah and then said, "This day is this scripture fulfilled in your ears" (Luke 4:17-21). Peter on Pentecost quoted Joel and David and applied what they said to what was happening there that day. The sermon of Stephen before the council at Jerusalem and that of Paul in Antioch of Pisidia were reviews of the history of God's dealings with his people though the Old Testament with an application to the audience. In my own younger years, I have heard giants of the faith quote sometimes two or three chapters and then methodically, logically, and interestingly unfold the teaching before the audience with necessary applications. That is why they could hold their audiences for such long periods of time without any-one complaining or watching the clock. Such preaching produced faith, developed conviction, and molded character.

When I was a boy and my family was newly converted from the Chris-tian Church, the brethren generally regarded as weak or untaught any preacher who did not use much Scripture. It is not wrong to quote human authors. Paul did that at Athens, though it was a brief and passing com-ment. There is a place for humor and pathos. Illustrations from the speaker's own experience have their place. But strong churches are not built by elo-quence of expression, by snappy one-liners, endless stories about dogs, moth-ers, war heroes, or voyages into psychology. You know I speak the truth when I say that much preaching today is pure psycho-babble. Like grapenuts, it is neither grapes nor nuts. It is heavy on Lucado, Swindoll, McGregor, Baxter, and the like, but light on the prophets, Jesus, Peter, Paul, James, and John. A wondrous and ecstatic ignorance has settled in at all too many places. Young people in many places, considered the cream of the crop, have very little basic knowledge of the Bible. Get some of them in a Bible class and see what I mean. They have grown up with spiritual pep talks, have come home excited from Bible camps, yet they know little of basic Bible truth.

Preaching in the New Testament period dealt with basic doctrines such as grace, faith, repentance, baptism, the church, the difference in the Mosaic law, and the gospel. It was heavy on the need to grow in grace and knowledge of Christ and to transcribe that into "walking worthy of the vocation wherewith you are called" (Eph. 4:1). Christians were taught to "abstain from fleshly lusts, which war against the soul" (1 Pet. 2:11). John said they were to "love not the world, neither the things that are in the world" (1 John 2:15-17).

What is the result of this watered-down preaching of the present? Not only are churches vulnerable to error of all sorts but they have developed an aversion to any effort to refute error. Subtle changes are being seen in worship. Many today are ripe for the same errors which divided the people of the Lord over institutions and the sponsoring church. Can fellowship halls and gymnasiums be far behind? Dancing, social drinking, wearing immodest dress, gambling, and adulterous marriages are being tolerated, if not openly embraced, among churches which have welcomed this change in preaching. Look at the list of subjects announced for some meetings now and see how much basic Bible truth is being dispensed. Changed preaching grows out of changed attitudes. It shows a change in attitude toward the word of God on the part of the preacher and also reflects a change of attitude on the part of those who sit and listen week after week to such weak preaching.

Attitudes Toward Fellowship

In the New Testament, fellowship involved a sharing or joint participation in spiritual activity growing out of a spiritual relationship. Paul said the Philippians had "fellowship in the gospel" with him (Phil. 1:5). They had sent "once and again to his (my) necessities" while he was preaching at Thessalonica (Phil. 4:15-16). They gave and he received. Thus, they had a joint participation, a partnership in the work of the gospel. The brethren at Jerusalem extended to Paul and Barnabas the "right hand of fellowship" (Gal. 2:9). They shared in the common work of preaching the gospel — Paul and Barnabas unto the heathen and the others to the circumcision. Had the Philippians or the brethren at Jerusalem regarded Paul as a teacher of error they would not have extended to him the right hand of fellowship.

According to the word of God there are limitations on fellowship. Paul said, "Have no fellowship with the unfruitful works of darkness but rather reprove them" (Eph. 5:11). "No fellowship" does not mean a little now and then. Not only must we refrain from partaking in works of darkness, but must openly expose, censure, and refute them. That is the meaning of "reprove them." The teaching of John is just as clear regarding those who come bearing a different message than the doctrine of Christ. John said we are not to "bid them God speed" and that if we welcome them and forward them in their work, we have become "partakers of their evil deeds" (2 John 9-11).

Departure from these clear statements signals a change in attitude toward error and those who advocate it. It does not matter if the erroneous teacher is a friend of long standing, or a member of our own family. I am confident that some of the very influential men who continued their open fellowship with Homer Hailey, after he began to publicly preach and teach what for many years he claimed to be only a matter of private conviction, did so out of close personal ties with a beloved man who had long been a colleague and whom they wished to protect. But when men held in great respect are invited to preach in meetings or local work, their views will become known. If they hold to false positions which, if acted upon, would lead souls astray to their own condemnation, then their expression of those views, even in private settings, could very well undermine the faith of some. The danger is magnified when such men are knowledgeable and personable.

Changed attitudes toward fellowship have become evident when congregations cancel meetings with men known for soundness in the faith and courage in proclaiming it, and replace them with those of the "unity-in-diversity" crowd. When that happens, then a clear statement of fellowship has been made. They have shown to whom they will not extend the right hand of fellowship and, at the same time, have indicated their partnership is with another element, a changed viewpoint. This changed attitude toward fellowship is also seen when churches withdraw their support from gospel preachers who oppose what they wish to endorse. This happened recently with a very able and faithful preacher in the Philippines, brother Domie Jacob. His sin was that he wrote a lengthy treatise on the history of the church up to and including recent issues involving "unity-in-diversity." In it he quoted from Ed Harrell in *Christianity Magazine* and listed the editors of that magazine, one of whom was the preacher in a church which had been supporting him for a number of years. They decided to terminate his support and wrote him a haughty letter. His response was gracious and kind and respectful. But he could not, and did not, back down on what he said. It was well documented. We need more men whose souls are not for sale and who will carry on the Lord's work under hardship rather than compromise the truth.

This changed attitude toward fellowship is seen in the invitations extended for lectures at some congregations and at Florida College. Men known to teach error on divorce and remarriage, on the deity of Christ, on the creation days have been welcomed and defended. Men who like to take pot-shots at those whose great offense is that they love the truth and are not ashamed or afraid to preach it and to expose error arrayed against it, are not welcome. If occasionally one is invited, as was the case with Donnie V. Rader at the 2001 Florida College Lectures, he is subject to shabby treatment after his speech. What a change in attitude! For his trouble, his integrity was challenged by written statements handed out by Bob Owen, Ed Harrell, and Earl Kimbrough. Bob Owen was allowed to read his statement. Donnie was not allowed to respond. All these actions draw lines in the sand about fellowship.

Attitudes Toward Journalism
There can be no doubt that periodicals published by brethren have had great influence in shaping attitudes among their readers. The restoration plea was sounded forth in various publications from the *Christian Baptist*, *Millennial Harbinger*, *American Christian Review*, *Gospel Advocate*, *Firm Foundation* and others. But in 1866, the year of Alexander Campbell's death, the first issue of the *Christian Standard* was published, edited by Isaac Errett. J.S. Lamar wrote the *Memoirs of Isaac Errett* and in it commented on why this paper was started. He said:

> There were several weeklies, also, among them the *Review and Gospel Advocate, but* these were not satisfactory. They were regarded as being narrow in their views in many respects, hurtful, rather than helpful, to the great cause which they assumed to represent. I would say nothing here derogatory of the editors of these papers (Ben Franklin and David Lipscomb, CWA). They represented and fostered that unfortunate type of discipleship to which the leading minds among the brotherhood could have no sympathy. We may credit these writers with sincerity and honesty, but we cannot read many of their productions without feeling that we are breathing an unwholesome religious atmosphere. They seem to infuse an unlovely and earth-born spirit, which they clothe, nevertheless, in the garb of the divine letter, and enforce with cold, legalistic and crushing power. The great truth for whose defense the disciples are set, demanded a wiser, sweeter, better advocacy — an advocacy that should exhibit the apostolic spirit as well as the apostolic letter (I:300-301).

Ben Franklin and David Lipscomb both opposed the missionary society and instrumental music, pressing issues of the day. One of the purposes behind the founding of the *Christian Standard* was to blunt the force and influence of Franklin in the *Review* and Lipscomb in the *Gospel Advocate*.

In 1938 the *New Christian Leader* appeared, published in Nashville, Tennessee. Clinton Davidson and others who were behind it complained about the harsh, combative spirit of the *Gospel Advocate*, which for the past five years had been edited by Foy E. Wallace, Jr. During those years the *Advocate* vigorously opposed premillennialism. Some who openly advocated premillennialism, and some who said they opposed it, yet sympathized with the promoters of this doctrine, were upset by the writings of Wallace, Whiteside, C.R. Nichol, and N.B. Hardeman. They were thought to be too militant. They wanted a kinder, gentler, more positive approach in journalism. They thought they should address a wider need among brethren. The *Leader* did not fare so well. Meanwhile great pressure was brought on J.C. McQuiddy to choose a new editor for the *Advocate* with a gentler and more irenic spirit. The choice was B.C. Goodpasture and the rest is history. This gentler spirit called for a quarantine on brethren opposed to institutionalism.

In the 1950s the *Gospel Guardian* bore the brunt of the battle and took much heat for the effort. In 1951, *The Preceptor* began, edited first by James R. Cope, with able departmental writers. In 1956 *Truth Magazine* began, first to combat modernism in the Chicago area and then to add its weight in the fight against liberalism. In 1960 *Searching the Scriptures* began with its primary influence in the southeast, soon spreading over the nation. There can be no doubt that these papers did much to inform brethren and embolden many to take a stand for what was right. Against this background, it is no great wonder that when *Christianity Magazine* began announcing in the first issue that it would "accentuate the positive," the doubts of many were raised as to where this would lead. In a letter sent to writers about the format and content of articles, the editors said:

> We want to emphasize that our perspective is Biblical and not polemical. While you should feel free to say anything that you believe the scriptures teach, we hope you will be able to state it positively in scriptural terms (even if it is a negative point). In short, while there is much to be against, if we can get before our readers what is right, we think the wrong will be identified. We do not object to your pointing out things that are wrong, but we want to be sure that we end up with a positive alternative clearly before us. To say that this is the type of approach we are seeking in no way implies that other means are less useful. We have, however, determined that this will be the approach of *Christianity Magazine*.

The letter asked that articles be short, limited to a single major point, and that, "generally speaking, two or three passages should provide a sufficient base for such articles — perhaps even one." Then writers were told "obviously, what we are after is a piece of journalistic writing" with "interest-catching leads, sharp illustrations, and, if possible, sprinkle in a little wit."

Such a format represented a changed attitude among those who published it. Evidently, the offerings of the *Preceptor*, *Gospel Truths*, *Gospel Anchor*, *Searching the Scriptures*, and *Truth Magazine* did not sufficiently scratch this itch for a more positive approach. So they wanted and needed something different. But the sentiment which produced this magazine is reflected in the preaching of many who were its contributors, now in articles in other magazines (such as *Focus*) and from the platform at the Florida College Lectures. The most popular preachers among many today are those who bought into this "think, write, and preach" positive mentality. Since the gospel is both positive and negative in its makeup, any approach to journalism (or preaching) that features only one side of this equation is flawed from the beginning. From this well-spring has come the furtherance of unity-in-diversity, errors on fellowship, and Romans 14. The most negative things said in this magazine were aimed at those who took a strong stand on the issues which swirled around marriage, divorce, and remarriage, and fellowship with those who advocated error on these subjects. The positive gospel was not so positive when these writers took aim at those who opposed their loose views on these subjects.

But one cannot place all the blame on those who published *Christianity Magazine*. Had there not been a receptive audience to this approach, it would have died of its own weight. Many of our brethren are greatly influenced by the spirit of the age in which we live. Dogmatism has few friends. Relativism is on the throne. Tolerance is king. The most offensive person is the one who knows what he believes, is certain that it is right, and opposes whatever is contrary to it. Kindness is not reserved for him. He does not deserve it. Hold him up to scorn and ridicule. Speak and write charitably about all the rest. This is the spirit of our time and anyone who thinks that such attitudes are not found among the people of God has not been paying attention.

Conclusion

We are faced with uncertain times among us. It is a time for soul-searching, a time for conviction. A time to stand in the gap and "quit you like men." I close with these passages from the prophets:

> Thus with the Lord, Stand ye in the ways, and see, and ask for the old paths, where is the good way, and walk therein, and ye shall find rest for your soul. But they said, "We will not walk therein." Also, I set watchmen over you saying, hearken to the sound of the trumpet. But, they said, "We will not hearken" (Jer. 6:16-17).

> Now go, write it before them in a table, and note it in a book, that it may be for the time to come for ever and ever. That this is a rebellious people,

lying children, children that will not hear the law of the Lord: Which say to the seers, see not; and to the prophets, Prophesy not unto us right things, speak unto us smooth things, prophesy deceits: Get you out of the way, turn aside out of the path, cause the Holy One of Israel to cease from before us (Isa. 30:8-11).

Let our attitude be "Speak Lord, thy servant heareth" and let there be no change either to the right hand or to the left.

Unity of the Spirit or Unity-in-Diversity?

Tom M. Roberts

"I am a companion of all those who fear You, and of those who keep Your precepts" said David in Psalms 119:63. This longing for fellowship with all of God's people is a natural product of the "common salvation" of which Jude spoke (v. 3). We share a common Savior, a common church, a common hope of eternal life, and a common appreciation for spiritual life. There is a yearning to be together, to know one another, and to reach out to those who are unknown in a brotherhood that spans the globe. A traveler in a strange land is instantly at home when those of "like precious faith" (2 Pet. 1:1) are found. We are to "love the brotherhood" (1 Pet. 2:17), even all those who are of the "general assembly and church of the first-born who are registered in heaven" (Heb. 12:23). Each of us is en-nobled to share in the family of God, having God as our Father, being born by the Spirit whereby we cry "Abba, Father" (Rom. 8:15). "For as many as are led by the Spirit of God, these are the sons of God" (v. 14). "For by one Spirit we were all baptized into one body — whether Jews or Greeks, whether slaves or free — and have all been made to drink into one Spirit" (1 Cor. 12:13). The least of all the saints shares fully in this unity of the Spirit, being added by the Lord (Acts 2:47) as they are baptized into Christ (v. 38).

What is Meant by the "Unity of the Spirit"

The "unity of the Spirit" is "of" or "from" the Spirit of God. It was not brought into existence by man, but was divinely created when the church was brought into existence in order to weld "brothers" (individual saints) into a "brotherhood." But this unity of the Spirit also binds these brothers to God, as much as to one another. A single Christian may enjoy the unity of the Spirit as he relates, individually, to God (as the Ethiopian nobleman, Acts 8:39). He may enjoy the unity of the Spirit as he relates to the broth-erhood (Col. 1:12; Rom. 16:16; Heb. 12:23). And he may also enjoy this same unity in a local congregation in which talents are blended for the edification of all (Phil. 1:1; 1 Cor. 14:26).

Again, man does not create this unity; it is divine in origin, nature and scope. We do not enter this unity relationship except by the invitation of God, and we remain in it by his grace. We do not extend the unity of the Spirit beyond the scope of its Designer, nor do we change its parameters at our whim, wish, or circumstance. The unity of the Spirit, like the proud waves of the sea, is determined by God: "When I fixed My limit for it, and set bars and doors; When I said, 'This far you may come, but no farther, And here your proud waves must stop'!" (Job 38:10-11). Man can no more change the parameters of unity than he can change the tides of the ocean. It is folly for us to "extend" unity when God has not. It is useless for us to deny unity to those whom God has accepted. The unity of the Spirit, as an objective relationship, can only be shared in a manner described by the word of the Spirit. While we may make subjective decisions about fellowship with others, or with God, those decisions may not, in fact, correspond with God's decisions. The scriptures alone, as God's revealed, objective truth, determine who is, and is not, in this unity. No denominational council, papal decree, sectarian creed, "yellow tag of quarantine," or congregational overlord (such as Diotrephes, 3 John 9-10) can exclude a brother from the Spirit's unity. Nor can any council, creed, pronouncement, decision, or exaggerated generosity include a person in the Spirit's unity whom God has not included. It is, exclusively and particularly, the unity of the Spirit.

The unity of the Spirit takes its nature from the Godhead; the unity of the Spirit is *oneness*. Nothing could be more clear than the context wherein the unity of the Spirit is declared. "There is one body and one Spirit, just as you were called in one hope of your calling; one Lord, one faith, one baptism, one God and Father of all, who is above all, and through all, and in you all" (Eph. 4:4-6). The fragmentation of the denominational world is a denial of the same passage that exhibits the seven "ones" of the Spirit's unity. The concept of unity-in-diversity which undergirds the denominational platform certainly does not describe true oneness. When brethren who oppose the denominational platform embrace unity-in-diversity, it is a contradiction of terms, an oxymoron or "contradictory terms brought sharply together" (Funk & Wagnall's *Standard Dictionary*). There is dissimilitude regarding "unity" and "diversity" which seems lost in the familiarity of the phrase. The ideas conveyed in "unity" and "diversity" can never apply to "oneness" terms. The apostle James warned that "blessings and cursings" should not proceed from the same mouth (3:9). Why? Because each has a different source, nature, and character than the other. Even so with "unity" and "diversity." Similarly, the two phrases "unity of the Spirit" and "unity-in-diversity" are not describing the same concepts. The first is divine; the second is of human origin. The first posits a unity of mind and action; the second accepts diversity and contradictions. The first draws God and man together; the second splinters believers. The first defines a true unity; the second mocks unity even while encouraging division. The devil has not waged a more effective battle in leading people astray than when he convinced so many to substitute unity-in-diversity for the unity of the Spirit. It is a sad day for the sons of God when this shallow imitation of the Spirit's unity is foisted upon brethren as identical in form and substance. It is even sadder when notable brethren who know the history of unity-in-diversity among churches of Christ and its dire consequences capitulate to popular consensus and propose acceptance as though they are the same.

Man is to Maintain the Unity of the Spirit

Paul, as a prisoner of the Lord, admonished the Ephesians, as those "endeavoring ("giving diligence," ASV) to keep the unity of the Spirit in the bond of peace" (Eph. 4:1-3). The brothers in the fellowship of Christ have a responsibility to maintain what the Spirit has created. This must be done by no other means than the weapons supplied by the Spirit, the "whole armor of God" (Eph. 6:13-18). Such are the weapons that make peace, even as the "sword of the Spirit, which is the word of God" (v. 17). The armor of God enables Christians to fight against "principalities, against powers, against the rulers of the darkness of this age, against spiritual hosts of wickedness in the heavenly places" (v. 12), so allowing Christ to make peace between God and man, between Jew and Gentile (Eph. 2:13-22).

It must not escape our attention that true peace between God and man, as between man and man, is found in preaching the gospel, the "whole counsel of God" (Acts 20:27). A shallow imitation of peace may be found in unity-in-diversity as some eviscerate the truth and bury their convictions. However, the unity of the Spirit is a true unity between God and man that includes waging war against every vestige of error. There can be no peace where error exists; there can be no unity where truth is omitted. Unity-in-diversity is capitulation to Satan by which common consent is implicit in allowing a place for error — a facade without foundation. Thus, the unity of the Spirit recognizes that we must "contend for the faith" (Jude 3), making peace by using the sword of the Spirit (Eph. 6:17). Those who want peace without this sword are doomed to failure. Those who are willing to sheath the Spirit's sword in order to placate error or errorists will never achieve anything more than unity-in-diversity. How long will it take us to learn what Jesus taught two centuries ago: "Peace I leave with you; my peace I give unto you: not as the world giveth, give I unto you" (John 14:27)? Unity-in-diversity is peace which the world gives. The peace that Jesus gives is the unity of the Spirit.

Three Areas in Which to Maintain the Spirit's Unity

There are three areas of life whereby the Christian maintains the unity of the Spirit. First of all, as individual saints, we must maintain our personal unity with God. As we have seen, one who has not been born again does not share in the unity of the Spirit (John 3:5). Once accepted into this unity, he must "walk worthy of the calling with which he was called" (Eph. 4:1) or "walk in the light" (1 John 1:7). One who is not in unity with God will not be allowed in the unity of brothers, even though a superficial congregational unity may exist. Diotrephes appeared to belong to the church to whom John wrote. In fact, he controlled its membership, but he was not participating in the unity of the Spirit. Those who walk in darkness cannot participate in this unity, though they may wear the name of "Christian" and be "pillars" in a local church (Gal. 2:9).

Secondly, as individual saints, we share in the "brotherhood." As we interact with other individual saints in this brotherhood, we are to "do good," especially to "those who are of the household of faith" (Gal. 6:10). Beyond "loving the brotherhood" (1 Pet. 2:17), we are to respond to their needs, having fellowship in their sufferings (2 Cor. 9:13). It is certain that brothers can recognize those in the brotherhood, the household of faith. The qualifications that identify a faithful brother at home are the same criteria that will identify a brother anywhere in the world. Though some might wish to recognize a brotherhood more extensive than the Lord's church, we must abide by the Spirit's law. John recognized an "us" and "them," acknowledging that "none of them were of us" (1 John 2:19). Thus, on the basis of what is revealed, we can recognize our brethren and maintain brotherhood unity. The New Testament is replete with admonitions which tell brethren to know, love, admonish, and fellowship other brethren around the world, as far as the possibilities exist. Jesus' prayer, shortly before his ascension affirmed this: "I do not pray for these alone, but also for those who will believe in Me through their word; that they all may be one, as You, Father, are in Me, and I in You; that they also may be one in Us, that the world may believe that You sent Me" (John 17:20-21). While there can never be corporate consolidation of the brotherhood, there is a unity and fellowship that we are to extend to the limits of our abilities and knowledge as we relate to other individual saints around the world. Some have expressed a denial that brotherhood fellowship exists at all. But the unity of the Spirit encompasses a brotherhood that, while known in its totality only by God, is recognizable by its individual members as they interact. This brotherhood fellowship may be extended or withdrawn just as John did to "us" and "them." To deny this is to deny a portion of the unity of the Spirit.

Thirdly, we share in the Spirit's unity in the local church. Here, the corporate identity of a congregation demonstrates an oneness of faith and practice that proceeds from the Spirit's message as it is translated into congregational activity. As local saints submit to the elders' watchful oversight and are served by the deacons' concern for their physical welfare, a congregation is unified as a body. In work, worship, and daily life, the saints are to "continue steadfastly in the apostles' doctrine and fellowship, in the breaking of bread and prayers" (Acts 2:42). Even as the primitive disciples, we should have "one heart and one soul" (4:32). Clearly, this was Paul's intent when he admonished the Corinthian brethren for having something less than unity: "Now I plead with you, brethren, by the name of our Lord Jesus Christ, that you all speak the same thing, and that there be no divisions among you, but that you be perfectly joined together in the same mind and in the same judgment" (1:10). Being "perfectly joined together," and "speaking the same thing" and "having the same mind" were reinforced by the apostle John when he warned: "Whoever transgresses and does not abide in the doctrine of Christ does not have God. He who abides in the doctrine of Christ has both the Father and the Son. If anyone comes to you and does not bring this doctrine, do not receive him into your house nor greet him, for he who greets him shares in his evil deeds" (2 John 9-11). Yes, the unity of the Spirit is based upon doctrinal unity, not just unity by accepting the deity of Christ. Intra-congregational unity is possible by abiding in the doctrine of Christ. As a local church is the "pillar and ground of truth" (1 Tim. 3:15), it shares in the unity of the Spirit in a local sense and, concurrently, with every other faithful church. Without having inter-congregational ties, a faithful church may recognize other faithful churches by acknowledging their stance for truth (1 Thess. 1:6-7). This is possible because of a common truth, not only a common Savior. Those who teach unity in "the Man" but not "the plan" ignore Paul's advice to Timothy. He was to tell the Ephesians to remember Paul's "ways in Christ, as I teach everywhere in every church" (1 Cor. 4:17). Yes, there can be unity among churches of Christ even while each congregation remains independent of all the rest.

Just as a faithful congregation can be recognized because of its support of truth, an unfaithful congregation can be recognized when it begins to teach or practice unsound activities. Just as Jesus warned Ephesus that it was about to "lose its candlestick" (Rev. 2:5), present-day churches may be in the same danger. We may warn of that danger without violating congregational autonomy, just as Scripture does.

The Scriptures speak clearly about the unity of the Spirit. Nothing less is acceptable and nothing else is comparable. In every phase of a Christian's life, he must be dedicated to "maintaining the unity of the Spirit in the bond of peace." Our generation needs to appreciate this blessing and be clear when we speak of unity. But many have rejected the unity of the Spirit and sought to replace it with unity-in-diversity.

Unity-in-Diversity Is a Reality

Unity-in-diversity has been accepted as a fact among many brethren. It is in popular demand and has been broadly advocated by Ed Harrell in *Christianity Magazine,* as well as by others. Brother Harrell's fellow editors, Dee Bowman, Paul Earnhart, Sewell Hall, and Brent Lewis, allowed his advocacy of unity-in-diversity to go unchallenged and unanswered. In fact, they refused to allow dissent in the paper from reputable brethren who opposed the error. But, while being as silent as the tomb about the error, they have been extremely critical of those who opposed the doctrine. Though the paper no longer continues to be published, it has lent potent support to the movement to incorporate unity-in-diversity among churches of Christ. The sheer popularity and familiarity of the staff writers for *Christianity Magazine* has created a tidal wave of acceptance. A wave of intolerance has washed across the land toward any who would oppose unity-in-diversity. Meetings have been canceled, preachers have been boycotted, reputations have been assaulted, and churches have been divided over this issue. An apostasy is gathering steam and the momentum pushing it along is a new acceptance of an old denominational doctrine: unity-in-diversity.

As usual, there are some who are "on the fence," unable or unwilling to choose one or the other. As Elijah chided Israel of old, "How long will you falter between two opinions?" (1 Kings 18:21), the "good old boy" system is in place and working well, blinding many to the need to choose the right way over friendships. Some seem afraid to take a stand lest they be numbered among the "watchdogs" and "brotherhood dictators," names so easily thrown about. I am reminded of a man who went fishing. He had one foot on the pier and the other on the boat. As the boat began to drift, he was unable to choose between either the pier or the boat; thus, he fell into the water. Some brethren want to stand with one foot among those who teach unity-in-diversity with the other foot among those who teach unity of the Spirit. They have ties to both "sides," failing to remember that our allegiance must be to Christ, first of all. Some participate in lectureships in which ridicule and vituperation is broadly spread upon faithful brethren who oppose unity-in-diversity. They too, silent as the tomb, allow slander to be spread about without raising their voice to correct what they know to be false. As the division broadens among brethren, they must make their choice. Will it be unity-in-diversity and popularity or unity of the Spirit and infamy? Eventually, they will make the choice. And, dear reader, you must make it, as well.

Historical Defense of Unity-in-Diversity

Is the unity of the Spirit a viable option or must we settle for unity-in-diversity?

Some say it is impossible to have complete doctrinal unity, now or ever. A redefinition process has been underway for years in which attempts are made to substitute a diverse unity for the Spirit's unity. It is profitable to note at the outset what the consequences of such actions are. Historically (and easily verified), those who accept unity-in-diversity are tolerant of doctrinal error, tolerant of removing restraints from God's marriage laws, and tolerant of moral error (such as social drinking, immodest apparel, gambling, etc.). Eventually, those who adopt unity-in-diversity accept fellowship with sectarian bodies, deny the efficacy of baptism to salvation, and are permissive of innovative worship activities. At the same time, they are most intolerant of those who oppose unity-in-diversity, using sarcasm, prejudicial name-calling and vile epithets to isolate and separate. It is more than passing strange to see those who advocate unity-in-diversity reach out to sectarians in love and toleration while denouncing their own brethren with vitriolic diatribes. It is equally strange to see brethren who, at one time, walked with "us" now associate freely with "them" (cf. 1 John 2:19). The tolerance that comes with unity-in-diversity allows adherents to wander freely among denominational churches, having fellowship with those who accept doctrinal and moral error. What makes this possible is the redefinition process: unity of the Spirit is now seen only as unity-in-diversity. While it must be acknowledged that not every person accepting unity-in-diversity has reached the full departure encouraged by the error, it is a "slippery slope" with no stopping place once embarkation has begun. Once the redefinition has been accepted, it is a matter of individuality how long one takes to reach the full end of apostasy. Not all who accept it will rush out to incorporate instrumental music into the worship, but it will be a lot easier to accept the adulterer into fellowship. It will be a lot easier to criticize the teacher of truth. It will be a lot easier to extend fellowship to those who practice error. The leaven of error has already begun. The apologists are growing in number. To be sure, the dangers are not imaginary, but real.

These dangers can, and should be, documented with statements which reveal a progressive intrusion into the thinking of brethren:

> Some of those who mistake conformity for unity appear to be startled when they first learn that we suggest there may be unity-in-diversity. Actually we go much further than that. We assert that if there is any unity at all it must be unity-in-diversity (Carl Ketcherside, *The Twisted Scriptures* 71-72).

> The implications of all this to unity and fellowship are weighty. It means that the gospel itself, not our doctrinal interpretations, is the basis of our being one in Christ and in fellowship with each other. That is, when one

believes in Jesus and obeys him in baptism, he is our brother and in the fellowship . . . This is oneness and this is unity . . . That fellowship is strengthened and made joyful by doctrine, but it is the gospel and not doctrine that determines fellowship . . . In doctrinal matters there can be and will be diversity of opinion and interpretation. It was so with the apostles themselves. But this is good, for we stretch each other's minds and help each other to grow in knowledge in our mutual search for truth. . . (Leroy Garrett, *Restoration Review*, Ch. 17, 42-46).

The present frontier is the frontier of a grace-based fellowship with all our brothers and sisters in Christ. A truth began to dawn on us in the 1960s and 70s and increasingly through the 1980s. That truth is that God's grace extends not only to our moral imperfections but also to our doctrinal shortcomings (Gary Pearson, *Image Magazine*, Sept./Oct. 1993, 32).

There should be room in the Christian fellowship for those who believe that Christ is the son of God, but who differ on eschatological theories such as premillennialism, ecclesiological matters such as congregational organization, on soteriological matters such as whether baptism is "for" or "because" of remission of sins (Carrol Osburn, *The Peaceable Kingdom*, 1993, 90-91).

Having read this far, some might say that the quotations above are to be associated with radicals and liberals, not "conservative" or "sound" brethren. Truly, these quotations could be multiplied by quotes from many more. All the writings of Carl Ketcherside and Leroy Garrett, along with Cecil Hook and Edward Fudge, among others, are on the Internet and available to all. However, it is easy to come closer to "home" and note those who, at one time, were known as sound brethren who are now deeply entrenched in the unity-in-diversity approach to fellowship.

What is the basis of one's hope before God? Is it not that we sustain a right relationship with God through Christ? . . . In other words — if one is right about Christ, then that one can be wrong about some doctrinal instruction without being lost, can he not? (Arnold Hardin, *The Persuader*, XI:16).

On what basis do we establish the bounds of Christian unity? That is the crucial question that lies before us. Are individual fellowship and congregational unity based on total agreement? Historical reality denies that unanimity existed in New Testament congregations or that it exists today. Is there, then, a scriptural basis for maintaining unity when brethren disagree? If so, what are the limits of the concept of unity-in-diversity? (Ed Harrell, "The Bounds of Christian Unity," *Christianity Magazine*, March 1989, 6).

It is noteworthy here to contrast brother Harrell's statement about unity with previous Scriptures, used above. Brother Harrell asserts that "historical reality denies that unanimity existed in New Testament congregations or that it exists today." Compare this with Acts 2:42: "They continued steadfastly in the apostles' doctrine and fellowship, in the breaking of bread and prayers." The Holy Spirit recorded a "historical reality" of early disciples who were of "one heart and one soul" (4:32). Does "historical reality" deny that we can be "perfectly joined together in the same mind" (1 Cor. 1:10)? Is that possible today? Though Jesus prayed for all disciples to be one, brother Harrell says unanimity is not possible. Though Paul commanded that the Corinthians be of one mind, brother Harrell says it is not possible. What is the acceptable alternative to brother Harrell? — unity-in-diversity!

But let us be clear. Is brother Harrell suggesting a unity-in-diversity on purely judgmental matters, matters of personal conscience or matters of indifference to God? No, not at all. The unity-in-diversity advocated by Ed Harrell is the same principle of unity-in-diversity advocated by Fudge, Ketcherside, Garrett, and Hook, *et al.* Fudge and others are perfectly willing to put doctrinal matters, important moral matters, under the aegis of unity and fellowship those on all sides of the spectrum. Though brother Harrell would not go that far, he has espoused the same principle that would allow it! And many brethren are willing to concede the matter and accept that principle without looking at the conclusion. Once unity-in-diversity is accepted, it is academic how quickly one proceeds to the logical end. Just as one cannot be a "little bit pregnant," one cannot accept a "little" unity-in-diversity. That brother Harrell has accepted the principle should not be in dispute. His own words tell the tale.

> Within certain limits, God grants to Christians the right to a private conscience in matters of "faith." I believe that right is discussed in Romans 14. However, whether or not one accepts my exegesis of that passage, honest minds must acknowledge the reality of a past and present Christian world that tolerates contradictory teachings and practices on important moral and doctrinal questions (Ed Harrell, "The Bounds of Christian Unity," *CM*, May 1990, 134).

> It would be less than honest to argue that scriptural local churches always exist without imperfections and, indeed, without some diversity of belief. At least two chapters written by the apostle Paul, Romans 14 and 1 Corinthians 8 speak in detail of the proper approach to disagreement (Ed Harrell, "The Parameters of Fellowship," *CM* , March/April 1997, 20).

As leaven, this doctrine, once introduced, will continue to permeate until and unless it is purged (1 Cor. 5:6). However, it continues to be defended by different means and different brethren. We need to face the fact that an appeal for unity-in-diversity has been made and now it is being defended. If fully implemented, it will change the face of churches of Christ in our generation, just as it did to the Christian Church when it adopted the same philosophy. Are you ready for your children to embrace unity-in-diversity, with all its consequences? Notable brethren are defending it, lending their weight to its acceptability.

Defensive Arguments For Unity-In-Diversity

This is our tradition. During Jesus' earthly ministry, he opposed an error that was firmly entrenched: the tradition of the elders. "Then the scribes and Pharisees who were from Jerusalem came to Jesus, saying, 'Why do your disciples transgress the traditions of the elders?'" (Matt. 15:12). Something can become a law by long established practice, though without the authority of God.

When the unity-in-diversity error began, it was originally concerned with fellowship over the divorce-remarriage issue. As lines began to be drawn and as brethren were willing to have fellowship with brother Homer Hailey in spite of his acknowledged error on the divorce issue, some argued that we should not limit fellowship on that issue because earlier generations here in America had not done so. It is not "our tradition" to limit fellowship over disagreements about divorce, we were told. If our "elders" (earlier generations of restoration pioneers) did not make it a test of fellowship, neither should we. This approach was taken by Earl Kimbrough in his booklet, *How Shall We Treat Brethren With Whom We Disagree?* It was distributed by Bob Owen in his first lectureship at Temple Terrace, Florida in September 1993. In that lectureship, brother Owen presented his views on fellowship in the context of a series of lessons on divorce and remarriage. Though brother Owen clearly did not agree with brother Hailey and though brother Owen taught the truth on divorce, he was willing to accept brother Hailey into unity, using an argument (among others) from tradition.

Inconsistency. Another approach that is heard often in defense of unity-in-diversity is that "some of you do not agree among yourselves, but you fellowship each other. Therefore, if you fellowship each other and do not fellowship us, you are inconsistent."

I submit that a search for truth is not the same as a search for consistency. While it is true that all who uphold truth should be consistent in its application, it does not alter truth if a disciple is inconsistent. I must first understand and apply truth for myself. If a brother does not apply it the same way, this does not alter truth! For example, if a brother teaches against instrumental music in assembly worship, but uses the instrument in a private setting to worship, he would rightly be considered inconsistent: right in one instance, but wrong in the other. But his inconsistency has not changed the truth about singing (Eph. 5:19; Col. 3:16; *et al.*). Should I look for inconsistencies or should I look for the truth? If I am wrong and find an inconsistency in an opponent, does his inconsistency support my erroneous position?

The argument that is often fallaciously made against Mike Willis and Ron Halbrook is that they disagree about the divorce issue, but they continue to fellowship one another. If so, this is inconsistent. But if there is weight to the argument, what does it prove? Are not those who make the argument suggesting that "since Mike and Ron fellowship one another while disagreeing, we should be allowed to fellowship Jerry and Don Bassett, Homer Hailey, Harold Dowdy, Olan Hicks, *et al.* when we disagree?" If this is not the argument, then what is it? Do two wrongs make one right? I am at a loss to understand why inconsistency continues to be an argument since it only proves, in that context, that fellowship should be extended to all who hold error on the divorce issue.

The truth of the matter is that Mike and Ron do not disagree on what the Bible reveals about marriage, divorce, and remarriage. While they are capable of speaking for themselves and I am not an apologist for either one, it should be made clear that they both express agreement on Christ's teaching. They both believe "one man, one woman, for life, with one exception." They both believe that adultery must take place before the innocent mate may put away the guilty and remarry, and that adultery must be the *cause* of the divorce. It is a lie to teach otherwise about either of these brethren. There are areas of *unrevealed judgment* that all of us must decide about for ourselves yet refuse to bind on others. For example: Must the word "adultery" be in the divorce decree? Is the civil procedure the same as biblical putting away? Exactly when does putting away take place? Exactly when does marriage take place? What if the guilty party in a marriage gets the divorce before the innocent party? This list could be multiplied many times over. But we must learn to make a distinction between what God has bound and what our personal judgments might be in peripheral matters. In the past, we have understood that baptism is in water for the remission of sin (Acts 2:38). One brother tried to bind that the water must be "running water" and not in a pool (baptistery). While admitting the truth about baptism, he went beyond what was revealed and tried to bind his judgment. Some want to do the same thing with the divorce issue. But Mike and Ron are not inconsistent because they do not disagree on the revealed truth about divorce and remarriage. And they are willing to allow each brother to hold personal judgments about unrevealed matters. It is this latter willingness (which all should accept) for which they are being pilloried, but it is being twisted to suggest a disagreement over revealed truth. As a pebble dropped into a pond creates ripples that will reach unknown shores, this lie about Mike and Ron continues to spread. At this point, you know the truth of the matter and should not be guilty of causing more ripples of untruth.

You practice what we practice. Some of those who advocate unity-in-diversity contend that there is no other kind of unity. Thus, they attempt to charge all with practicing what they practice, labeling all with believing in unity-in-diversity whether we acknowledge it or not. Nothing could be farther from the truth.

The argument is made that every congregation has in its membership those who differ in "important doctrinal and moral questions." Since this will always be so, we are told, the only way to handle it is to allow unity-in-diversity to take place. Usually, Romans 14 is used at this point to buttress their argument.

First of all, it is acknowledged that every congregation of any size has in it those who hold "contradictory teachings and practices on important moral and doctrinal questions." In most congregations, there will be babes in Christ, ignorant brethren, some who are untaught on certain issues, as well as some possible rebels (teachers of error) who deny truth openly. Is Romans 14 the proper way to deal with all these situations? Certainly not!

Romans 14 does not pose a catch-all for "receiving one another" (v. 1) when we disagree on "contradictory teachings and practices on important moral and doctrinal questions." There is nothing inherently sinful in Romans 14 about which brethren differ. "Important doctrinal and moral questions" could cover instrumental music, premillennialism, institutionalism, homosexuality, adultery, social drinking, and other things, all of which are inherently sinful. Unity-in-diversity suggests that we "accept one another" in such matters. But the context of Romans 14 discusses matters of personal scruples, personal judgment, and matters that are "clean" (v. 14), "good" (v. 16), and "pure" (v. 20). Romans 14 discusses the proper use of *authorized liberties* (1 Cor. 8:9; 10:23), not inherently sinful practices. It is a violation of the text to suggest that doctrinal sin and moral impurities be included in a discussion of Romans 14.

Further, the immediate context around Romans 14:1-15:7 cannot be used to violate other passages in the same Roman letter. Note that Romans 13:12-14 condemns *moral sins* and demands that we "make no provision for the flesh, to fulfill its lusts." But advocates of unity-in-diversity teach that it is permissible to put moral sins in Romans 14 and to "receive" those who teach and practice such. Note also that Romans 16:17-18 (the chapter following 14:1-15:7) warn against *doctrinal error.* "Now I urge you, brethren, note those who cause divisions and offenses, contrary to the doctrine which you learned, and avoid them. For those who are such do not serve our Lord Jesus Christ, but their own belly, and by smooth words and flattering speech deceive the hearts of the simple." How can anyone be so simpleminded as to argue that Romans 14-15 allows fellowship with doctrinal and moral sins while the passages that surround it so clearly teach the opposite?

The truth of the matter is that Romans 14 does not discuss "contradictory teachings and practices on important moral and doctrinal questions." Rather, the chapter discusses matters that are indifferent to God because they are not bound. The danger for the weak brother was his attitude: to bind where God had not bound (v. 4), or to violate his own conscience (vv. 21-23); there was nothing inherently sinful to which the weak brother could object. The danger for the strong brother was his attitude: to show contempt for the weak (vv. 10, 14-19); there was nothing inherently sinful in the passage which condemned him if he indulged.

Brother Bob Owen has taught otherwise. He maintains that sinful matters were to be considered in the instruction of Romans 14, thus "received," because the "weak brother" thought it was sinful. Hear what he had to say:

> Now the fellow who thought it could be a sin to eat those meats had to look at the other fellow and think he was sinning. Had to. In Rome, the fellow who thought it was a sin to eat any kind of meat would have thought you sinned if you ate a piece of meat. And yet Paul taught them that they should accept one another (Bob Owen, "We Differ, Can We Fellowship?" Concord, NC, Feb. 19, 1995).

Yes, the weak brother thought it was sinful, but his knowledge was faulty (1 Cor. 8:7). The fact that the weak brother thought a practice to be sinful did not make it so! It was a matter of indifference to God whether or not one ate meat (1 Cor. 8:8) and whether or not one observed days (Col. 2:16). It was a matter of indifference to God if one practiced circumcision (1 Cor. 7:19; Gal. 5:6). Eating meats, observing days, and circumcision were all examples of liberties. Liberties are not things commanded, liberties are not things condemned, they are things that are allowed to be practiced or not, depending on personal conscience (1 Cor. 8:9; 10:23).

Some brethren do not like the expression, "Matters of indifference to God." It is precisely that, however. It does not matter to God whether or not one eats meat, observes days, or practices circumcision. One is not made a better Christian either way, and God is indifferent to such things. But, to put this is biblical terms to which none may object, Paul described matters of "liberty" in 1 Corinthians 8:9; 10:23. They were matters of personal conscience (1 Cor. 10:28-29), not commandments or condemnations. Romans 14 discusses matters of liberty, of personal conscience, not sinful matters. With this before us, we can see that it is wrong to put "important doctrinal and moral differences" in Romans 14 and just "receive one another" in the their practice. *We do not practice the same thing* if you mean putting sinful matters in Romans 14.

The next part of this question is: "Well, if you don't put sinful matters in Romans 14, how do you deal with sinful differences in a local church?" This is not a hard question at all, and it is surprising that seasoned Christians do not know the difference.

"Contradictory teachings and practices on important moral and doctrinal questions" are handled in Ephesians 4:11-16; 1 Thessalonians 5:14; 2 Thessalonians 3:5-6; Jude 22-23, etc. There is a vast difference between one defending a false teacher (as Ed Harrell did with Homer Hailey) and edifying a babe in Christ who has recently obeyed the gospel and is untaught on many (even sinful) issues. *Neither support for false teachers nor edifying untaught babes in Christ should be put in Romans 14.* However, such widely disparate brethren are not ignored in Scripture. Thankfully, God has addressed the proper manner in which to deal with teachers of error even while edifying untaught brethren. Careful attention to the truth will provide the answer which has escaped those advocating unity-in-diversity.

The Lord has provided a local church with the ability to bring its members to a "unity of the faith and the knowledge of the Son of God, to a perfect man, to the measure of the stature of the fulness of Christ" (Eph. 4:13). This is done by the structure given to the local church (vv. 11-12), for the "equipping of the saints." Yes, it is true that in any growing church there might be babes in Christ, the ignorant and untaught, as well as the rebel and false teacher. Within the framework of a local church at work, God has made provision for edification, for perfection, for "instruction in righteousness" (2 Tim. 3:16-17), as the word of God is brought to bear in their lives. When the truth is fully taught, it brings pressure to bear on all who hear it. Preach the truth from the pulpit. Preach the truth in classes. Preach the truth "publicly and from house to house" (Acts 20:20). The "whole counsel of God" leaves no person behind. Babes in Christ will be brought to maturity, to perfection. The ignorant will be taught. The rebel and false teacher will be disciplined and brought to repentance or cast out.

This is all done with patience, longsuffering, and love, but "contradictory teachings and practices on important moral and doctrinal questions" are not tolerated, received and accepted into the fellowship with an open-ended, never ceasing fellowship. *We do not practice the same thing!* Unity-in-diversity is willing to put "important doctrinal and moral differences" in Romans 14 and "receive one another." The unity of the Spirit accepts that there will be "contradictory teachings and practices on important moral and doctrinal questions," but they are placed in the context of a growing church that utilizes the word of God, through its God-given structure, to bring people to maturity and perfection, to repentance, or to discipline and withdrawal. This is a vital difference between unity-in-diversity and the unity of the Spirit. Notice this distinction in the chart on the following page.

Accentuate the positive-Eliminate the negative. Serving as a thematic for *Christianity Magazine,* this catch-phrase became the vanguard for unity-in-diversity. From the first issue to the last, notice was served that no dissension was to be allowed when controversial subjects were discussed. It was the policy of the paper that few Scriptures were to be used in each article, but that pithy journalism was to be the norm. Restrictions were placed upon "reproving, rebuking, and exhorting" (2 Tim. 4:2) by an editorial policy that put an emphasis on a "positive" gospel. False teachers found an open door for their writings so long as they "accentuated the positive" and did not include the false teachers' error in the articles. Predictably, the non-controversial policy of the paper was controversial itself. But more to the point, a rejection of the "whole counsel" of God (Acts 20:27) made it impossible for the journal to deal completely with issues that affect sinful people. Coupled with Ed Harrell's defense of Homer Hailey and his proposal for unity-in-diversity in "contradictory teachings and practices on important moral and doctrinal questions," along with the stony silence of his fellow-editors, a wholesale approach for apostasy was put into place.

Beyond the magazine itself, the attitude of "accentuate the positive and eliminate the negative" has changed the complexion of preaching that is demanded in many churches. Preachers are constantly challenged to be more "positive" and less "negative." A heritage from *Christianity Magazine* is the tendency for members to excoriate plain and bold preaching. It is anathema for a preacher to identify false teachers by name, to preach against sin, to deal with issues. Now, brethren want shorter sermons, sermons with more jokes and anecdotal tales, sermons that make one "feel good about oneself." *Christianity Magazine* cannot escape its legacy: it has fostered weak preaching and a thematic that is the death knell of gospel preaching that includes the whole counsel of God. It has been the handmaiden to unity-in-diversity.

Unity of the Spirit	Unity of the Spirit	Unity-in-Diversity
"Contradictory teachings and practices on important moral and doctrinal questions."	Matters of indifference to God; Liberties; Matters of Personal Conscience (Rom. 14:1-15:7)	"Contradictory teachings and practices on important moral and doctrinal questions."
The Practice No fellowship (Eph. 5:11; 2 John 9-11; Rom. 13:12-14; 16:17-18).	**The Practice** Open ended, never-ending fellowship.	**The Practice** Open ended, never-ending fellowship. Toleration.
Things Considered Inherently sinful practices; Things commanded or forbidden.	**Things Considered** "Clean," "Good," "Pure" (Rom. 14:14, 16, 20). Matters of authorized liberty.	**Things Considered** Inherently sinful practices; Things commanded or forbidden.
How to React With love and patience, bring to maturity, repentance, knowledge or withdrawal (Eph. 4:11-16; 2 Tim. 3:16-17; Jude 3, 22-23; 1 Thess. 5:14).	**How to React** Receive one another. Do not judge one another. Be fully convinced in own mind. Do not violate conscience. Do not bind where God has not bound. Do not cause brother to stumble (Rom. 14:1-15:7).	**How to React** Receive one another (Rom. 14:1).
Result Sin is purged, knowledge is increased, church is purified.	**Result** Personal consciences are respected; peace and harmony continues.	**Result** Sin continues; leaven influences whole lump (1 Cor. 5:6-7).
Unity of the Spirit	**Unity of the Spirit**	**Unity-in-Diversity**

Destroy the opposition by castigation and vilification. It is absolutely amazing what things are done under the guise of unity, in the name of Christ, under the banner of love. Because some of us have opposed unity-in-diversity, those who advocate it have resorted to the role of assassins, murder by slander, and wanton fratricidal attacks. Calls for open discussion are met with derision and scorn. Motives are questioned and spot-less reputations are besmirched rather than keeping doors open for broth-erly avenues of study. It is worthwhile to note that this has been one-sided. Among those who oppose unity-in-diversity, there is a willingness to meet and discuss the issues that separate us. There has been no rush to name-calling. While those who favor unity-in-diversity have been named openly, it has been with respect and kindness. We want unity to continue. We want open discussion of the growing number of issues that are acceptable to unity advocates. We want to continue as brethren.

But we are met with vilification. The type of language used against us includes:

> "A pack of snarling curs, suspicious and paranoid, biting, snarling and snapping in all directions. . ." ". . .a paranoid frenzy of biting and devour-ing one another. . ." ". . . slander in the name of the gospel. . ." ". . . journalistic and pulpit jingoism. . ." (Paul Earnhart, "Watch Them Dogs," *CM*, July 1996; *With All Boldness,* Dec. 1996).

> "Extremists who have their own cause to promote. . ." ". . . reckless and irresponsible. . ." (Editor's Report, *CM*, Nov. 1992).

> "Unrighteous and dishonorable. . ." ". . . sectarianism," "jingoists"(Harry Pickup, Jr., University Heights, Lexington, KY, July 14, 1998; Forest Hills, Tampa, FL, Dec. 1998, Q&A session, audio tape); "scavengers" "looking for carrion," "perennial gossips and fault-finders (often 'nit-pickers'), vultures," "unreasonable scrupulosity," "witch hunters" and "brotherhood inquisitors" (James Adams, *With All Boldness,* July 1996, 5; *Ibid.*, August 1994, 1-2).

Such language against brethren has never been retracted and hangs as an impediment against future relationships. While some have reported that private statements from some brethren have expressed regrets about such volatile language, nothing as public as the pronouncements has ever been stated. If, indeed, regret exists that brethren have been so pilloried, it would be most helpful for apologies to be extended in plain terms. Such would go a long way toward opening doors that are now slammed shut.

Brethren, doors need to be opened. Discussions need to resume. Issues need to be examined in the light of God's word. While we are aware of the vicious name-calling such as that listed above, it will not be returned in kind. We are brethren and will continue as brethren until doors are com-pletely shut and locked against us. We hope such will not be the case and offer every opportunity to meet with disputants and talk. We will do it formally in debates, if that is desired. We will meet informally in small groups or one-to-one, as opportunity presents itself. We see a growing distance between those advocating unity-in-diversity and those who oppose it. Before we reach that sectarian plateau of irretrievable division, let us make every effort to open doors, not close them. Let us call one another brethren, not vile names. Let us remember the Lord who bought us and "do unto others as we would have them do unto us" (Matt. 7:12).

Conclusion

In our generation, unity-in-diversity is a growing danger. It is not going away unless and until faithful brethren meet it head on and defeat it by the unity of the Spirit. It is part and parcel of the thinking of the religious world at large, but it has not always been a part of churches of Christ. We hear some say that "you watchdogs" are doing it all wrong, that we are "too unloving and unkind." Clearly, we understand that Jesus was the only Master Teacher and that he said everything perfectly, with the right attitude and at the right time. It may be that many of us have made mistakes in our approach to issues. But if every "watchdog" and "jingoist" died today, the problem of unity-in-diversity would still be here. The problem of easy divorce will still be here. The problem of a changing church that does not like bold preaching will still be here. The problems of worldliness, materialism, itching ears, soft preaching, and many other of Satan's devices will still be here if we disappear.

What are you going to do about it? If I, and my brethren, have done it all wrong, will you take up the challenge and do it right? Where is your voice speaking out against the evils of divorce and those who advocate it? Where is your voice crying out against unity-in-diversity? Where is your voice speaking out against fellowship with "contradictory teachings and practices on important moral and doctrinal questions"? If you do speak out, you may find yourself vilified, as we have been. To be sure, there is room in the kingdom of God for different voices, with different styles, who, at different times, deal with sin and Satan. If it is a matter of judgment as to how and how much sin is opposed, why is your judgment better than ours? But if your judgment is better, we will not strive about methods and details. You will be gladly received as you add your voice to those already in the battle.

The Creation Issue and the Authority of Scripture

Daniel H. King, Sr.

If you have made a study of the book of Job, you are well aware that Job 32:6-10 represents a transition in the material of the debate.

Young Elihu had listened carefully and patiently while Job's friends accused him of evil despite his godly life, and while Job (not able to discover any better solution to the problem of his suffering) accused God of unfairness in his dispensing of justice and punishment. Elihu here declares that human wisdom, gained by experience and by the passing of years, is inferior to "the breath of the Almighty," which he declares "giveth them understanding." So, "it is not the great that are wise, nor the aged that understand." Job's young associate declares that divine revelation is superior to man's speculations about such high matters.

God-Breathed Scripture Furnishes Completely, Then, Now, and Always

Friends, it is that critical distinction which makes the difference in all human opinions. The differentiation Elihu made is one we must make also. Job and his three friends were frustrated without the benefit of it in their wrestlings with spiritual questions. We will also find ourselves "running around in circles chasing our tails" if we permit such distractions to avert our attention from what God-breathed Scripture says and to fix our eyes upon some other object than its lofty wisdom.

Paul spoke of "Holy Scripture" which is "able to make thee wise unto salvation," which is "God-breathed" and "profitable for teaching, reproof, correction, for instruction which is in righteousness, that the man of God may be complete, furnished completely unto every good work" (2 Tim. 3:15-17). It was the answer for his age, and it is the answer for our own.

Is God-breathed Scripture the true, the real, the actual formative basis of our opinions on a given issue? Or, is our opinion, our position, our stance based upon other considerations? Are we, even unwittingly, being forced into the mold of our own particular culture, and the straightjacket of the intellectual assumptions of our time? Unquestionably, in every age some are.

We could certainly argue, for example, that Gnostics and Docetists of the early centuries of the church were being influenced by the intellectual presuppositions of their time when they created an apostate religious movement that troubled the church for several centuries. The apostle John lived long enough to write in opposition to their perverse teachings, but not long enough to see the full fruition of their absurd speculations. Their theologies involved complex philosophical beliefs that were in vogue at the time and were inconsistent with traditional Christianity. In the end they chose the contemporary culture over God-breathed Scripture. John blasted them with the plain truth that they were "not of God," but "of the world," and the "world heareth them" (1 John 4:3, 5).

We could just as readily establish, of course, the same phenomenon in the form of reticence on the part of religious folk to accept scientific facts, which are wholly consistent with the Bible but inconsistent with religious presuppositions that have no basis in biblical truth. Galileo's experiences with the Roman church are illustrative. But this fact is often used as "cover fire" for those who would push scientific theories as truth, when in reality they are no more than faddish guesses about things which science is not equipped to address.

In both of these instances, however, God-breathed Scripture was given a back seat to other factors: in the first case, precedence was given to philosophical or theosophical prejudices, in the second, to religious traditions of human origin. Both are condemned by the Word of God in many different places, but nowhere more specifically or forcefully than in Paul's renunciation of these spiritual alternatives found in Colossians 2:8. There he wrote: "Take heed lest there shall be any one that maketh spoil of you through his philosophy and vain deceit, after the tradition of men, after the rudiments of the world, and not after Christ."

The bottom line is that faithfulness to God-breathed Scripture is equated with faithfulness to Jesus Christ, and disrespect for Scripture is equated with disrespect for God and his Son.

Rethinking Our Approach to Scripture:
A Sign of the Times and A Sign of Apostasy

Some will immediately cry "Foul!" when we make the connection regarding our views of Scripture over the creation issue. The opposition will no doubt ascribe our differences to matters of opinion and of spiritual indifference. On the part of some that may actually be the case. But nothing could be further from the truth or more apparent than this in a few instances, in spite of the hue and cry that may arise when the issue is raised.

Historically, it is the general softening of attitudes toward Scripture and how it is to be viewed which makes way for any "new reading" of the Bible regarding fundamental issues of faith and practice in the church. This is a fact that is so obvious and clear-cut that it needs no real proving.

Every past apostasy has been attended by some sort of re-evaluation or rethinking of how Scripture ought to be approached, how it should be read, or how it is to be applied. Apostasy needs justification, and that justification can only come from Scripture. So, Scripture must be approached in a different manner than formerly, or read in a different way than before, or applied differently than previous generations of faithful Christians have tended to apply it. This is a clear mark of apostasy as it develops in any age. However, it needs to be noted that it always begins in a subtle way and over several decades becomes ever more obvious and grossly offensive in its methodology.

Over the last several years numerous warnings have been sounded by men of good reputation and long experience in the body of Christ. The thrust of their words of caution have been identical to the old adage from a past generation, "Brethren, we are drifting."

These words of caution have not been taken seriously by most of our brethren in the non-institutional churches of Christ. In fact, words of scorn and derision have been heaped upon these veteran preachers. Many of these men lived through the last division, and again are seeing many of the identical attitudes being demonstrated which made way for those departures from the New Testament pattern of faith and action which proliferated in the churches a half century or so ago.

This is to be expected. Paul warned that when apostate movements begin, the first order of business is to sweep aside those conservative influences that present obstacles to the "new order of things." He wrote, "The one who now holds it back will continue to do so till he is taken out of the way" (2 Thess. 2:7, NIV).

Along with the other associated problems which arise during such momentous and yet troubling times, there is the inevitable "rereading" and "rethinking" of our approach to Scripture. The subtlety of this process can at first be deceiving because it is not being trumpeted from the pulpits in just those terms. It is rather evident to the discerning ear and eye in the form of changing attitudes and disturbing nuances of language and questionable actions. Something seems not to be quite right, but it is difficult to put one's finger on it specifically. And then an issue arises which brings it all out into the open. The "creation days" discussion is precisely such an issue. Now we can put our finger on it.

Creation Days and Scriptural Authority

Momentarily, let us return to our original proposition: What has made us distinctive as a people is our obsessive adherence to the Bible as our authority in all matters religious. God-breathed Scripture furnishes us completely unto every good work. "God said it, I believe it, that settles it." Argumentation, attempted justification, or reasoning which does not begin and end with Scripture is vacuous, empty, and a waste of time and energy. Worse than that, it may prove to be a veiled effort to provide cover fire for modernism as it erects its tent among us.

Any view set forth in our midst that challenges that basic approach to Scripture is bound to lead to alienation, and eventually, division among us. Paul declared that it is an heartbreaking inevitability: "There must be also factions among you, that those who are approved may be made manifest among you" (1 Cor. 11:19). This is most unfortunate, but unavoidable. As Amos said, "How can two men walk together except they be agreed?" (Amos 3:3).

It is precisely that sort of thing that has characterized the controversy over the creation. Those who ought to know better, and assuredly have done better in the past, have spewed forth the most vacuous rhetoric that one may imagine. Men who are accustomed to giving book, chapter, and verse for their religious faith and practice, and who have demanded the same from denominational preachers and priests — suddenly have become carbon-copies of the very spiritual weaklings whom they once opposed.

But now, let's allow you to be the judge. Consider in your own mind the following quotations from those who are pressing for alternative views of the creation to be embraced, or at least tolerated among us. Is this the sort of approach to God-breathed Scripture which the movement to restore New Testament Christianity has promoted for the past 200 years? And if it is not, then does it not undercut the centrality and authoritative nature of the Holy Bible? I aver that it does.

Together, let's meander through the "poppy fields of poppycock" through which many of us have had to wade in the last three years. Note just a few select quotations from the rationalizations and justifications of those who are promoting this new openness to "creation alternatives." Time and space will permit only a sampling from the literature.

The Big Bang

Hill Roberts has likely become the most conspicuous name associated with this issue. In our brotherhood Hill had been a controversial figure for a number of years, but came to be the center of this particular storm after his invitation to speak at the Florida College lectures in 1999.

Brother Roberts is convinced that God used the Big Bang as his *modus operandi* for creating the material universe. In our Open Letter (written in response to Hill's invitation and the Florida College faculty and administration's staunch self-justification) we provided proof from Hill's essays that he is a proponent of this notion. On page 7 of *Genesis and the Time Thing*, Hill asks the reader to "consider just how much of Genesis 1 is paralleled by empirical data using the premise that Genesis 1 is true, but very simplified." Of the first four similarities suggested, Brother Roberts cites Big Bang supporting hypotheses as his corroborating "empirical data." He then notes the following on page 18:

> This **Big Bang theory is now the standard explanation** for how the energy and matter resulting from the beginning came to be distributed as it is today. . . . **Genesis affirms the fact of the beginning but not the process**. Therefore there can be no conflict between Genesis and science as to process. However, the physical data does argue strongly for a beginning consistent with Genesis. In this, **the data supporting the Big Bang theory is the Bible believer's friend and the atheists' nemesis**.

According to Hill "Genesis 1 is true, but very simplified." He informs us that Genesis "affirms the fact of the beginning but not the process." His conclusion is, "Therefore there can be no conflict between Genesis and science as to process." So, in the thinking of Hill Roberts, whatever scientific theory is in vogue at any juncture in history cannot possibly conflict with or contradict anything in Genesis 1! Whatever the evolutionists cook up, now or in the future, should give us no cause for alarm.

At every turn, brother Roberts reshapes the creation account in Genesis 1 to fit this evolutionary, humanistic, godless theory of the origin of the inanimate universe. The biblical account is made to "fit" the theory by the insertion of vast amounts of time between the "days" of the narrative. Furthermore, in doing so, he makes ample use of the writings of theistic evolutionists like Hugh Ross and others, evidencing both where his affections lie and from whence he derives his ideas.

What is the authority here? Is the Bible the authority, or does Hill derive his authority from scientific speculations about the origin of the inanimate universe and the compromising theories of other theistic evolutionists? You be the judge.

Do You Believe In Evolution?

The *Huntsville Times* (Sept. 23, 2000) Religion Editor Yvonne Betowt reported regarding a "Skeptics Forum" held by the Reasons to Believe group in their city, beginning the article with these two paragraphs:

> Did God create the heaven and the Earth as it says in the first verse of Genesis? Or, was there a "Big Bang" in which the universe was set into motion? Or, could it have been a little of both?

> When people ask me if I believe in evolution, I reply, "Yes, no and maybe," said Dr. Hill Roberts, a local physicist and a deacon at Weatherly Road Church of Christ *(Local Group Hopes to Bring Science and Faith Together: Scientists, Tech Workers in Reasons to Believe Hold "Sceptics Forum")*.

We might note as an aside, that Hill does not have a doctorate, and he is now an elder at Weatherly Road; it seems that the church there has seen fit to reward him with the title of a "shepherd" of that flock since this firestorm of controversy has surrounded him. It is just this sort of double-speak that has put Hill into hot water all around the nation. We would inquire of the reader: Does this sort of talk conform to Paul's admonition in his writings to Timothy: "Hold the pattern of sound words, which thou has heard from me . . ." (2 Tim. 1:13); or, "If any man teacheth a different doctrine, and consenteth not to sound words, even the words of our Lord Jesus Christ, and to the doctrine which is according to godliness, he is puffed up, knowing nothing" (1 Tim. 6:3-5); and, finally, "O Timothy, guard that which is committed unto thee, turning away from the profane babblings and oppositions of the knowledge (science) which is falsely so called; which some professing have erred concerning the faith" (1 Tim. 6:20-21)?

Brother Roberts bristles when he is alluded to as a "theistic evolutionist." But his own words betray him. He cannot say "No, no, no!" He says, "Yes, no, and maybe." This is the reply of a theistic evolutionist, irrespective of whatever else he may say.

Primary Revelation of God Through Nature

Brother Roberts also has much to say about the concept of God's special revelation through nature. He describes it as God's "primary revelation from God in that area":

> Where we have failed when it comes to biblical contexts concerning nature is to ignore the exceptions above by excluding the primary revelation from God in that area — nature itself (*Genesis and the Time Thing,* 15).

Thus, the supposed revelation in the rocks is given precedence over the written revelation from the Bible in understanding the creation. When an apparent conflict exists, brother Roberts accepts the interpretations of current scientific thought as literal and makes the literal statements of the Holy Spirit figurative. How far afield this is from the normative scriptural attitude regarding such matters, is illustrated by the following texts: "Open thou mine eyes, that I may behold wondrous things out of thy law" (Ps. 119:18); "I have more understanding than all my teachers; for thy testimonies are my meditation. I understand more than the aged, because I have kept thy precepts. I have refrained my feet from every evil way, that I might observe thy word" (Ps. 119:99-101); "Through thy precepts I get understanding: Therefore I hate every false way" (Ps. 119:104); "My heart standeth in awe of thy words" (Ps. 119:161); "The sum of thy word is truth; and everyone of thy righteous ordinances endureth forever" (Ps. 119:160); "Thy law is truth" (Ps. 119:142); "Sanctify them through thy truth; thy word is truth" (John 17:17).

Again, you are the judge: Is Holy Scripture given precedence in Hill's argument, or something else? Where does the authority lie with Roberts and those who agree with him?

Natural Action Over Vast Eons of Time
Made the Physical Earth

Brother Roberts claims that, after the initial "Big Bang," natural action over vast eons of time made the physical earth. His article, "A Harmonization of God's Genesis Revelation with His Natural Revelation," details this concept paralleling the doctrine of uniformitarianism. He repeatedly speaks of the changes needed to the Earth's initial state as "a blob of clay-gas" hot from the Big Bang which must be "cooled" and "stabilized" by natural means over vast periods of time so that it could be prepared for God's next action (1-6).

What is his authority for these vast periods of time? It is certainly not the Bible, because it says just the opposite: the time was brief for creation in the Bible, just six days.

Again, quoting from our Open Letter, "The psalmist declared that, 'By the word of Jehovah were the heavens made, and all the host of them by the breath of His mouth' (Ps. 33:6). Did God speak his will and then let the natural forces take over and accomplish it through natural, uniformitarian change over billions of years? No! The following words of the psalmist preclude such an interpretation: 'For He spake, and it was done; He commanded, and it stood fast' (Ps. 33:9)."

We could go on with many other quotations from the pen of Hill Roberts dealing with the Universal Flood, "gradual" miracles, the historicity of Adam and Eve, etc., but all of this has been treated extensively in the available literature, written by many fine preachers and Bible scholars. The simple fact is, that brother Roberts deals heavily in speculation and at every turn attempts a *rapprochement* with scientific theory at the expense of the biblical text. In all of this the Bible takes a back seat to theistic evolutionary presuppositions.

Justification of the Hill Roberts Invitation at Florida College
When Florida College was questioned about its choice of Hill Roberts as a speaker at the 1999 lectureship, brother Ferrell Jenkins was chosen as chief spokesman to reply, since he was at the time the head of the Bible department. Ferrell pled ignorance regarding many of Hill's views, and then noted two particulars: (1) The school does not claim to agree with every speaker on every lectureship, and (2) The invitation actually resulted in good, because it led to brethren studying these questions.

To a certain degree we could of course sympathize with Ferrell's first point. It is indeed unrealistic to expect any school to endorse everything that anyone they invite as a speaker might possibly believe. This does not, however, leave the school or the Bible department with no obligation at all regarding such things. And this certainly does not clear the way for them to invite anyone to speak no matter what his views are on anything. No false teacher ought to be invited unless his views are under review by faithful men and he is being given the opportunity to respond (Eph. 5:11; 2 John 9-11). Nor can it be justified on the basis that it provides "education" on these issues. If this is an appropriate justification, then all false teachers should be invited to Florida College all the time. We would all be appropriately challenged and get a really good education in false doctrine then!

Given this assumption, Timothy could have invited Hymenaeus and Philetus (2 Tim. 2:17, 18) to Ephesus to discuss "The Home" (or perhaps, "using advanced technology to reach a skeptical world") and then rejoiced when the church was thus offered the opportunity to discuss whether "the resurrection is past already" for the next three years (as we have been doing since the Hill Roberts speech at Florida College)!

Does this kind of justification of our actions elevate the Bible in our thinking? Or, does it make some of us take it less seriously?

Taking Genesis 1 at Face Value Is A Mere Prejudice

While stating in his speech that he believed in a six consecutive twenty-four hour day creation period, Ferrell left many questions unanswered. Because he wanted to leave plenty of room for alternative views of the creation, he placed his convictions about the matter in the realm of his "prejudices." He said:

> I want to start this morning by giving you my prejudices. I want to give you what I believe about this subject so you'll know where I'm coming from, as the old expression goes. I believe that God created the heavens and the earth. I believe that. I am inclined to think that this was in six periods of 24 hours each, just like we've got an hour here today. But I recognize some problems with this view and I'm not going to go into all of those ("Making Sense of the Days of Creation," 2000 Florida College Lectures, 2).

It is strange indeed to hear the Bible being taken at face value, and then to describe that as mere "prejudice." On the other hand, brother Jenkins' view of the creation days clearly is not as settled as it might be, for he admits that he recognizes "some problems with this view." What are these problems to which he refers? Why does he not go into them?

What other critical issues would brother Jenkins classify as among his "prejudices"? Is the notion that the Bible is inerrant a "prejudice"? Does he also see problems with it? I do not mean to imply that Ferrell would feel this way about inerrancy. But the very fact that he has so conveniently fitted so important an issue as the creation of the universe in the time span described by the author of Genesis into the category of one's "prejudices" and that he sees problems with taking the text as it is written, gives us pause to ask, "What other issues would he fit into this same category and refuse to take a solid stand about, because he 'sees problems'?"

Does this kind of talk lift up Scripture in our thinking? Or are we left wondering about what sort of authority it possesses to speak to our age or any other about this controversy?

Days of Genesis 2 Cannot Be Literal

In *Sentry* magazine (Vol. 21, No. 1), brother Shane Scott argued the case for the Day-Age Theory of Creation. He said, "Some Bible believers insist that the world, according to Genesis 1, was created in six twenty-four hour days. I believe, however, that the days of Genesis 1 should not be interpreted literally." The next section of his article was entitled, "The Days Cannot Be Literal."

In his article in *Sentry*, on his web site, as well as in discussion with others, brother Scott maintained his view that brother Roberts' timetable of the universe being about 15 billion years old and the earth being 4+ billion years old is in complete harmony with the Scriptures.

In the same essay, Shane also affirmed, "What happened on the fourth day was that the sun, moon, and stars became visible to the earth's surface." However, to brother Scott, that is not a literal fourth day, but a fourth group of vast ages. When he affirms that the earth's atmosphere changed over long ages to become clear enough for the sun, moon, and stars to be visible, what is the basic assumption? It is the same assumption made by brother Roberts — uniformitarian change over vast amounts of time by natural law to account for the present order of the physical universe.

Brother Scott cannot find justification for such affirmations in Scripture itself. There is nothing in all the Word of God that makes reference to such long aeons of time. The only way on the face of this earth to read Genesis 1 and maintain that the days of that chapter "cannot be literal" is to approach the text assuming evolutionists are correct when they posit the universe is astoundingly old. In other words, you must *bring this assumption to the text. You cannot read it out of the text! That is eisogesis (the opposite of exegesis), and it always makes the Bible secondary to other considerations.*

Men Who Signed the Open Letter
Intend to Divide the Church

The remarks of Tom Couchman would not be taken seriously by most of us, except that his material has been published on the *Bibleworld.com* web site of Ferrell Jenkins, so is very clearly viewed as valuable by Ferrell and others.

Brother Couchman's remarks are both judgmental and unkind, and unbecoming of any child of God, but they are indicative of the sentiments of a number of people, or else they would not have been publicized. Apparently brother Jenkins, in particular, agrees with these sentiments since he posted them on his web site. Couchman wrote:

> I cannot see why anyone who values unity would participate in a discussion initiated for the express purpose of dividing brethren over an issue which has nothing to do with obedience to the gospel message, the imita-

tion of Christ or the ministry of the New Testament church. . . . To the NT
requirements for salvation and fraternity, the Sixty-Seven have with absolutely no authority from Scripture, added the acceptance of their interpretation of Genesis 1-2 ("A Response to the Creation Account and Florida
College," page 1, paragraph 4; page 2, paragraph 2).

Couchman wishes to avoid an honorable discussion of issues by doing two
things: (1) Judging the motives of those preachers who signed the Open
Letter (Imagine the assumption contained in this allegation: Sixty-seven
preachers have gotten together and decided to divide the church! Somehow or other, I missed that meeting!), (2) Charging sixty-seven preachers
with making their interpretation of Genesis 1-2 a requirement of salvation. It
is nothing short of amazing to see brother Couchman ascribing to himself
divine attributes, since only God can know what is in the hearts of men.

Speaking for myself, though, I can assure him that I have no interest in
causing division in the church. The Open Letter was intended to stop division by making others aware that we were not willing to stand by quietly
and allow such doctrine to be taught without fighting it fiercely and openly.
For those who signed the letter this matter is not one of indifference, and
none of his judgmental and insulting remarks will make it so, nor will they
silence us.

As to the latter point, quite frankly, I was under the impression there was
no part of Sacred Scripture that could be misapplied without the "twister"
being in dire jeopardy. Peter said that when the ignorant and unsteadfast
"wrest" or "twist" the Scriptures, they do so "unto their own destruction"
(see 2 Pet. 3:16).

What Couchman's material represents ideologically is a move away from
honest discussion of issues and open debate of differences toward insult,
hateful speech, name-calling, and a reprehensible judging of motives, all
of which does no honor to anyone. It certainly does not move us closer to
the Bible or show much respect for its absolute authority. It is, however,
indicative of a weak position scripturally and logically.

The same sort of unkindness and hateful speech, along with judging of
motives and misrepresentation of positions, is apparent in the article by
Bill Robinson, Jr. titled "The 29th Question and Beyond." Robinson says
the real problem here is an "age of the earth" issue, when the Open Letter
specifically declared that it was not. He says the letter is "an instrument
that undermined the all-sufficiency of the scripture whether intentional or
not. Both instruments are trying to define the lines of fellowship and as

such (whether intended or not) are attempts to say 'line up' or else. Furthermore, the 'Open Letter' like the questionnaire smacks of partyism." Then, to cover what is a transparent fallacy in his own reasoning that almost anyone would readily detect, he attempts to say that he is not opposed to us asking questions about such matters: "No one is opposed to asking questions any more than one is opposed to writing a reasoned and rational critique of another's position." As the old saying goes, "O consistency, thou art a jewel!" The Lord said, "By thy words shalt thou be justified, and by thy words shalt thou be condemned" (Matt. 12:37). His own words are the best refutation of his position.

Brother Robinson knows that John was suggesting just such questions be directed at those who denied that Jesus had come in the flesh in 1 John 4:2, 3. How else could they have "confessed" one way or the other? If brethren then were to ask questions in order to determine whether someone was sound in faith or "lined up" with the heretics, there is nothing unscriptural about our doing so today. The truth of the matter is that brother Bill is sensitive about this issue because he agrees in the main with Shane Scott about his view of the creation and resents our vocal opposition to their theory. He told me as much in a telephone conversation a year and a half ago. All of the rest of this is mere window-dressing!

Another Florida College Bible Teacher Goes On Record Defending Evolutionist's Assumptions on the Creation Days

We do not have the time here to summarize the arguments made by Phil Roberts in the private summer study program at Florida College last year sponsored by Harry Pickup Jr., but we do recommend that you read our responses to his materials published in *Watchmanmag.com* in the December issue of 2001 and January of 2002 (Vol. 4, No. 12; Vol. 5, No. 1).

Phil, a brother to Hill Roberts, valiantly defended his brother's position at the study. Now this ought to surprise many people. They have defended the Florida College Bible Faculty, saying that Hill's views were his own and were not shared by the members of the Faculty. Further, they have contended that the Bible faculty was ignorant of Hill's views when they invited him to speak at the school. It is rather hard to swallow this notion now that we know Hill's brother is on the faculty and defends the doctrine he holds. These folks were wrong. In our response to Phil's lecture presentation (we had access only to the outlines and charts), we summarized the written materials as follows:

> Phil divides his rationalization for accepting alternative approaches to
> the literal view of creation into several parts. First, he questions whether

the normal sense of the word "day" is confined to a literal 24 hour time period. Next, he protests our contention that the use of the word *yom* with numbers indicates the "days" of Genesis 1 must be consecutive 24 hour days. Third, he challenges the idea that the qualifying phrases surrounding the word "day" indicate that it is used in the sense of a 24 hour day. Fourth, he doubts that usage of the word elsewhere in Scripture indicates that the days must be literal and consecutive. Fifth, he suggests that contextual clues may be indicative of unusual usage of the word by the writer. Finally, brother Roberts makes the case that non-literal interpretations of the days of the creation account predate the rise of modern views about the age of the earth ("Genealogies, Genesis and the Days of Creation: Responding to Florida College Bible Teacher Phil Roberts; Phil's View of Days").

We went on to comment that "It is obvious from such sophisticated argumentation as brother Roberts sets forth in these documents, that he is squarely in the camp of those who refuse to believe the Genesis account of creation is literal. Clearly he wishes these words and phrases to have something else in mind than a series of consecutive 24 hour days.

There is little wonder that the Bible faculty at Florida College was so unmoved by the strong popular sentiment against Hill Roberts' invitation to speak at the school and Shane Scott's retention as a teacher in the Bible department — apparently there were others on the Bible department who shared their views. . . . Now we know that one of those people was Phil Roberts.

The Plain Sense of Scripture
One of the most disturbing aspects of Phil Robert's presentation came in the form of his paper on "Do You Accept The Literal Sense?" Phil persisted in his argument against believing the Genesis account of creation is to be taken literally with evidence which he gleaned from two passages. Regarding Genesis 1:7 and Joshua 10:12-13, he wrote, "What would a person who knew nothing about modern astronomy assume that the passages were saying? What is the 'plain sense' of the passages? Would somebody who rejected the 'plain sense' in favor of an interpretation adjusted to fit modern knowledge of astronomy be a false teacher?"

From the book of Joshua, brother Roberts cited 10:12-13 to assert, "This passage was the primary proof-text against Copernicus and his theory that the earth revolved around the sun rather than the sun revolving around the earth. Copernicus was condemned as a heretic." Then, Phil quotes Genesis 1:7, "And God made the firmament, and divided the waters which were under the firmament from the waters which were above the firmament." Regarding this text he promulgates an extensive argument which we shall attempt to summarize. He says that "flood geologists generally, and at least one brother who has written extensively and prominently on the necessity of interpreting the days of Genesis literally, say that this verse may be describing a vast blanket of water vapor encompassing the earth prior to the flood. But that is not at all what the Bible says, at least not in the plain-sense natural interpretation of the words. The Bible says that the firmament was something that separated between bodies of water, with water below and water above (Genesis 1:7). Furthermore, the Bible says that the sun, moon, and stars are located in that firmament (Genesis 1:14, 15, 17)" (Phil Roberts, *Further Notes on the Firmament*).

Brother Roberts continues, "Flood geologists and the brother cited above reject that interpretation for an explanation that, according to the evidence we have, would never have occurred to anyone prior to the time of the Copernican revolution in astronomy. Only since the time of Copernicus have people generally understood (some ancient Greeks excepted) that the sun and stars stand at such a great distance from the earth, and that there is no vault holding back some reservoir of waters beyond. Indeed this understanding of the firmament as a domed vault holding back the waters above was the standard interpretation right down to just before modern times." After offering a few illustrations of this point, he persists: "No doubt someone who proposed that there was no reservoir of waters out beyond the sun, moon, and stars would have been denounced as a heretic who just refused to accept the plain sense of the Bible. But the discoveries of modern science have ruled that possibility out for those of us who believe that the Bible is the word of God" (*Ibid.*).

Does brother Roberts intend for us to believe that "the plain sense of the Bible" is that "the firmament was something that separated between bodies of water," "that the sun, moon, and stars are located in that firmament," "that the sun, moon, and stars were relatively close to the earth — somewhere up in the sky just beyond the clouds," that it was "a domed vault holding back the waters above," and "that there is a reservoir of waters out beyond the sun, moon, and stars"? Are we to believe that "all these people were accepting the text in its plain-sense, natural meaning, at least as they understood it" when they believed these gross scientific errors? Please do not accuse me of misrepresenting our brother, for each of these is a direct quotation of his own words!

Can one honestly say that when he reads remarks of this kind he is brought to a higher appreciation for the authenticity, integrity, and authority of Holy Scripture? You be the judge.

What Is This Controversy *Really* About?

This entire controversy was never a matter of misrepresentation by radical conservatives, as many have been led to believe by the administration of the college. These men were not innocent of the charges. They believed and taught what was alleged of them. The reason the Bible Department was reluctant to admit wrong was because there were others on the faculty who wished their own views not to be challenged! Ferrell Jenkins was not too confident about his own view that the days were literal and wished others to be able to hold with impunity theories like the ones Shane Scott and Phil Roberts embrace. Moreover, Phil Roberts is able to make an even better case for alternative approaches to Genesis 1 than his brother! He proved that at the private meeting with preachers and Florida College Bible Department staff in Temple Terrace.

In our written response to Phil Roberts, we reminded brother Phil of several principles of biblical interpretation, which he and others have been ignoring as they pressed for toleration of alternative views of the creation narrative. One of those was particularly important, we believe. It was the last one we listed, and quote from our remarks below:

> A final principle of interpretation which is neglected by those who, like Phil and Hill, mishandle the days of the Genesis creation narrative, comes in the form of a warning which goes unheeded as they go about their task. It is found in the work of Walter M. Dunnett. He advises: "Beware of reading modern ideas into a biblical passage. If we 'read into' a text something that is not there, we substitute our own authority for the authority of the author" (*The Interpretation of Holy Scripture: An Introduction to Hermeneutics* 94, 95).

Those who wish to "read into" the text of Genesis 1 the modern view of earth history in order to make it consistent with theories of geology which are current today, and which may be rejected tomorrow, are attempting a compromise which is neither needed nor necessary. Moreover, by so doing "we substitute our own authority for the authority of the author" of Holy Scripture. Is this not what Hill does when he argues for the Big Bang, gradual uniformitarian change of the inanimate creation, stellar evolution, etc.? He "reads into" the Genesis account what cannot be found there. When Phil argues in defense of Hill's postulates, even if he does not agree in every detail with his brother's positions, he makes himself a *"partaker with him"* in his work (2 John 9-11). Tom Couchman and Bill Robinson do likewise as they offer a defense of the errors of Shane Scott and others.

Where Do We Go From Here?

In our estimation it does not look bright for the years ahead. The truth of God is being watered down and compromised in order to conciliate humanistic theories of the origin of the universe. Some very respected men among us have compromised their faith with the theory of evolution. That is a fact. All of the empty rhetoric in the world will not cover it up. Many others are sympathetic toward them; they feel that it will do us no harm. To their minds the real enemies are those of us who are challenging these men whom they love and respect so highly.

I, for one, think they are dead wrong. Only time will "tell the tale," as to who is right. Make no mistake about it, though, the stakes are astronomically high.

But for now, Paul's stern warning to a past generation is worthy of our consideration: "Evil men and imposters shall wax worse and worse, deceiving and being deceived, but abide thou in the things which thou has learned" (2 Tim. 3:13). That was excellent advice to the men of another generation. It would be well for us to heed it also.

Discussions of the Age of the Earth in Restoration History

Steve Wolfgang

Discussions of the age of the earth, arising from various interpretations of the opening chapters of Genesis, have occurred periodically in the history of attempts to restore New Testament Christianity. This paper attempts to chronicle some of those efforts to grapple with the meaning of the opening verses of the Bible by those professing to be "Christians only."

Alexander Campbell

In the fall of 1838, shortly after his 50th birthday celebration, Alexander Campbell left his prosperous farm in Bethany, Virginia, embarking on an extended six-month tour of the southern United States.[1] Accompanied by one of his daughters, he went first to Charlottesville, where he visited Jefferson's home and grave and made contacts at the University of Virginia, to which he would return the following year as an invited speaker. Capitalizing upon his increasing prestige stemming from his Cincinnati debate with Roman Catholic Archbishop Purcell the preceding year, Campbell was contemplating the beginning of his own higher educational enterprise, Bethany College, and used this trip to support efforts to establish it. Following stops in Charleston and Montgomery, Alabama, he wintered in New Orleans before proceeding to the state college, then located at Jackson, where his friend James Shannon was president. Continuing upriver by steamboat, Campbell disembarked at Louisville, where he was met by brethren who accompanied him to Frankfort. Following several other speaking appointments, he came finally to Maysville, where his close friend Walter Scott would spend much of the last part of his life. Just prior to boarding another steamer for the last leg of the trip to Wheeling and up to Bethany, Campbell received an invitation to address the local Lyceum. The soon-to-be college president chose as his topic, "Supernatural Facts."

---

[1] This expedition is recounted in Robert Richardson, *Memoirs of Alexander Campbell* (Philadelphia: J.B. Lippincott & Company, 1868), II:446-462.

In this same address, Campbell rejected not only the popular "nebular hypothesis" of La Place, but also a strictly literal reading of Genesis which demanded 24-hour days of creation.[2] To Campbell, arguing that the Genesis phrase "evening and morning" was necessarily 24 hours was "unwarranted from the Bible" or science. In Campbell's view "the last days of the creation week may have been no more than twenty-four hours . . . (but) the first two or three may have been twenty-four thousand years, for any thing which science or the Bible avers on the subject."[3] In the fashion of true Baconian science, so popular in his day, Campbell would not be theory-driven to any conclusions not clearly discerned in nature or Scripture.[4]

Fully twenty years later, during the 1859-1860 academic year, Campbell delivered a series of Lectures on the Pentateuch to Bethany College students. In the course of these addresses, he argued that the description in Genesis 1 of the Spirit of God moving upon the face of the waters before

---

[2] Campbell, "Supernatural Facts," *Popular Lectures and Addresses* (Philadelphia: James Challen & Son, 1864), 152-153. Campbell also included some reflections on science in his address at New Athens College in 1838 ("Literature, Science, and Art," *PLA*, 125-141); see also Campbell's "Is Moral Philosophy an Inductive Science?" in *PLA*, 95-124.

[3] In so arguing, Campbell in many ways was following the scientific thought of his age, particularly in the case of Isaac Newton's friend, Thomas Burnet. See the recent discussion by Stephen J. Gould, in one of his last works, in *Rocks of Ages: Science and Religion in the Fullness of Life* (New York: Ballantine, 1999).

[4] The influence of Baconianism, a highly empirical or inductive approach to science and other ways of knowing, on nineteenth century religious thought is the subject of much recent research. See the discussion in James Stephen Wolfgang, "Science and Religion Issues in the Restoration Movement" (Ph.D. dissertation, University of Kentucky, 1997), from which much of this account is derived. Probably the standard work, and a good place to begin, is Theodore Dwight Bozeman, *Protestants in an Age of Science: The Baconian Ideal and Antebellum Religious Thought* (Chapel Hill: University of North Carolina Press, 1977). A recent work which places Baconianism in the context of pre-Civil war religious thought is Mark A. Noll, *America's God: Jonathan Edwards to Abraham Lincoln* (New York: Oxford University Press, 2002).

the six days of creation "might have been for millions of years, for what we know."[5]

Robert Milligan

Other examples of the influence of Baconian principles among Restoration thinkers may be seen in Robert Milligan's *Reason and Revelation*. Milligan had a distinguished academic career at Indiana University, where he taught "natural philosophy" (as what we call "science" was then known) before coming to Bethany College.[6] Following a stint as co-editor of Campbell's *Millennial Harbinger*, Milligan taught for many years, eventually becoming president, at Lexington's College of the Bible, formerly a division of Transylvania University, now Lexington Theological Seminary. *Reason and Revelation* contains chapters on "Inductive and Deductive Methods of Exegesis" as well as "Harmony of the Bible and Science." A companion volume, *The Scheme of Redemption*, was released the following year. In the first chapter of that work, Milligan considered both several ways in which geological evidence for the earth's antiquity could be reconciled, concluding that "geology makes it quite probable, if not indeed absolutely certain" that creation occurred "many ages previous to the historic [present] period." Having advanced what would come to be known as the "gap theory," Milligan argued that "during these intervening ages, many distinct orders of vegetables and animals were created and destroyed at the beginning and close of each geological formation."[7]

David R. Dungan and Clark Braden

One example among many of the popularity of Baconian, inductive science is David R. Dungan's *Hermeneutics*, which contains short sections on "common sense" and "Bacon" (although Roger Bacon, rather than Francis,

---

[5] Campbell, "Supernatural Facts," *PLA* 152-153; Campbell, "Lecture XII," in *Familiar Lectures on the Pentateuch* (Cincinnati: W.T. Moore, 1867), 140-141. Campbell also included some reflections on science in his address at New Athens College in 1838 ("Literature, Science, and Art," *PLA* 125-141).

[6] The "non-denominational" religious character of Indiana University in the early nineteenth century is described in Gayle Williams, "Andrew Wylie and Religion at Indiana University, 1824-1851: Nonsectarianism and Democracy," *Indiana Magazine of History* XCVI (March 2003).

[7] Milligan quotations are from *Reason and Revelation* (Cincinnati: R.W. Carroll & Co., 1868), 180-205, 341-343.

is discussed). This simple substitution speaks inadvertently but eloquently to the magical power Bacon's name held among some nineteenth-century Disciples. In fact, the only name which might outrank that of Bacon was Jesus Christ, to whom Dungan attributes the inductive method. From Dungan's perspective, "it is everywhere apparent that when the Lord would conduct an investigation on any subject, he did it by the inductive method." Largely self-educated except for brief periods at Kentucky University and Drake University, Dungan reminded his readers that deduction and inference "may be used in the ascertainment of facts and also in the conclusions reached from them." Nonetheless, the inductive method was still preeminent, since "the great teachers in the science of medicine have long held to this method of investigation" and "have for their main object the increase of knowledge by the induction of facts." Dungan rejected a hyper-literal interpretation since it is "most commonly employed by dogmatists, in order to maintain a view that can not be supported in any other way." Dungan cautioned his readers that "figures (of speech) are the exception" and that the correct rule should be that "all words are to be understood in their literal sense, unless the evident meaning of the context forbids."[8]

The views of one of Dungan's contemporaries, Clark Braden, deserve further investigation in the context of the nineteenth-century Baconian orientation toward science and biblical interpretation. Dungan, president of a succession of short-lived Disciple colleges in Southern Illinois from 1876-1900, argued in *The Problem of Problems and Its Various Solutions*, that "it matters not whether the six days in Genesis be six periods or six literal days."[9]

Tolbert Fanning and David Lipscomb
For a variety of reasons, it is apparent that Christians in the post-Civil War South took a more conservative view of many issues than did their counterparts in the North, who increasingly affiliated with the Disciples of Christ. Still, many of their views on this question are not dissimilar to their

---

[8] David R. Dungan, *Hermeneutics: A Text-book* (Cincinnati, 1888; reprint; Delight, AR: Gospel Light Publishing Company, n.d.). Dungan biographical information in John T. Brown, *Churches of Christ* 454; and J.H. Painter, ed., *The Iowa Pulpit of the Church of Christ* (St. Louis: John Burns, 1884), 105-108.

[9] Clark Braden, *The Problem of Problems and Its Various Solutions* (Cincinnati: Chase and Hall, 1877), 84-85.

Northern brethren.[10] Tolbert Fanning, a student of Tennessee geologist
Gerard Troost, and later president of Nashville's Franklin College and one
of the founders of the *Gospel Advocate*, was obviously influential on an
entire generation of preachers in churches of Christ throughout the south.
In several articles, produced prior to the appearance of Darwin's *Origin of
Species*, Fanning argued that the entire geological column could have been
formed before the six days of creation.[11]

Fanning's student, David Lipscomb, founder of the Nashville Bible
School and long-time *Gospel Advocate* editor, took a similar view.[12] In
1876, Thomas Henry Huxley (popularly known as "Darwin's bulldog")
visited Nashville to lecture publicly and in classes at Vanderbilt University.[13] Responding to Huxley, Lipscomb published several articles in the
Nashville American, a secular newspaper. Lipscomb's articles were later
reprinted by reader request in the *Gospel Advocate*, and are perhaps most
accessible in J.W. Shepherd's edited version of Lipscomb's articles.[14]

Reminding readers that both natural science and the Bible are subject to
interpretation and misunderstanding, Lipscomb invoked the example of
heliocentricity: "For a long while men thought the sun moved around the

---

[10] Ronald L. Numbers and Lester D. Stephens, two of the leading historians of
science, dispute the notion that reactions to Darwinism differed markedly in the
South compared to the North. See especially chapter 3 in Numbers, *Darwinism
Comes to America* (Cambridge, MA: Harvard University Press, 1998).

[11] Tolbert Fanning, "Geology and the Bible," *Christian Magazine* 2 (July, 1849),
272; and "Science and the Bible," *GA* 3 (June 1857), 164.

[12] See James R. Wilburn, *The Hazard of the Die: Tolbert Fanning and the Restora-
tion Movement* (Austin, TX: R.B. Sweet Publishing, 1969), 35, 73-74, and Robert
E. Hooper, *Crying in the Wilderness: A Biography of David Lipscomb* (Nashville:
David Lipscomb College, 1979), 256-257.

[13] On Huxley's visit, consult James M. Smith, "Thomas Henry Huxley in Nashville," *Tennessee Historical Quarterly* 33 (1974):191-203, 322-431; and Lipscomb's
articles in the *Gospel Advocate*, 1873 (515-521) and 1899 (56, 72-73).

[14] David Lipscomb, "Evolution and the Bible," and "Geology and the Bible," in
J.W. Shepherd, ed., *Salvation from Sin* (Nashville: McQuiddy Printing Company,
1913), 347-364 and 365-375.

earth; they interpreted the Bible to say so. . . . The theory that the earth revolves around the sun is universally accepted by Bible students now, and none think the theory contradicts any statement of the Bible." Using similar reasoning, Lipscomb pointed out that "for a great while men understood the first chapter of Genesis said that the world was created in the six days enumerated in this chapter. The truths of geology led to the study of this matter, and -lo!- the Bible does not say this. It says 'In the beginning [an indefinite period, antedating the six days' work, in which Jesus, as the Word, existed with God before the worlds were made — see John 1:1] God created the heavens and the earth.'" Lipscomb concluded, "A truth in the material world thus helps us to understand the great foundation and far-reaching truths of the spiritual world."[15]

Regarding the role of the flood, Lipscomb observed:

> For a great while people who saw the remains of shells and sea animals embedded in the rocks of our highest mountains, as well as through the broad plains of earth, took this as clear evidence that the waters of the flood covered this land and our highest mountains, and that the great masses of stratified rocks, with their shells and imbedded remains of water animals, were deposited by the waters during the flood. A serious study of the facts would have satisfied any one of common sense that all the deposits, with their fossils, could not have taken place during the prevalence of the flood. . .

Still, Lipscomb was open to further investigation, qualifying the above statement by adding, "Yet I am not sure but a comparison of the Bible account with these geological truths will not yet show they bear evidence of the flood."[16]

In "Geology and the Bible," Lipscomb argued that "the word *made* does not always mean to create out of nothing; but it frequently means to mold, shape, or introduce into new relations and change to new ends and purposes. 'In the beginning God created the heavens and the earth' (Gen. 1:1) refers to the calling of these into existence." Arguing that "this was at a period of time indefinite before the six days' work [when] 'The earth was

---

[15] Lipscomb, "Evolution and the Bible," 349-350.

[16] *Ibid.* 351.

waste and void.'" Lipscomb explained, "This carries the idea that there had been a change, sudden or violent, that had left the earth a waste, without living creatures or plants or animals. It carries the idea, too, that the whole earth was covered with water. Geology teaches this."[17]

Regarding the statement, "Let there be light" in Genesis 1:3-5, Lipscomb observed, "This scripture does not say there was no light in existence, but that light did not reach the earth, because the Bible is giving here a generation of the earth in its present state." Lipscomb argued, furthermore, that "*Made*, as applied to sun, moon, and starts, does not mean *created*; but the arrangement of the firmament was such that now they shone upon the earth, and so regulated day and night, summer and winter, and all the changing seasons." In Lipscomb's view, "the earth's surface gives ample evidence that an order has prevailed for a time, run its course, and closed, sometimes suddenly, sometimes gradually." Unwilling to be dogmatic about such matters, Lipscomb emphasized, "I suggest these as possibilities, but more to show our inability to comprehend some of the great facts given to us in Gen. 1, and that we may see how little we know of the conditions heretofore existing, out of which the present condition of the earth has resulted."[18]

Alfred Fairhurst and Sir John William Dawson
One notable character in the nineteenth century restorationist discussions of Darwinism, evolution, and related topics, was long-time Kentucky University science professor Alfred Fairhurst, who would play a large role in the evolution controversies at that institution. Fairhurst became an ally of McGarvey, making common cause in the College of Arts and Sciences with the College of the Bible president to prevent the infiltration of evolutionary theories and other forms of modernism.

Born in Indiana in 1843, Fairhurst graduated from Northwestern Christian University in Indianapolis, and pursued advanced work in science at Harvard University during the time that both Louis Agassiz and Asa Gray

---

[17] Lipscomb, "Geology and the Bible," 368.

[18] *Ibid.* 368, 370.

[19] Biographical information on Fairhurst is found in an official Transylvania University Board resolution passed at its June 6, 1921 meeting (Special Collections, Transylvania University Library); and in the Preface, written by his daughter, Mary Fairhurst Baughn, in Alfred Fairhurst, *Atheism in Our Universities* (Cincinnati: Standard Publishing Company, 1923), 9-14.

were on the Harvard science faculty. He then returned to teach at his alma mater, by then renamed Butler University, in 1866.[19] In 1881, Fairhurst became professor of natural history in Kentucky University, where he remained for more than thirty years. Partly due to his urging, the university obtained funds from Andrew Carnegie for the construction of a new science building in 1908. Fairhurst retired from teaching in 1914 at age 70. He published three books examining evolutionary theory, beginning with *Organic Evolution Considered*, published in 1897, re-issued in a revised edition in 1911, and reprinted in 1913. These were followed by *Theistic Evolution* (1919) and *Atheism in Our Universities*, which was published posthumously, two years after Fairhurst died in 1921.[20]

Fairhurst's approach to evolutionary theory was similar to many other conservative Christians who struggled with the reception of Darwinism in the late nineteenth century. While he rejected theistic evolution as destroying the authority of Scripture just as surely as atheistic or materialistic evolution, Fairhurst interpreted the "days" of Genesis as indefinite periods of time, thus allowing for the possibility of the age of the earth in millions of years.[21] Although his works are studded with quotations from a wide variety of both pro- and anti-evolutionary writers, Fairhurst frequently cited renowned Canadian geologist John William Dawson.

A native of Nova Scotia, Dawson had studied geology at the University of Edinburgh in the 1840s and had become a devotee of Charles Lyell. Returning to his native Canada, Dawson taught geology at McGill University.[22] A devout Presbyterian, he regularly taught Sunday School classes at a Presbyterian church in Montreal, and became a popular lecturer in reli-

---

[20] Alfred Fairhurst, *Organic Evolution Considered* (St. Louis: Christian Publishing Company, 1897; revised 1911); *Theistic Evolution* (Cincinnati: Standard Publishing Company, 1919).

[21] Alfred Fairhurst, Gradebooks, 1884-1913, in Special Collections, Transylvania University Library; A. Fairhurst, *My Good Poems* (St. Louis: Christian Publishing Company, 1899), 220, 222; Fairhurst, "The Little Tin Gods" (Typescript, Special Collections, Transylvania University Library). Note especially sheets 44-57.

[22] On Dawson, see Charles F. O'Brien, *Sir William Dawson: A Life in Science and Religion* (Philadelphia: American Philosophical Society, 1971); John F. Cornell, "From Creation to Evolution: Sir William Dawson and the Idea of Design in the Nineteenth Century," *Journal of the History of Biology* 16 (1983), 147-170.

gious circles on issues of science and religion. In 1878, Princeton University president, James McCosh, invited Dawson to join the faculty there. During the 1880s he served as president of both the American Association for the Advancement of Science and the British Association for the British Association for the Advancement of Science, "a unique achievement." Dawson was quite willing to grant that the "days" of Genesis chapter 1 might have been long eras, that the biblical flood was local rather than universal, and that the earth (though not mankind) was perhaps of considerable antiquity. Indeed, special creation meant to him only that "all things have been produced by the supreme Creative Will, acting either directly or through the forces and materials of His own production."[23] As far as Dawson was concerned, creation was not necessarily miraculous. Furthermore, his concept of special creation "does not even exclude evolution or derivation to a certain extent" since "anything once created may, if sufficiently flexible or elastic, be evolved in various ways."[24]

Fairhurst and other nineteenth-century religious thinkers were also influenced by the works of George Frederick Wright, including a widely read five-part series, "Recent Books Bearing upon the Relationship of Science to Religion," which later were compiled into book form as *Studies in Science and Religion*.[25]

---

[23] The quotation is from Ronald L. Numbers, *The Creationists: The Evolution of Scientific Creationism* (New York: Alfred A. Knopf, 1993), 10. See also William R. Shea, "Introduction" to J. William Dawson, *Modern Ideas of Evolution* (New York, Prodist, 1977). On the AAAS, see Sally Gregory Kohlstedt, *The Formation of the American Scientific Community* (Urbana: University of Illinois Press, 1976).

[24] See Dawson, *The Story of Earth and Man* (New York: Harper and Brothers, 1873), 340-341; Dawson, *The Meeting-Place of Geology and History* (London: Religious Tract Society, 1874), 147. Some of Dawson's other published works include *Nature and the Bible* (New York: Robert Carter and Brothers, 1975); *The Origin of the World According to Revelation and Science* (London: Hodder and Stoughton, 1877, 1886); and *Modern Ideas of Evolution as Related to Revelation and Science* (London: ReligiousTract Society, 1890, 1900).

[25] *Studies in Science and Religion* (Andover, MA: Warren F. Draper, 1882). See "No. 1 — The Nature and Degree of Scientific Proof," *Bibliotheca Sacra* 32 (1875), 548; and "No. 2 — The Divine Method of Producing Living Species," *Bibliotheca Sacra* 33 (1876), 459.

Studies of Wright include Michael McGiffert, "Christian Darwinism: The Partnership of Asa Gray and George Frederick Wright, 1874-1881" (Ph.D. disserta-

Hall L. Calhoun

At the dawn of the twentieth century, unwilling to see his beloved College of the Bible fall prey to Darwinism or other forms of modernism, J.W. McGarvey had set about to plan the institution's future. These plans included the hope that the College of the Bible "shall eventually become the greatest seat of Biblical learning in the world." His annual report for 1908, submitted in his eightieth year, contained some of McGarvey's provisions for accomplishing the task:

> I have had a conference with my junior colleagues on this subject, and have charged them each to select a branch of Biblical learning in which to make himself a specialist and a master, so that in this no man anywhere shall be his superior.[26]

Indeed, according to one of the College's historians, McGarvey had the vision to see that Disciples would inhabit a "new world," and thus, besides strengthening the existing faculty, he encouraged several of his best students to pursue graduate training at reputable universities and divinity schools in the country, including Harvard and Yale.[27] To facilitate this transition to the future, McGarvey helped make arrangements for his hand-picked successor, Hall Laurie Calhoun, to attend Yale Divinity School beginning in 1901. Under a financial arrangement approved by McGarvey and the Board of Trustees, Calhoun, an 1892 graduate of the College of the Bible in Kentucky University, was to pursue graduate education and return to teach in Lexington. Calhoun went first to Yale Divinity School, where he received a B.D. He then went to Harvard University, becoming both a Hopkins Fellow and a Williams Fellow and working with the renowned Biblical scholar,

---

tion, Yale University, 1958), and William James Morison, "George Frederick Wright: In Defense of Darwinism and Fundamentalism, 1838-1921" (Ph.D. dissertation, Vanderbilt University, 1971). See also G.F. Wright, "The Revision of Geological Time," *Bibliotheca Sacra* 60 (1903), 580, 582; Wright, "The Uncertainties of Science and The Certainties of Religion," *Homiletic Review* 46 (1903), 413-415.

[26] Quoted in Dwight E. Stevenson, *Lexington Theological Seminary, 1865-1965* (St. Louis: The Bethany Press, 1964), 134.

[27] Richard M. Pope, *The College of the Bible: A Brief Narrative* (Lexington: The College of the Bible, 1961), 20-21.

George Foot Moore. After receiving his Ph.D. in 1904, Calhoun returned to Lexington to join the faculty.[28]

Conservative by nature and background, Calhoun was irenic enough that when invited to give the alumni address at the centennial celebration of Harvard Divinity School in 1916, he emphasized areas of common agreement and suggested ways in which conservative and liberal approaches to biblical study might co-exist.[29] But circumstances and conviction would soon force Calhoun into a more confrontational stance. Calhoun had become Dean when W.C. Morro left the College of the Bible for Butler University in 1911.[30] When McGarvey died later that year, Calhoun fulfilled his and McGarvey's expectations, becoming President of the College of the Bible, albeit on an interim basis. Institutional changes would thwart McGarvey's best-laid plans, and result in Calhoun leaving not only the College of the Bible, but the Disciples of Christ as well.[31]

A complex series of events, including a full-fledged "heresy trial," resulted in Calhoun resigning, chemistry professor Ralph Records leaving the college of Arts and Sciences under protest, the forced resignation of Alfred Fairhurst from the College of Bible board, and of COB board chair-

---

[28] For biographical information on Calhoun, see Adron Doran and J.E. Choate, *The Christian Scholar: A Biography of Hall Laurie Calhoun* (Nashville: Gospel Advocate, 1985); Biographical file Disciples of Christ Historical Society, Nashville, TN.

[29] Richard L. Harrison, Jr., "Disciples Theological Formation: From a College of the Bible to a Theological Seminary," in Williams, *A Case Study of Mainstream Protestantism*, 288-295.

[30] Morro later wrote a biography of McGarvey; see W.C. Morro, *Brother McGarvey: The Life of President J.W. McGarvey of the College of the Bible* (St. Louis: Bethany Press, 1940). For a conservative view of McGarvey, see Richard O.N. Halbrook, "J.W. McGarvey: His Role in Communicating the Conservative Approach to Scripture During the Rise of Liberalism, 1865-1911" (M.A. thesis, Vanderbilt University, 1979).

[31] See Doran and Choate, *The Christian Scholar*, chapters 6 and 7; and John D. Wright, *Transylvania: Tutor to the West* (Lexington: University Press of Kentucky, 1980), 336-342, for sharply contrasting versions of the controversy. Doran, former president of Morehead State University and Speaker of the Kentucky House of Representatives, was also a minister among churches of Christ. Choate was a professor or history at David Lipscomb University in Nashville.

man Mark Collis, a long-time McGarvey friend and ally.[32] Calhoun left Lexington to teach at Bethany College, which had begun a graduate program in religion. Although that program was planned before the problems in Lexington became apparent, it was seen by some as a rival to the College of the Bible. At Bethany, Calhoun's career floundered in the sense that after the unexpected death of T.E. Cramblett, the president who recruited him to Bethany, support for the newly established graduate program in religion evaporated, and Bethany College moved toward strengthening its role as an undergraduate institution.[33] After eight years at Bethany, Hall was teaching strictly undergraduate courses. Most significantly, he was becoming all the more disillusioned by the direction in which he saw the Disciples heading.[34]

Returning to his native Tennessee, he made a clean break with the Disciples, and did the one thing that even the most broad-minded Disciple might abhor: he affiliated with the non-instrumental churches of Christ. After leaving Bethany, Calhoun taught at Freed-Hardeman College and then at David Lipscomb College in Nashville. Beginning in the late 1920s, he served as minister for the Central Church of Christ in downtown Nashville. The Central church offered an array of social and outreach services, including a kitchen and dining room for the needy, a library, and reading room. The church also had a short daily service at noon each day, and in 1925, in the infancy of radio, began broadcasting that service, soon expanding to other broadcasts on station WLAC. Calhoun thus unintention-

---

[32] Details of these events are recounted in Wolfgang, "Science and Religion Issues" (85-90), based on research in the primary documents locate in several files marked "Evolution Controversy," Special Collections, Transylvania University, Lexington. Several of those who left began more conservative rival institutions to the College of the Bible, McGarvey Bible College at Louisville, and Cincinnati Bible College. After a few years, the Louisville school merged with Cincinnati. See James DeForest Murch.

[33] Biographical file, Disciples of Christ Historical Society, Nashville.

[34] On these developments, see James B. North, *Union in Truth: An Interpretive History of the Restoration Movement* (Cincinnati: Standard Publishing Company, 1994), esp. pp. 312ff. That work is based in part on North's "Fundamentalism and Modernism Among the Disciples of Christ in the 1920s" (Ph.D. dissertation, University of Illinois, 1973). North teaches church history at Cincinnati Christian Seminary.

ally became one of the first mass media evangelists — possibly the only one in history with a religion Ph.D. from Harvard.[35]

That same year, Calhoun contributed a chapter on "The Two Accounts of Creation," the *Gospel Advocate's* book *The Bible Versus Theories of Evolution*, published in the wake of the Scopes Trial (see below).[36] In that article, Calhoun argued, "How long it was from 'the beginning' till the first one of the six days, the Bible nowhere says. There is time here for all the geologic ages." Furthermore, Calhoun contended that "What existed on the earth and what changes took place in it between 'the beginning' and the first of the six days is nowhere stated in the Bible." Calhoun also observed, "It is a very common thing for evolutionists to misrepresent the Bible by claiming that it that the heavens and the earth were created about six thousand years ago, and then they proceed to claim that this contradicts the science of geology. Even some persons who claim to believe the Bible do not know what the Bible story of creation is."[37]

---

[35] On early religious broadcasting, see Dennis N. Voskuil, "Reaching Out: Mainline Protestantism and the Media," in William R. Hutchison, ed., *Between the Times: The Travail of the Protestant Establishment in America, 1900-1960* (Cambridge: Cambridge University Press, 1989), 72-92; Voskuil, "The Power of the Air: Evangelicals and the Rise of Religious Broadcasting," and Quentin J. Schultze, "The Invisible Medium: Evangelical Radio," in Schultze, ed., *American Evangelicals and the Mass Media* (Grand Rapids, MI: Zondervan/Academie Books, 1990), 69-95 and 171-195; Schultze, "Evangelical Radio and the Rise of the Electronic Church," *Journal of Broadcasting and the Electronic Media* 32 (Summer 1988), 301ff.; and Eric Barnouw, *A Tower of Babel: A History of Broadcasting to 1933* (New York: Oxford University Press, 1966). For further information see the extensive annotated bibliography in the section, "The Modern Electronic Era: 1920 to the Present," in Leonard I. Sweet, ed., *Communication and Change in American Religious History* (Grand Rapids, MI: Eerdmans, 1993), 452-479.

[36] Unquestionably the best account of the Scopes Trial, and the context in which it occurred and followed it, is Edward J. Larson, *Summer for the Gods: The Scopes Trial and America's Continuing Debate Over Science and Religion* (Cambridge, MA: Harvard University Press, 1998), winner of the 1998 Pulitzer Prize for History. In many ways, Calhoun and other Christians like him were following the lead of William Jennings Bryan, who during the trial disavowed belief in a young earth or a 6,000-year-old creation.

[37] Calhoun, "The Two Accounts of Creation," in E.A. Elam, ed., *The Bible Versus Theories of Evolution* (Nashville: Gospel Advocate Company, 1925), 297-301.

William Webb Freeman

Perhaps the most telling event regarding creation-evolution issues in early twenthieth-century churches of Christ was the controversy at Abilene Christian College regarding William Webb Freeman, son of a well-known minister and protégé of J.N. Armstrong. After studying at one of Armstrong's colleges, Freeman matriculated in 1913 at the University of Louisville, graduating in 1916, and then studied under the respected Greek grammarian, A.T. Robertson, at the Southern Baptist Theological Seminary in Louisville. There he encountered a fairly conservative brand of biblical criticism under men like Robertson and E.Y. Mullins.[38] Freeman received a Th.M. in 1917 and completed the coursework for a Th.D. during 1917-1918, ultimately finishing his dissertation and receiving the degree in 1926. After teaching three years at Abilene, Freeman sought further academic credentials, and was accepted at Yale Divinity School to work toward a Ph.D. in New Testament. At the conclusion of his first year at Yale, Freeman submitted a series of articles to the *Firm Foundation* on the relationship of science and the Bible.[39] Freeman was responding to articles such as one in the *Gospel Advocate* which equated the six days of creation with literal, 24-hour days.[40]

Freeman's articles touched off a firestorm of controversy. Insisting that Christians should accept the truth in any area of study, Freeman demon-

---

[38] See William E. Ellis, *"A Man of Books and A Man of the People": E.Y. Mullins and the Crisis of Moderate Southern Baptist Leadership* (Macon, GA: Mercer University Press, 1985).

[39] See G.H.P. Showalter, "The Bible, The Word of God," *FF* 36:19 (May 13, 1919), 2; A.B. Lipscomb, "Edifying as the Need May Be," *GA* 61 (April 17, 1919), 301-302. A.B. Barrett, "Notes of Travel," *FF* 40:22 (May 29, 1923), 3. Kelly's article was taken directly from *The Fundamentals*.

[40] Ernest C. Love, "Christian Education," *GA* 64 (May 4, 1922), 409-410. On Freeman, see C.R. Nichol, *Gospel Preachers Who Blazed the Trail* (Austin, TX: Firm Foundation Publishing House, 1911; n.p.; alphabetical listing of biographical sketches, unnumbered pages); Lloyd Cline Sears, *For Freedom: The Biography of John Nelson Armstrong* (Austin, TX: R.B. Sweet Publishing, 1969), 126; and "Preface" in Freeman, "Was Paul A Sacramentarian?" (Th.D. dissertation, Southern Baptist Theological Seminary, 1926). On the Southern Baptist Theological Seminary, consult James J. Thompson, Jr., *Tried As By Fire: Southern Baptists and the Religious Controversies of the 1920s* (Macon, GA: Mercer University Press, 1982).

strated that the Baconian fact-theory dichotomy was alive and well among churches of Christ.[41] Arguing that the conflict between religion and science was "caused by this false claim of the Bible as infallible in every dictum," he contended that the Bible was not a scientific text, but a work of religion which should not be used as a guide to science. Such extreme literalism was dangerous according to Freeman, since it might cause readers to believe in "the four corners of the earth" or "the rise of the sun."[42]

Firm Foundation correspondent U.G. Wilkinson attacked the interpretation of the word "day" in Genesis 1 as periods of time longer than 24 hours as he answered the question, "Is the Story of Creation, Fall and Redemption of Man a Legend or Myth?" Accepting Bishop Ussher's literalistic approach to Old Testament genealogies, Wilkinson affirmed that "the world is now 5921 years old . . . according to the Bible, according to Moses and the prophets and Christ and the apostles."[43]

G.C. Brewer, one of the best known preachers among churches of Christ and a staunch supporter of Abilene Christian College, responded to Freeman's articles in a manner no doubt representative of most church members. Addressing the Abilene Christian College president, Brewer demanded, "Brother Sewell, if there are any ideas of theology in Abilene

---

[41] Showalter, "The Bible and Science," 2. This "Baconian" comparison between the mere "theory" of evolution and the self-evident "fact" of Divine creation was a common staple in many articles by members of Churches of Christ. See A.B. Lipscomb, "A Theory and a Fact," *GA* 61:11 (March 13, 1919), 1. A.B. Lipscomb, a graduate student in sociology at Vanderbilt University, was a nephew of David Lipscomb and served briefly as editor of the *Gospel Advocate*.

For parallel developments in Fundamentalism generally, see Ronald L. Numbers, "The Dilemma of Evangelical Scientists," in George Marsden, ed., *Evangelicalism and Modern America* (Grand Rapids, MI: William B. Eerdmans, 1984), 150-160; Marsden, "Understanding Fundamentalist Views of Science," in Ashley Montagu, ed., *Science and Creationism* (New York: Oxford University Press, 1984).

[42] Freeman, "Use and Abuse of the Bible, No. 1," *FF* 39:24 (June 6, 1922), 3; G.H.P. Showalter, "The Bible and Science," *FF* 39:29 (July 18, 1922), 2; Freeman, "Use and Abuse of the Bible, No. 2," *FF* 39:28 (July 11, 1922), 4.

[43] U.G. Wilkinson, "Is the Story of Creation, Fall, and Redemption of Man a Legend or Myth?" *FF* 34 (June 19, 1917), 2.

Christian College, get them out or dynamite the premises and blow the school to gehenna." Brewer, possibly the most colorful and certainly one of the most visible spokesmen for churches of Christ during this period, gained notoriety by debating Judge Ben B. Lindsey of Denver on the subject of companionate or trial marriage in 1928 at Memphis. One result of that debate was that by 1931 churches of Christ in various locations around the country were trying to arrange a debate between Clarence Darrow and Brewer, now billed as "the Bryan of the Southwest."[44]

But the most telling response to Freeman was the terse message, cabled to the *Firm Foundation* office by Abilene Christian College president Jesse P. Sewell, announcing to members of churches of Christ that W.W. Freeman would no longer be teaching at that institution.[45] H. Leo Boles, president of David Lipscomb College (as Nashville Bible School had recently

---

[44] G.C. Brewer, "Some Observations on W.W. Freeman's Recent Remarks," *FF* 39:40 (October 3, 1922), 4; and Brewer, "Clarence Darrow and Debates," *GA* 73:19 [May 7, 1931], 538). See also Brewer, "The Christian Evolutionist," *GA* 77:39 (September 25, 1935), 914. For biographical information on Brewer, consult Ron Halbrook, "Grover Cleveland Brewer: Perennial Protagonist," in *They Being Dead Yet Speak: The Florida College Annual Lectures, 1981* (Temple Terrace, FL: Florida College, 1981), 198-219; and Warren S. Jones, "G.C. Brewer: Lecturer, Debater, and Preacher" (Ph.D. dissertation, Wayne State University, 1959).

[45] Jesse P. Sewell, "Just What Do You Mean, Brother Freeman?" *FF* 39:33 (August 15, 1922), 2; Freeman, "Use and Abuse of the Bible, No. 4," *FF* 29:37 (September 12, 1922), 4; Showalter, "Concerning the Use and Abuse of the Bible," *FF* 29:36 (September 5, 1922), 2.

Freeman never finished his Yale degree, but while teaching classics at East Texas State University at Commerce, completed in 1933 an M.A. at Southern Methodist University in Dallas, producing a thesis entitled, "The Background of Education in the Campbell Movement" (interview, Jean Freeman Bly, Denton, Texas, March 4, 1989). I thank Mrs. Bly (W.W. Freeman's daughter) for allowing me to examine and photocopy much of Freeman's personal papers and correspondence, which is soon to be donated to Abilene Christian University, and from which the information about Freeman is derived. A greatly expanded version of Freeman's SMU thesis, brimming with information on the "Restoration Movement," is in the Special Collections Department of the Abilene Christian University Library in Abilene, TX.

been renamed) and editor of the *Gospel Advocate*, concurred with his fellow college president. He entered the fray, alleging that Freeman's views were "calculated to discredit the inspiration of the Bible."[46] Boles cautioned, "Unless he comes clear on the subject of higher criticism . . . the churches should be warned against him."[47]

Bible vs. Evolution

Immediately after the Scopes trial, the *Gospel Advocate* noted "the general interest manifested at this time in evolution" as well as "the opportunity now open to impress the Bible account of creation." Thus, the Nashville-based company published a 320-page book, *The Bible Versus Theories of Evolution*, edited by E.A. Elam, whose career included a stint as president of David Lipscomb College as well as editor of the *Gospel Advo-*

---

[46] H. Leo Boles [unsigned], "Evangelistic Notes," *GA* 64:41 (October 12, 1922), 968. Boles wrote frequently on various aspects of evolution. See "Evolution," *GA* 64:35 (August 31, 1922), 826; "Evolution — Its Limitations," *GA* 64:36 (September 7, 1922), 853; "Evolution and Faith," *GA* 64:37 (September 14, 1922), 877; "Evolution and the Bible," *GA* 64:38 (September 21, 1922), 900; and "Evolution and Education," *GA* 64:41 (October 12, 1922), 971. In the last article, Boles reproduced correspondence between himself and Vanderbilt University English professor Edwin Mims in which Mims disparaged the biblical account of Noah and the flood. To Boles, this was enough "to substantiate the statement that rank infidelity is taught in our schools and colleges" (971). Mims was a favorite target of *Advocate* writers; see F.W. Smith, "Dr. Edwin Mims in Washington," *GA* 70:6 (February 9, 1928), 132. See also F.W. Smith, "The Cole Lectures at Vanderbilt," *GA* 64:19 (May 11, 1922), 448; Robert Moats Miller, *Harry Emerson Fosdick: Preacher, Pastor, Prophet* (New York: Oxford University Press, 1985), 89, 102, 114, 119, and 124-148. See also Paul K. Conkin, with Henry Lee Swint and Patricia Miletich, *Gone With the Ivy: A Biography of Vanderbilt University* (Knoxville: University of Tennessee Press, 1985), 306-307. Fosdick's Cole Lectures at Vanderbilt were published as *Christianity and Progress* (New York: Fleming H. Revell Company, 1922).

[47] Following his dismissal from ACC, Freeman became professor of classics at East Texas State University, and later an elder in the church at Commerce. Freeman eventually was at least partially reconciled with Sewell, Showalter, and Brewer, all of whom published eulogies following Freeman's death in 1954. See Willis G. Jernigan, "William Webb Freeman — A Tribute," *Gospel Guardian* 6 (May 27, 1954), 54; Elmer L'Roy, "He Was My Teacher," *Ibid.* 54, 59; and Fanning Yater Tant, "A Gentle Man Has Gone," *Ibid.* 60. Tant commented: "Suffering cruelly and unjustly at the hands of his brethren some thirty years ago, he came through the ordeal with his faith in God unshaken — and, what's more, with his faith in man (his brethren) not embittered. . . . We honor his memory."

cate. The authors of the book's chapters read like "Who's Who" of the best-known ministers among churches of Christ in the 1920s. Included were two reprinted articles by David Lipscomb himself, who had died in 1917, and by H. Leo Boles, then president of David Lipscomb College and editor of the *Gospel Advocate*. Also contributing articles were A.G. Freed, N.B. Hardeman, and Batsell Baxter — presidents of colleges in Tennessee, Texas, and California which were financially supported by churches of Christ. Hall Calhoun and other well-known preachers such as F.W. Smith, A.B. Barrett, S.H. Hall, James A. Allen, and the young B.C. Goodpasture, who would edit the *Advocate* from 1939-1977, also appeared.[48]

Following the Scopes trial, if not before, members of churches of Christ frequently made "common cause" against evolutionary theories with a wide variety of conservative denominational or even fundamentalist religious leaders (that is, both groups concurrently fought evolution). For example, articles by leading anti-evolutionists like William Jennings Bryan and Dr. Howard A. Kelly of Johns Hopkins University Medical School frequently appear in the "brotherhood journals" of the 1920s. Hall L. Calhoun favorably reviewed Wheaton College professor Glenn Gates Cole's *Creation and Science* in the *Advocate* in 1929. The *Firm Foundation* and the *Gospel Advocate* both called readers' attention to Alfred Fairhurst's books.[49]

A.B. Barrett
In fact, for a short while, former Abilene Christian College president A.B. Barrett edited a journal, designed for circulation among churches of

---

[48] E.A. Elam, ed., *The Bible versus Theories of Evolution* (Nashville: Gospel Advocate Company, 1925). The book was reviewed and endorsed by David Lipscomb, Jr. ("Evolution," *GA* 68:12 [March 25, 1926], 270-271).

[49] F.W. Smith, "A 'Double-Barreled Answer,'" *GA* 70:2 (January 12, 1928), 35-37; and "A Convention of Evolutionists," *GA* 70:4 (January 26, 1928), 84-85). The AAAS Nashville meeting was reported extensively in *Science*, volumes 66 and 67. See also Smithson, "Dislike Antievolution Laws," *GA* 71:7 (February 14, 1929), 148; and Hall L. Calhoun, "Book Reviews," *GA* 71:30 (July 25, 1929), 718. Biographical information on Calhoun is found in Adron Doran and J.E. Choate, *The Christian Scholar: A Biography of Hall Laurie Calhoun* (Nashville: Gospel Advocate Company, 1985).

[50] Barrett's journal in some ways paralleled S.O. Pool's periodical, the *Biblical Educator*, which was published from 1909-1912, almost exactly at the time The Fundamentals were being published. See James Stephen Wolfgang, "Fundamentalism and Churches of Christ" (M.A. thesis, Vanderbilt University, 1990), for details regarding S.O. Pool, a protégé of Daniel Sommer.

Christ and devoted entirely to the discussion of modernism, evolution, and the so-called "higher criticism" of the Bible.[50] Published from 1925 to 1927, while Barrett was living in Fayetteville, Tennessee, and Austin, Texas, *The Contender* included reprints from publications of the Moody Bible Institute and other Fundamentalists sources, as well as correspondence between Barrett and leading Fundamentalists including William Jennings Bryan, George McCready Price, W. Graham Scroggie, and others. Regular features included articles by various pro-evolutionary authors, advertisements for a variety of books by avowedly Fundamentalist, anti-evolutionary, and anti-modernist authors. Also appearing was a column on "Biblical Criticism" by Hall L. Calhoun, and a news column detailing developments in opposition to anti-evolution legislation and accounts of Barrett's activities, among other things. A typical entry reports,

> Among the churches: I have recently lectured on evolution at [various Tennessee churches], David Lipscomb College, Tennessee; Harding College, Morrillton, Ark., and I am now in Texas for six weeks lecture tour among the churches of this state, directed by the church in Austin. This work is being done in the interest of the Bible Chair at the State University.

William Wesley Otey

One of the best-known evangelists among churches of Christ, W.W. Otey was quite comfortable using the word "creationist" to describe himself and his views. But as with many other avowed creationists of the time, he was unwilling to specify any particular estimate of the age of the earth. Otey seemed to see no point in insisting on a "young-earth" version of creationism. Commenting on the contentions of evolutionary theorists that the fossil record demonstrated that extinct animals lived on earth millions of years before man, he remarked, "if that be true, it in no way disproves the history of creation as recorded in Genesis."[51] Without using the term, Otey then advanced a modified form of the "gap theory," popular among many conservative Christians as a means of reconciling Genesis and geology. While allowing for a "gap" of millions of years between the creation of matter and the creation of human life, Otey contended that the latter was much more recent. In good Restorationist fashion, he insisted upon observing the

---

[51] W.W. Otey, *The Origin and Destiny of Man* (Grand Rapids, MI: William B. Eerdmans, 1938), 107. Otey's significance among churches of Christ, and his production of these works, is explored in Cecil Willis, *W.W. Otey, Contender for the Faith* (Akron: 1964).

[52] *Ibid.*

silence of Scripture, maintaining that "What may have existed before this order of life was created, is not stated."[52] Quoting the Genesis affirmation, "In the beginning, God created the heavens and the earth," he argued,

> That is one part of creation, and how long ago that was measured in years, the Bible does not give a hint. . . . How much older the material world may be than man, is a matter of pure speculation. Nor does "creating the heavens and the earth" necessarily mean bringing these into existence out of nothing. It simply means bringing order out of chaos; organizing material substances into an orderly system.[53]

As far as he was concerned, "if it be argued that the progenitors of the present order of plant and animal life now on earth were created a long period before man, I would not waste time arguing the contention."[54] By contrast, for Otey and for many conservative Christians, the vital question at issue was that "man has no ancestors such as fishes, reptiles, and apes."[55]

Foy E. Wallace, Jr.

In a frequently-quoted section of his 1945 Houston Music Hall lessons on premillennialism, Foy E. Wallace, Jr, stated: "There is no statement in the Bible which indicates the age of the earth. 'In the beginning God' is a phrase that defines a period of remote antiquity, hidden in the depths of eternal ages. If the scientists . . . want to ascribe to the earth the age of a million, a billion, or 300 billion years, I will not pause to argue the question with them now. . . . 'In the beginning God.' That is all the Bible affirms on the question."[56] One should note that Wallace is not stating a position on the issue, nor endorsing any old-earth view. He is simply arguing that such an issue is not, perhaps, the most pressing or effective place to pitch a battle over such questions.

Douglas Dewar and James D. Bales

Douglas Dewar, a British naturalist whose writings influenced several

---

[53] W.W. Otey, *Creation or Evolution* (Austin, TX: Firm Foundation Publishing House, 1930), 71.

[54] Otey, *Origin and Destiny of Man*, 107.

[55] Otey, *Ibid.* 123.

[56] Foy E. Wallace, Jr., *God's Prophetic Word* (1946), 6-7.

American creationists (notably the young James D. Bales), had his *Transformist Illusion* published in an American edition by George DeHoff. Although personally committed to an inerrant Scripture, preferred even if it seemed contradictory to geological evidence, Dewar nonetheless omitted any religious references in his book. His intention was to communicate to readers "on purely scientific grounds." Privately, he dealt with geological evidence of the earth's antiquity by an unusual version of the "gap theory."[57] This attempt to reconcile science and the Bible, sometimes known as "ruin and restoration," placed a "gap" after the first two verses of Genesis, allowing for successive Divine creative acts within the framework of long geological eons.[58] Dewar, however, theorized a gap between the first two chapters of Genesis. His work attracted the attention of the amateur American geologist, George McCready Price. Price, led by his Seventh-Day Adventist religious views to insist on a young earth, was happy to hear of his fellow evolution opponent from across the Atlantic. Ultimately, however, Dewar remained unconvinced of Price's young earth views.[59]

Bales was also taken with Dewar's work, and correspondence between the two resulted in Dewar asking the young American to merge his new organization with the Evolution Protest Movement. Bales accepted with

---

[57] Information on Dewar derived from *Who Was Who, 1951-1960* (London: Adam & Charles Black, 1961), 302; see also Dewar, "The Limitations of Organic Evolution," *Journal of the Transactions of the Victoria Institute* 64 (1932), 142ff.; and Dewar, "Current Theories of the Origin of Living Organisms," *Journal of the Transactions of the Victoria Institute* 76 (1944), 59-93.

[58] The terms "gap theory" and "ruin and restoration" are often used interchangeably, but are not exactly or necessarily synonymous. To posit a "gap" between, say, Genesis 1:1 and 1:2 does not necessarily commit one to a fanciful theory during that "gap" of an earlier creation and its destruction, or a succession of creations and their subsequent demise. Of course, there are other meanings and uses of "gap" theory, in addition to Dewar's "gap" between Genesis 1 and 2, not its "normal" location. Ron Numbers, in *Darwinism Comes to America*, documents Wesleyan and Pentecostal uses in the 1920's evolution controversy of "gaps" between the literal 24-hour days of Genesis.

[59] Douglas Dewar and Frank Flinn, *The Making of Species* (London: John Lane, 1909), ix, 26; Dewar, *Difficulties of the Theory of Evolution* (London: Edward Arnold, 1931), and *More Difficulties of the Evolution Theory: And a Reply to "Evolution and Its Modern Critics"* (London: Thynne, 1938). Dewar is quoted in Numbers, *The Creationists*, 145-146.

alacrity, taking up the task of imitating it by publishing a journal titled *The Thinking Christian*. But the journal was short-lived, ceasing publication after just a few issues. Bales did arrange to publish an American version of Dewar's works. Entitled *The Transformist Illusion*, the book combined material from *Difficulties* and its sequel, *More Difficulties of the Evolution Theory*.[60]

The Creation Research Society and Churches of Christ

An emerging group of scientifically-credentialed teachers which developed in colleges supported by churches of Christ in the post-World War II era showed an increasing willingness to work with other creationists, while not always sharing young-earth views. Jack Wood Sears, son of long-time Harding College dean Lloyd Cline Sears (himself J.N. Armstrong's son-in-law),[61] earned his Ph.D. in genetics from the University of Texas in 1955. His book, *Conflict and Harmony in Science and the Bible*, was the first to bring to the attention of members of churches of Christ the crucial distinction argued by British biologist G.A. Kerkut of the University of Southampton between the "general theory" and "special theory" of evolution (now commonly called "macro-evolutions" and "micro-evolution").[62] Published by a leading evangelical publisher, Baker Book House, and containing an introduction by well-known Evangelical commentator Merrill C. Tenney of Wheaton College, Sears' book was among the first to popu-

---

[60] Dewar, *The Transformist Illusion* (Murfreesboro, TN: DeHoff Publishing Company, 1957). Information on Dewar derived from author interviews with Bales and from Numbers, *The Creationists*, 149-153. On the background of British Evangelicalism and their scientific views, see David Bebbington, *Evangelicalism in Modern Britain: A History from the 1730's to the 1980's* (London and Boston: Unwin Hyman/Routledge, 1989); James R. Moore, "Evangelicals and Evolution: Henry Drummond, Herbert Spencer, and the Naturalization of the Spiritual World," *Scottish Journal of Theology* 58 (1985), 383-417; and George M. Marsden, "Fundamentalism as An American Phenomenon: A Comparison with English Evangelicalism," *Church History* 46 (June, 1977), 215-232.

[61] See Lloyd Cline Sears, *The Eyes of Jehovah: The Life and Faith of James Alexander Harding* (Nashville: Gospel Advocate Company, 1970), and L.C. Sears, *For Freedom* 126.

[62] Information in this section is derived in part from author interviews with Sears at Searcy, AR, November 1, 1996 and July 17, 1998, and G.A. Kerkut, University of Southampton, England, November 5, 1990. Kerkut's book is *Implications of Evolution* (New York: Pergamon Press, 1960).

larize what would become a critically important distinction used by many creationists. Years later, in a debate with young-earth creationist Bert Thompson, Sears explicitly affirmed that "the biblical account of creation allows for a very ancient earth."[63]

Harding University chemistry professor Donald England, like his colleague, Jack Wood Sears, summoned the testimony of British non-creationist biologist, G.A. Kerkut, who argued that, "It is therefore a matter of faith on the part of the biologist that biogenesis did occur" because "the evidence for what did happen is not available."[64] But England was also willing to live with a faith based upon the ambiguity of scientific evidence when it

---

[63] Jack Wood Sears, "How the Worlds Were Framed (Hebrews 11:3): The Biblical Account of Creation Allows for a Very Ancient Earth," and Bert Thompson, "How the Worlds Were Framed (Hebrews 11:3): God Created the Universe and all that is in it in a Mature State in Six Literal Days of Approximately 24 hours each," in Dub McClish, ed., *Studies in Hebrews* (Denton, TX: Valid Publications, 1983), 405-434. Sears and Thompson had discussed the same issue in Zimbabwe (then Rhodesia) in December 1977 (cited by Thompson, 433).

[64] Kerkut, *Implications of Evolution*, 150; Donald England, *A Christian View of Origins* (Grand Rapids, MI: Baker Book House, 1972). The most authoritative study of this issue is John Farley, *The Spontaneous Generation Controversy from Descartes to Oparin* (Baltimore: Johns Hopkins University Press, 1977). See also NYU chemistry professor and DNA researcher Robert Shapiro's *Origins: A Skeptic's Guide to the Creation of Life on Earth* (New York: Simon and Schuster, 1986), 98-131; and Klaus Dose, "The Origin of Life: More Questions Than Answers," *Interdisciplinary Science Reviews* 13 (1988), 348f. The famous Miller-Urey experiments are described in S.L. Miller, "Production of Some Organic Compounds Under Possible Primitive Conditions," *Journal of the American Chemical Society* 77 (1955), 2351. See also S.L. Miller and H.C. Urey, "Organic Compound Synthesis on the Primitive Earth," *Science* 130 (1959): 245-251. Miller describes the circumstances surrounding the experiment in "The First Laboratory Synthesis of Organic Compounds under Primitive Earth Conditions," in J. Neyman, ed., *The Heritage of Copernicus: "Theories Pleasing to the Mind"* (Cambridge, MA: MIT Press, 1974), 228-242. A fascinating summary of the likelihood of biotic-soup origins of life on earth, and a "creative" proposal of directed panspermia as an alternative hypothesis, is found in Sir Francis Crick, *Life Itself: Its Origin and Nature* (New York: Simon and Schuster, 1981), 15-16, 79-88 and *passim*. An informative examination of origin of life experiments and theorizing is found in the work of Charles B. Thaxton, Walter L. Bradley, and Roger L. Olsen, *The Mystery of Life's Origin: Reassessing Current Theories* (New York: Philosophical Library, 1984).

came to the age of the earth. Clearly renouncing flood geology, he could see no reason "to suppose that a few catastrophic events over a relatively short period of a few thousand years could have given the earth its general overall appearance of great antiquity." Hinting at the doctrinal presuppositions of some young-earth advocates such as Adventists or premillennialists, England argued that:

> There is no specific and well-defined statement in Biblical revelation as to the age of the earth or to the age of life on earth. Furthermore, we should resist the temptation to take a general impression which we get from Biblical revelation and crystallize it into an absolute truth that we bind on others. Some religious groups have done this in areas of Biblical revelation, to their great harm and apostasy.[65]

In a later book, published in 1983, England was even more outspokenly critical of flood geologists. In *A Scientist Examines Faith and Evidence*, he identified "'young earth' advocates who invoke the flood of Genesis 6 to explain all geological phenomena and impose that belief upon others" as taking "unwarranted liberties with the Genesis account."[66]

By publishing their work with reputable evangelical publishing concerns, Sears and England attained access to a much wider audience than if they had limited themselves to one of several publishing houses operated by members of churches of Christ. Some of these later publishing ventures no doubt demonstrate the growing affinity felt by some in churches of Christ for many in the wider evangelical community.

Indeed, whatever reservations some members of churches of Christ may have had regarding the Flood Geologists, they were comfortable enough with their fellow creationists to cooperate with them on various projects. When the Creation Research Society produced a biology textbook designed for use in secular classrooms, four of fifteen editorial committee members were members of churches of Christ. The four included Sears, David

---

[65] England, *A Christian View of Origins*, 105-106; see also 101-102 and the sections of Chapter 5 entitled "The Age of the Earth" and "Why Do Some Insist on a Young Earth?"

[66] England, *A Scientist Examines Faith and Evidence* (Delight, AR: Gospel Light Publishing Company, 1983); interview, author with England (Searcy, Arkansas, September 30, 1991).

Lipscomb College biology professor, Russell Artist, Pepperdine University biology professor, Douglas Dean, and an El Paso high school biology teacher, Rita Rhodes Ward.[67] In 1965, Ward had written *In the Beginning: A Study of Evolution versus Creation for Young People*, designed for use in churches or parochial school classrooms. Ward published her book with Baker Book House, and it was largely through her efforts that Sears, Artist, and Dean became affiliated with the textbook project. Dean had received his Ph.D. from the University of Alabama. He then relocated to Southern California, a hotbed of "scientific creationism." There he not only taught biology at Pepperdine but also became vitally involved in the active creationist movements which existed in Orange County, home of many CRS members, and San Diego, where Morris' and Gish's Institute for Creation Research was located.[68] The new CRS text bore the title, *Biology: A Search for Order in Complexity*. According to one history of creationist movements, Ward herself "outlined the volume" and assisted in other ways, including "lining up over a dozen contributing authors, including three biologists from church of Christ colleges."[69]

Despite her experience in having already produced a high-school level book on the subject, Ward was in some ways a peculiar choice for the CRS. In her own book, she repeatedly warned students against adopting any position on the age of the earth on the basis of some biblical doctrine or

---

[67] John N. Moore and Harold S. Slusher, eds., *Biology: A Search for Order in Complexity* (Grand Rapids, MI: Zondervan Publishing Company, 1970, 1974), xvi, xxiv. The papers of Walter E. Lammerts, renowned geneticist and long-time secretary of the Creation Research Society, are located in the Bancroft Library at the University of California at Berkeley. They contain a number of files pertaining to the work done by Ward and others on the preparation of *Biology: A Search for Order in Complexity* (photocopies in author's possession). On the relationship of Churches of Christ to modern Evangelicalism, see Richard T. Hughes, "Are Restorationists Evangelicals?" in Donald W. Dayton and Robert K. Johnston, *The Variety of American Evangelicalism* (Knoxville: University of Tennessee Press, 1991), 109-134.

[68] Douglas Dean biographical information from author interview (Malibu, CA, June 10, 1991). Dean died in 1992.

[69] Numbers, *The Creationists*, 289; author interview with Nell Segraves (Yucaipa, CA, June 12, 1991).

statement. Pointing out several problems with the chronology of Bishop Ussher's date of creation, Ward argued not only that "the commonly held 4004 B.C. has no reliable scriptural basis" but that "scripture gives no date for either the creation of the materials of the universe or for the creation of living things." Furthermore, Ward adamantly declared that "Scripture does not say when the universe was created and science has no way of finding out. Christians will do well to leave the matter there." Suggesting both the gap theory and the day-age theory as possibilities for an understanding of Genesis, she concluded, "It is important that we believe that God did create both the universe and life, not that we know when or how such creation took place."[70]

While Ward and other scientifically credentialed members of churches of Christ were thus willing to collaborate with creationists of various denominations, they formed enough of a critical mass to conduct their own programs. In 1972, Bales, Sears, England, Dean, and other credentialed scientists or philosophers of science who were members of or taught at colleges related to churches of Christ, assembled in Atlanta for a public conference which was widely advertised in the local media.[71] The conference was organized by Robert Camp, a church of Christ minister who, according to historian of science, Ronald Numbers, endorsed George McCready Price's anti-evolutionary views. Also included on the program was Thomas B. Warren, fresh with a philosophy Ph.D. from Vanderbilt University, who over the next decade would make a career of debating theism and atheism with an array of world-class philosophers, including England's A.G.N. Flew and Wallace Matson of the University of California at Berkeley.[72]

---

[70] Rita Rhodes Ward, *In the Beginning: A Study of Creation versus Evolution for Young People* (Grand Rapids, MI: Baker Book House, 1965), 37-39, 42, 66-67. See also Ward, "A Study of English Micraster Research," in Walter E. Lammerts, ed. *Scientific Studies in Special Creation: Selected Articles from the Creation Research Society Quarterly, Volumes I through V (1964-1968)* (Nutley, NJ: Presbyterian and Reformed Publishing Company, 1971, 184-197).

[71] Robert S. Camp. ed., *A Critical Look at Evolution* (Atlanta: Religion, Science, and Communication Research and Development Corporation, 1972); Numbers, *The Creationists*, 315. On Price, see Numbers, chapter 5 and *passim*.

[72] Thomas B. Warren and Antony G.N. Flew, *The Warren-Flew Debate on the Existence of God* (Jonesboro, AR: National Christian Press, 1977); Warren and Wallace I. Matson, *The Warren-Matson Debate on the Existence of God* (Jonesboro,

Flood Geology Dissenters

However, several scientifically-credentialed members of churches of Christ were suspicious or disenchanted enough to register open dissent from the "flood geology" espoused by the increasingly visible work of Morris, Gish, and the Institute for Creation Research. In 1970, David Koltenbah, a physics professor at Ball State University in Muncie, Indiana, published two lengthy articles in *Truth Magazine*, then edited by Cecil Willis. Warning that parts of Whitcomb and Morris' *Genesis Flood* "constitute a distortion of the evidence and a misunderstanding of scientific laws and theories," Koltenbah described the material in chapter 7 dealing with the supposed effects of cosmic ray radiation on rates of radioactive decay as "simply a piece of science fiction." Even with regard to the more general aspects of the Whitcomb-Morris approach to science and religion, Koltenbah sounded an urgent cautionary note, reminding readers that if "'Flood Geology' is a matter of Biblical truth, then it can hardly be merely a scientific hypothesis for the Bible believer. But if it is a scientific hypothesis to be treated on the same footing with other scientific theories in the gladiatorial arena of science, then it is not a matter of clearly revealed Scriptural truth." Koltenbah also admonished readers, as well as committed "Flood Geologists," that "one has no right to invent miracles to bolster 'scientific' conjectures."[73]

A behind-the-scenes exchange between the journal's editor and a senior staff writer to whom Koltenbah's manuscript was sent for pre-publication review is as telling as Koltenbah's articles. The senior staffer, James W. Adams, recalled that "while a student at Freed-Hardeman [College], I was taught the 'Gap Theory,' and I see nothing in it contradictory of Bible teaching." Adams went on to explain that "by 'Gap Theory,' I mean that the text would allow a long period or periods of time between creation in Genesis 1:1 and the beginning of the first day's work of 'renovation' in verse 3." He reminded the editor that "Robert Milligan takes this view in *Scheme of Redemption*." He also recalled that H. Leo Boles, who had been editor of the *Gospel Advocate* and twice president of Nashville Bible School, ar-

---

AR: National Christian Press, 1978); see also Matson, *The Existence of God* (Ithaca, NY: Cornell University Press, 1965).

[73] David Koltenbah, "Concerning the Creation Research Society, the Book *The Genesis Flood*, and 'Flood Geology,'" *Truth Magazine* 15 (November 19 & 26, 1970), 39, 51, 53.

gued that "to recognize the possibility that the 'days' of Genesis 1 were long periods of time" was not "contradictory of Bible teaching."[74]

Agreeing with Koltenbah that "we should not tie ourselves irrevocably to 'flood geology,'" Adams proceeded to question "whether the Genesis flood alone was catastrophic enough or cataclysmic enough to have produced all of the scientifically observable characteristics of the earth's crust. It appears to me that this would be at least scientifically debatable."[75]

Emphasizing that "brethren of ability and sound judgment have through the years recognized several alternatives to an acceptance of the theory of evolution," he expressed an opinion that the "Gap Theory" is "very probably the view assumed by some brethren (preachers particularly) than any other." Koltenbah's articles were published without editorial criticism, and elicited no negative response from the over 4,000 subscribers, mostly ministers among conservative churches of Christ, who read the journal.

Flood Geology Dissenters in the "Mainstream"
Because of Koltenbah's relatively small reading audience, however, his cautions lacked the impact of the continuing efforts of a number of other dissenters from "Flood Geology." Probably the most visible such dissenter was John N. Clayton, a high school science teacher in South Bend, Indiana. With master's degrees in earth science from Indiana University and in geology from the University of Notre Dame, Clayton had been an outspoken atheist before his conversion to Christianity. In the 1970s, he began conducting intensive weekend seminars on creation-evolution issues all over the United States, often in churches of Christ, but frequently on college and university campuses as well. Vocally critical of flood geology and its advocates, Clayton in 1976 published a book, *The Source*, which espoused an agnostic position with reference to the age of the earth.[76] Clayton's monthly publication *Does God Exist?* deals occasionally with broader issues but nearly always contains several articles examining evolutionary theory as well as broader science/religion questions.

---

[74] James W. Adams to Cecil Willis [editor], August 1970 (copies of this correspondence are in author's possession).

[75] *Ibid.*

[76] John N. Clayton, *The Source: Eternal Design or Infinite Accident?* (Mentone, IN: Superior Printing, 1976, 1978, 1993). See also regular issues of Clayton's monthly paper, *Does God Exist?*

Some of his critics among churches of Christ have pointed to differing, possibly even contradictory, statements in Clayton's writings over the years, and frequently have turned such differences to their own polemic uses. Possibly the clearest summary of Clayton's basic views of creation is provided by a well-known anti-creationist, Tom McIver. In lengthy review of the "Gap Theory," McIver described Clayton's argument that:

> The Genesis order of creation is the same as the geological record (reinterpreting some of the Bible terms) but also maintains that there were long ages before the six days of creation. . . Clayton's hybrid scheme thus allows for some day-age interpretation and also perhaps some theistic evolution in addition to its modified gap theory.[77]

Indeed, in *The Source*, Clayton discusses a number of theories proposed over the years to attempt harmonization between geology and Genesis. After eliminating several such theories, partly by labeling them as the "Anti-Science" and "Deception" positions, he commented on two others, namely, the so-called "day-age" and "gap" theories. While noting "inconsistencies" in those theories, these two, according to Clayton, "can be more easily justified in terms of the language of Genesis 1." Insisting that "there is absolutely no evidence of the kind of global destruction proposed in the gap theory," Clayton went on to propose a sort of conflated view, or modified gap theory described by McIver.[78] As *The Source* was in production late in 1975, Clayton wrote to the elders of the South Bend church which sponsored his work. He explained to them that:

> We did not espouse either the day age theory or the gap theory. We did point out that those theories are more consistent with the record than other theories denominations have advanced. . . .We have simply tried to

---

[77] Tom McIver, "Formless and Void: Gap Theory Creationism," *Creation/Evolution* 8 (1988:1-23, quotation from p. 22). See also McIver's useful book, *Anti-Evolution: A Reader's Guide to Writings Before and After Darwin* (Baltimore: The Johns Hopkins University Press, 1992), and McIver, "Creationism: Intellectual Origins, Cultural Context, and Theoretical Diversity" (Ph.D. dissertaion, University of Southern California, 1989).

[78] Clayton, *The Source,* 136-138 [1976]; 154-158 [1990].

get people to realize that the Genesis account is not a detailed historical account.[79]

While some "mainstream" church members found Clayton's views unacceptable, others not only agreed but were openly more vocal, and Clayton gladly publicized their writings.

For example, Clayton reprinted an article by Pepperdine University biology professor, Norman Hughes, which sought to disabuse readers of false dichotomies. It was "a fallacy," Hughes argued, to believe that accepting "evolutionary explanations" meant that "one has eliminated God's role in the creation of life." The Pepperdine biologist encouraged Christians to accept "both natural and supernatural explanations at the same time" when confronted with apparent conflicts between evidence from natural science and Scripture.[80] While such statements resulted in both Hughes and Clayton being labeled "theistic evolutionists," so negative was the word "evolution" as a description of their beliefs that its use drew protests even when modified by the word "theism." Hughes' paradoxical comments in the *Journal of the American Scientific Affiliation* illustrate the problem of definitions and labels when the words themselves become polemically value-laden. "I am a theist," he said, adding in the next sentence, "I am an evolutionist — I find many biological phenomena which are not explainable except by the theory of evolution." He concluded, however, with the fervently curious plea, "But please, don't call me a theistic evolutionist!"[81]

Not everyone was quite so reticent. At least one biologist, who was an elder of an Arkansas Church of Christ, seemed willing to unabashedly embrace evolutionary theory. Neal Buffaloe, less restrained possibly because he taught at a state university rather than a "Christian college," willingly affirmed that "the concept of evolution is neither degrading to man, detrimental to human dignity, nor in conflict with the Bible." Unabashedly em-

---

[79] Clayton to Donmoyer Avenue Church of Christ elders, September 5, 1975, quoted in Wayne Jackson and Bert Thompson, *In the Shadow of Darwin: A review of the teachings of John N. Clayton* (Montgomery, AL: Apologetics Press, 1992), 84.

[80] Norman Hughes, "Monism, Belief, and Scientific Explanations," in *Does God Exist?* (September/October 1984),12-18; quotation from p. 16.

[81] Norman Hughes, "Letters," *Journal of the American Scientific Affiliation* 38 (December 1986), 282.

bracing a position of theistic evolution, Buffaloe asked, "What do we care that man the animal is a product of evolution as long as man the spirit is begotten of God?"[82]

Bert Thompson

It would be erroneous, however, to conclude that there is no recent support for flood geology among members of churches of Christ. Soon after Clayton's work began to circulate widely among church members, Wayne Jackson, a Stockton, California minister formed an alliance with young Texas A&M professor, Bert Thompson. Together, they began a publishing and lecturing enterprise similar to Clayton's with a primary goal of blunting the influence of Clayton and others, and promoting young earth views similar if not identical to those of Henry Morris, Duane Gish, and others associated with the Institute for Creation Research.[83]

By 1985, however, Thompson reeled in bigger fish when repeated complaints about the teaching of theistic evolution at his alma mater, Abilene Christian University, brought his full attention to bear on that problem. Early in 1985, Thompson received a letter from a student at ACU alleging the teaching of theistic evolution at that institution. The student, a biology major, wrote to Thompson in part because he knew Thompson had also been a biology major at Abilene before going on to earn a Ph.D. in food microbiology at Texas A&M University. The student, Mark Scott, enclosed some of the handouts from a course he was taking, required of all biology majors, in which the professor had required as a text the book *Science and Creationism* by Ashley Montagu. The handouts included chapters from Philip Kitcher's *Abusing Science: The Case Against Creationism* and Dou-

---

[82] Neal Buffaloe, "God or Evolution?" in *Mission* 3 (April 1969), 17-21. *Mission* was an avant-garde journal for the expressions an emerging and more ecumenical outlook by some members of churches of Christ in the 1960s. For Buffaloe's views, see also Buffaloe and N. Patrick Murray, *Creationism and Evolution* (Little Rock, AR: The Bookmark, 1981).

[83] Wayne Jackson and Bert Thompson, *Evolutionary Creationism: A Review of the Teaching of John Clayton* (Montgomery, AL: Apologetics Press, 1979). See also Thompson, *Theistic Evolution* (Shreveport, LA; Lambert Book House, 1977); Thompson, *The Scientific Case for Creation* (Montgomery, AL: Apologetics Press, n.d. [ca. 1990]); Jackson, *Creation, Evolution, and the Age of the Earth* (Stockton, CA: Courier Publications, 1989); and issues of *Reason and Revelation*, Thompson and Jackson's monthly journal.

glas Futuyma's *Science on Trial* as well as an essay, "A Clock of Evolution" by Stephen J. Gould. Worse, as far as Scott and Thompson were concerned, were the professor's own handout notes which excoriated creationists and labeled Genesis 1 as "myth."[84]

Within weeks, Thompson had received similar letters from two more students, including handout materials from a course taught by a second professor. The handouts included material from Gould and Isaac Asimov. Over the course of the next year, Thompson corresponded and met with teachers and administrators at ACU, keeping documents and notes which he later published in excruciating detail in a book, *Is Genesis Myth?* While several in the ACU administration attempted to deny that any thoroughgoing evolution had been taught, the professors themselves acknowledged through several sources that evolution was indeed taught at ACU and that "the biology class is no place to refute evolution." The incident ended in a sort of Mexican stand-off with neither side pleased by the outcome, demonstrating that there was no unanimity of opinion in "mainstream" churches of Christ on evolutionary theory. Indeed, different church members in influential positions held seemingly diametrically opposite viewpoints while remaining in good standing, at least in some quarters. At the very least, the incident demonstrated that teaching evolutionary theory was at least tolerated if not received enthusiastically by some members of churches of Christ.

Ultimately, to bring this portion of the story full circle, Thompson's disapproval of anything less than full acceptance of strict young-earth creationism brought him into public discussion with a retiring church of Christ biology professor, Jack Wood Sears, who had first debated the issue more than twenty years before in Little Rock, while Thompson was still a high school student.[85] In 1983, the Christian Student Center at the University of Mississippi, which had provided the forum in which the substance of Sears

---

[84] Bert Thompson, *Is Genesis Myth? The Shocking Story of the Teaching of Evolution at Abilene Christian University* (Montgomery, AL: Apologetics Press, 1986). One result of Thompson's expose was the publication of a volume of essays edited by long-time ACU religion professor J.D. Thomas, *Evolution and Faith* (Abilene: ACU Press, 1988). The various chapters on science and religion subjects are contributed by several faculty members at ACU, including Bert Thompson's mentor, Clark Stevens, and concluding with an appendix by John N. Clayton.

[85] See Wolfgang, "Science and Religion Issues," pp. 200-204 for a description of the 1965 "Debate of the Century" which pitted Sears and Bales against two rising stars of the American scientific community, Carl Sagan and Richard Lewontin, as well as well-known Roman Catholic philosopher of science Ernan McMullin.

and England's books had been presented, proposed to devote another annual lectureship to creation-evolution issues. They planned a panel discussion which included not only previous participants such as Donald England, but also provided for a discussion of "Theistic Evolution" by Neal Buffaloe, "Creation Science" by Bert Thompson, and "An Argument for Antiquity and Classical Geology" by John Clayton.[86] Thompson declined to participate, and ultimately neither he, Clayton, nor Buffaloe appeared. Jack Wood Sears was subsequently invited and appeared on the program. Sears also agreed to a debate with Thompson, and the two met at Denton, Texas in November 1983. Sears affirmed that "the biblical account of creation allows for a very ancient earth," while Thompson opposed Sears, affirming that:

> God created the Universe and all that is in it in six literal days of approximately 24 hours each; He did not employ a system requiring vast periods or long ages of time to bring the material universe to its present state.[87]

Perceiving a marked anti-creationist bias among the scientific community, and failing to publish their views in the refereed scientific journals, many modern creationists chose the more populist appeal to public opinion through debating various evolutionists. Modern day restorationists were no less fond of appealing to popular opinion through the tactic of debating (which has, of course, a long and storied history among restorationists). In March 1984, just a few months after the Thompson-Sears exchange, another public debate occurred at Clark College in Atlanta. Moderated by Andrew Hairston, a local judge, civil rights leader, and minister of the Simpson Street Church of Christ near downtown Atlanta, the debate featured Rubel Shelly, minister of Nashville's Ashwood Church of Christ and recently graduated from Vanderbilt University with a philosophy Ph.D. His opponent for the evening was Charles V. Powell, a self-described "independent researcher" who held a doctorate in experimental psychology from the University of Georgia and had taught at several colleges in Georgia. The debate, televised before a studio audience, concentrated specifically upon the question of whether creationism should have alternate-theory, equal-time status in public schools. However, the debate was largely in question-and-

---

[86] Thompson, *Creation Compromises* (Montgomery, AL: Apologetics Press, 1995), 245-250.

[87] Jack Wood Sears, "How the Worlds Were Framed" (*op.cit.*), 405-434.

answer format and therefore proved to be wide-ranging and relatively un-focused. Among other things, Shelly attempted to disconnect creationism from biblical doctrines by denying that creationism was a religion or had any necessarily religious content. For his part, Powell attempted to portray all creationists as disciples of "the leading creationist," Henry Morris, whose writings he repeatedly referenced and quoted. In rebuttal, Shelly distanced himself from any young-earth geological position, saying, "I certainly don't think that it is characteristic of intelligent creationists today to make the claim that the universe and all of the galaxies of it were created 10,000 years ago."[88]

Thus, creationism in all its varied forms had spread widely among restorationists in the intervening years, and by the 1980s no single institution, group, or person, could claim to represent *the*, or even a majority, creationist viewpoint. And so it was among churches of Christ. In addition to the faculties of the better-known "Christian colleges," there were many other credentialed individuals who had staked out a position on the issue.

Conclusions

Several years ago, writing under the pressure of an impending deadline, I wrote the following paragraph:

> One item of personal curiosity for me before beginning this study emerged as a contrast to the diversity emphasized above. I speak of the nearly unanimous views of Restoration preachers and scientists who declined to demand or accept a "young-earth" view of creation. Indeed, the list of those willing to at least tolerate, if not stipulate an earth millions of years old reads like a virtual Restoration "Who's Who." It includes editors and college presidents from Campbell, Milligan, and Fanning to Lipscomb and Boles. They are joined by their science faculty and others with scientific credentials, including Fairhurst, Sears, England, Koltenbah, and others, including well-known preachers from Dungan to Otey. Thus, it would appear that any attempt by twentieth-century creationists within the Restoration Movement to achieve a young-earth orthodoxy will succeed only at the cost of declaring many of the movement's earlier leaders heretical on the question.[89]

Upon further reflection, some qualification seems in order. First, while

---

[88] Charles V. Powell and Rubel Shelly, *Of Human Origins: A Debate* (Nashville: 20th Century Christian Foundation, 1984), 11-12,16.

[89] Wolfgang, "Science and Religion Issues," 243. Consult chapter six of this work for more information on creationist controversies among churches of Christ.

it is clear that there was a range of diversity and a lack of enforced "ortho-doxy" on the question of the age of the earth, most of those quoted above, as James W. Adams noted, used the "gap theory" as a means of finding a "fit" between what Scripture seems to say, and what modern scientific evidence seems to report. One would be hard pressed to find examples of anyone among churches of Christ seriously attempting to stretch the meaning of "day" to mean eons of time.[90] Certainly one hears no brash assertions to the effect that days of Genesis "cannot be literal" or that they "must be figurative."[91]

---

[90] This is true at least of those who came to regard themselves as members of churches of Christ as opposed to the Disciples. Exceptions to this can occasionally be found among those who eventually affiliated with the Disciples of Christ. As the disciples came to adopt more liberal views on many issues in the late nineteenth century, one can find diverging opinions and teachings not only on the age of the earth, but on broader evolutionary issues and philosophies as well.

[91] The quotations "cannot be literal/must be figurative" are the headings in a written debate by Shane Scott, opposing Greg Gwin's affirmation of a "young earth" position in *Sentry Magazine* in 1995.

Sentry Magazine has continued a general trend of publishing articles by defenders of an old-earth position. See, for instance, the latest installment in which a vocal old-earth advocate lifts quotations extensively from my copyrighted Ph.D. dissertation, based upon literally decades of research, without citing it as the source of the material, without comment or correction from the editors (Tom Couchman, "Not Anything New," *Sentry* 29 [March 31, 2003], 10).

Others have cited my work as implying that the variety of Restorationist views somehow provides authority for similar stances in the present day. I have seen such instances on a variety of websites, including those operated by Shane Scott and Ferrell Jenkins. An extensive discussion of such issue occurred on the Watchman.org website.

Extensive discussions of age-of-the-earth issues include (to cite merely a sample), Daniel H. King, Sr., "The Days of Genesis," a four-part series in *Truth Magazine* during June and July 2000; Connie W. Adams, "The Days of Creation," *Truth Magazine* 44 (July 6, 2000), 387; followed by an exchange between Adams, King, Harry Osborne, Colly Caldwell, and Shane Scott in the July 20 issue (C.G. "Colly" Caldwell, "The Days of Creation: Some Things to Consider," 454; Shane Scott, "Response to Connie Adams," 456; Connie W. Adams, "Response to Brethren Caldwell and Scott," 457; and Daniel H. King, Sr. and Harry Osborne, "An Open Letter: The Creation Account and Florida College," 460. See also articles by Mike Willis, "In the Beginning God" (*Truth Magazine* 44 [February 27, 2000], 98; "The

Second, it is difficult to imagine most of those cited above finding any comfort in attempts to allow the "assured results of modern science" to dictate the interpretation of Genesis or any other portion of Scripture. Re-translating Genesis to make it more palatable to their generation of scientists seems not to have been on their agenda. While many of them lived in a time when an earlier version of "science," or "natural philosophy" — with its Baconian emphasis on empiricism and the collection, accumulation, and arrangement of "facts" — seemed to them to be hospitable to Biblical enterprises, they would have abhorred attempts to place the ever-changing conclusions of science in a place of primacy over revelation expressed in Scripture. This is one of the broader themes emphasized in my dissertation, "Science and Religion Issues," cited above.

Third, for whatever it may be worth, it seems clear that many, if not most, "restorationists" have followed the prevailing climate of opinion in the larger American religious culture on this question.[92] During the late nineteenth and early twentieth centuries, most religious conservatives used either the "gap theory," or occasionally the "day-age theory" or some combination to attempt a reconciliation of the Bible and modern science. During that period, members of churches of Christ frequently used such arguments in their own discussions. After about 1960, when the "Flood Geology" of Seventh-Day Adventist George McCready Price was given a veneer of scientific credibility through the work of Henry Morris, Duane Gish, and the Institute for Creation Research, "young-earth" advocates pre-empted the use of the term "creationism." Specifically, the term "scientific creationism" came to mean almost exclusively a "young-earth" view of Genesis — even though "old-earth" creationists were more numerous

---

Flood, " (*Truth Magazine* 44 [November 2, 2000], 642; "Genesis One vs. Pagan Cosmologies" (*Truth Magazine* 45 [October 4, 2001], 45; and a four-part series on "The Chronology of the Bible" in *Truth Magazine* 46 (September 19, 2002, 546 through October 27, 2002, 614); and another Daniel H. King, Sr., "Do We Have Theistic Evolutionists Among Us?" in *Truth Magazine* from November 15, 2001 through the January 17, 2002 issue; as well as David Dann, "Did God Create the World in One Literal Week?" (*Truth Magazine* 45 [September 6, 2001], 519; and Harry Osborne, "The Creation Account: Literal or Non-Literal?" (*Truth Magazine* 46 [August 1, 2002], 454).

[92] A case study of how churches of Christ have related to the broader conservative religious environment is found in James Stephen Wolfgang, "Fundamentalism and Churches of Christ" (M.A. thesis, Vanderbilt University, 1990).

(though perhaps less vocal).[93] It is also true that many who insist on "young-earth" creationism frequently invoke the work of those who accept an old-earth view (e.g., Michael Behe or Phillip Johnson and other "intelligent design" advocates) despite their acceptance of the earth's antiquity.[94]

Of course, enterprises such as this raises questions such as, "Why study the opinions of past generations?" since we disavow any authoritative role for them. The truth often is, we quote them with approval when they agree with us (or we with them), and when they do not, we ignore or dismiss them. In the same manner, future generations will no doubt disregard, discount, and dissent from our recorded opinions. If "turnabout is fair play" — or, more importantly, if our devotion is to the word of God rather than the thinking of humans — perhaps that is as it should be.

---

[93] This theme is explicit in Numbers' massive history, *The Creationists,* as well as in Numbers, *Darwinism Comes to America* (Cambridge: Harvard University Press, 1998), especially chapters 5 and 6, which expand the scope of Numbers' study to include Seventh-Day Adventism, Wesleyan, Holiness, and Pentecostal groups which attempt to understand the Bible literally.

[94] A useful discussion among a variety of young- and old-earth creationists is J.P. Moreland and John Mark Reynolds, eds, *Three Views on Creation and Evolution* (Grand Rapids: Zondervan, 1999). There is an explosion of literature on the "Intelligent Design" ideology; for an introduction, consult William A. Dembski, ed., *Mere Creation: Science, Faith, and Intelligent Design* (Downer's Grove, IL: InterVarsity, 1998), and Robert T. Pennock, ed., *Intelligent Design Creationism and Its Critics* (Cambridge, MA: MIT Press, 2001).

The Chronology of the Bible
Mike Willis

(Reprinted from *Truth Magazine* [September 19, October 3, 17, and November 21, 2002] with some revisions.)

In recent years, brethren have opened discussion about the creation account and this has subsequently triggered discussion about the age of the earth. Brother Shane Scott conducted a discussion in *Sentry* magazine (XXI:1) in which he argues that the days of creation cannot be six twenty-four hour days and accepts the timetable of the universe being 15 billion years old and the earth being 4+ billion years ("An Open Letter: The Creation Account and Florida College," *Truth Magazine* [August 3, 2000], 19). Brother Hill Roberts also presents the old earth theory in CD-ROM articles entitled "A Harmonization of God's Genesis Revelation With His Natural Revelation" and "Genesis and the Time Thing." That a few brethren have accepted the big bang/old earth position is not nearly so alarming as is the number of brethren who have indicated that holding that position is inconsequential. To my understanding, the old earth position undermines the teaching of Scripture and ultimately denies the inspiration of Scripture.

Those who are denying a literal interpretation of Genesis 1-2 appear to be influenced by what they see as unanswerable scientific evidences of an old earth (4.5 billion years old). The approach to Bible interpretation which allows the pronouncements of science to determine Bible exegesis results in science having superior authority to the revealed word of God. What science says about the age of the earth is to be believed rather than what the Bible teaches about the same subject. If this approach is followed on the age of the earth, it must also be followed on the following:

- The pronouncements of science must be believed over what the Bible says about a universal flood.
- The pronouncements of science must be believed over what the Bible says about the virgin birth.

- The pronouncements of science must be believed over what the Bible says about Joshua's long day.

Every miracle related in the Bible will eventually be suspect on the very same grounds that the literal interpretation of Genesis 1-2 is rejected.

Efforts to harmonize the pronouncements of science with the Bible always begin at the wrong end. The starting point that is adopted is this: The pronouncements of science are true and, therefore, one must restudy the Bible to see how it can be interpreted to fit what present day science affirms. Certainly this is true in the discussions about the age of the earth. Never does one begin by stating the following: The Bible is divinely inspired and, therefore, inerrant when it speaks about science. We must therefore restudy the scientific evidences to see wherein the interpretation given to them is mistaken.

In the beginning of this series of articles, I want to present my outline of study. I do not intend to look at scientific evidences of a young earth, although others have gathered scientific data to argue for a young earth. Their evidences should not be lightly dismissed by those who argue the age of the earth from a scientific point of view. There are limitations to arguing for a young earth on the grounds of scientific data, including that virtually every statement by one qualified scientist can be countered by a quotation from an equally qualified scientist who disagrees. Most of us, including me, are not qualified to sift through the technical scientific data. However, my belief in a young earth is not based on scientific data. I have an interest in the age of the earth discussion only as it relates to what the inspired word of God teaches. Consequently, this presentation is entitled "The Chronology of the *Bible*" because it is based on what God has revealed to us in his word. The Bible claims to be a revelation from God, an inspired document. I intend to show what the Bible teaches about the age of the earth and call upon men to believe, teach, and defend what the Bible teaches on the grounds that it is a revelation from God.

The Bible and the Age of the Earth

Does the Bible tell how old the earth is? Yes and no. The answer is, "No," if one wants a specific age of the earth. Nowhere does the Bible say that the earth is "x" years old in the same way that it says Jesus was in the tomb for three days (Matt. 12:40), the children of Israel wandered in the wilderness for forty years (Num. 14:33), and there were 480 years from the time of the Exodus to Solomon's fourth year (1 Kings 6:1).

However, the answer is, "Yes," if one means, "Does the Bible give an approximate age of the earth?" Certainly the Bible records the history of man from the creation and is very careful to put this in a chronological framework. There are limits on what the framework of Bible history will tolerate and, in this sense, the Bible does define the age of the earth.

Common Agreement on Bible Chronology
The Bible and all Bible historians have common agreement on 99% of the chronology of the Bible. Let's consider what the Bible says about chronology and see where there is agreement. As we write this in A.D. 2002, we can look back and see these areas of agreement:

We are agreed on the time when Christ lived. The Scriptures place the life of Christ in the framework of the first century. Luke 3:1-2 records the beginning of Jesus' ministry, placing it within the framework of history: "Now in the fifteenth year of the reign of Tiberius Caesar, Pontius Pilate being governor of Judaea, and Herod being tetrarch of Galilee, and his brother Philip tetrarch of Ituraea and of the region of Trachonitis, and Lysanias the tetrarch of Abilene, Annas and Caiaphas being the high priests, the word of God came unto John the son of Zacharias in the wilderness." Historians are agreed with these dates for the life of Christ. Jesus is thought to have been born about 6 B.C. and to have lived to A.D. 27. Though there may be a variation of as much as 1-2 years, there is no serious disagreement with these dates. This means that there is no problem of chronology in the New Testament.

We are agreed on the time of King Solomon. Chronologists usually date the reign of King Solomon at approximately 970-930 B.C. Though there may be disagreements ranging to about five years, there is no serious disagreement about the period at which any of Israel's kings ruled. These dates are accepted by non-believing archaeologists, modernists, and Evangelicals. The agreement on these dates takes us back to the reign of King Solomon and, therefore, of King David and King Saul. There is no disagreement on chronology as far back as 1 Samuel; men are agreed about the chronology of 1 Samuel through Malachi.

We are agreed back to Abraham. There are small problems of biblical chronology between Solomon and the Exodus. Regarding the date of the Exodus, the two different positions are the early date of 1440 B.C. (based on 1 Kings 6:1, 480 years to 966 B.C. = 1446 B.C.) and the late date of 1250-75 B.C. The early date is supported by the following texts of Scripture: (a) 1 Kings 6:1, "And it came to pass in the four hundred and eightieth year after the children of Israel were come out of the land of Egypt, in the fourth year of Solomon's reign over Israel, in the month Zif, which is the second month, that he began to build the house of the Lord." The dating of Solomon is generally agreed upon (970-930 B.C.). His fourth year (966

B.C.) is said to be 480 years after the Exodus. The face value of Scripture leaves the impression that the Exodus occurred in 1446 B.C. (b) Acts 13:19-20, "And when he had destroyed seven nations in the land of Chanaan, he divided their land to them by lot. And after that he gave unto them judges about the space of *four hundred and fifty years*, until Samuel the prophet." (c) Judges 11:26. During the time of Jephthah, the Ammonites made war against Israel. In desperation, the Israelites turned to Jephthah to deliver them from the Ammonites. Jephthah tried to reason with the Ammonites about attacking Israel, asking why they were attacking Israel. The Ammonites charged that Israel had taken their land during the conquest of Canaan (taking the area on the east side of Jordan between the Arnon and the Jabbock). Jephthah replied that Israel had occupied that land for 300 hundred years saying, "While Israel dwelt in Heshbon and her towns, and in Aroer and her towns, and in all the cities that be along by the coasts of Arnon, three hundred years? Why therefore did ye not recover them within that time?" This figure poses a serious problem for those who take the late date for the Exodus (966 [date of Solomon] + 40 reign of David + 40 years reign of Saul + 300 years [remember that Jephthah was not the last judge] = 1346 B.C.). Those who take an late date for the Exodus face serious problems of Bible interpretation.

While there is heated argument about the late and early date, a difference of a mere 200 years is nothing in terms of the discussion of the earth being 4.5 billion year old. Whichever date is taken, there is a disagreement of only about 200 years with reference to the Exodus.

This disagreement in Bible chronology affects when Abraham lived. Evangelical scholars who take the 1446 B.C. date for the Exodus add the ages of the Patriarchs to arrive at 2166 for the birth of Abraham.

Abraham was 100 years old when Isaac was born (Gen. 21:5)	100
Isaac was 60 years old when Jacob was born (Gen. 25:26)	60
Jacob was 130 years old when he went down into Egypt	130
Total:	**290**

Adding these together one arrives at the following figures:

Date at Solomon's fourth year	966 B.C.
Years from Exodus	480

Years in Egypt	430
Years to time of Abraham	290
Date at the birth of Abraham	**2166 B.C.**

Other scholars date the Exodus about 1250 B.C. and the time the Israelites were in Egypt to 215 years, resulting in a date for Abraham at about 1750-1800 B.C. Their dating system relies more heavily on the conclusions of archaeology, harmonizing the list of kings in Egypt and in other surrounding countries, and the Bible itself. The differences that Bible chronologists have for the date of Abraham is a mere 300-400 years maximum, which again is a mere pittance of time when one is speaking of an earth that is dated 4.5 billion years old. Basically one can say that Bible scholars are agreed on the chronology of the Bible from Genesis 12 through Revelation 22.

That leaves a mere eleven chapters of the Bible in which one is trying to find 4.5 billion years! About the rest of the chronology of the Bible there is relatively little difference in dating because all are generally agreed about those dates within a range of 200-300 years.

The Bible Material in Genesis 1-11

The evidence for the chronology for Genesis 1-11 must center on three chapters: (a) The creation narrative in Genesis 1; (b) The ten generations between Adam and Noah (Gen. 5); (c) The ten generations between Noah

Textual Versions								
Massoretic Text			LXX Version			Samaritan Pentateuch		
Man	Age at Son's Birth	Remaining Years	Age at Death	Age at Son's Birth	Remaining Years	Age at Death	Age at Son's Birth	Remaining Years	Age at Death
Adam	130	800	930	230	700	930	130	800	930
Seth	105	807	912	205	707	912	105	807	912
Enos	90	815	905	190	715	905	90	815	905
Cainan	70	840	910	170	740	910	70	840	910
Mahalaleel	65	830	895	165	730	895	65	830	895
Jared	162	800	962	162	800	962	62	785	847
Enoch	65	300	365	165	200	365	65	300	365
Methuselah	187	782	969	167	802	969	67	653	720
Lamech	182	595	777	188	565	753	53	600	653
Noah	500	450	950	500	450	950	500	450	950

and Abraham (Gen. 11). We will begin by looking at the two chronology/ generation charts.

The Bible is very careful in providing the chronology from creation to Abraham. The text of Genesis 5 follows this pattern: "**A** lived **x** number of years, and begat **B**. And the days of **A** after he had begotten **B** were **y** number of years." There are ten generations between Adam and Noah and the above chart gives the information recorded in Genesis 5 (Chart 1).

One notices a pattern to the variants between the Massoretic text and the LXX which, with three exceptions, adds 100 years to the age of the patriarch before the birth of the firstborn and subtracts 100 years from his life after the birth of the firstborn. The exceptions are Jared, Methuselah, and Lamech, in two of which (Jared and Methuselah) the LXX agrees with the Hebrew. The Samaritan Pentateuch disagrees with the Hebrew text in the lives of Jared, Methuselah, and Lamech, but never agrees with the LXX against the Hebrew text. According to the Hebrew text, the Flood occurred 1656 years after creation; according to the LXX it occurred 2242 years after creation and according to the Samaritan Pentateuch in 1307 (Wevers 68). Scholars are disagreed on how trustworthy the Samaritan Pentateuch is.

Of those who accept the Hebrew text as the superior reading, there is universal agreement that the flood occurred 1656 years after creation if one adds up the relevant information in the Hebrew text. The text also gives the following chronological sequence (Chart 2).

The ten generations of Genesis 11 are also given according to the pattern of Genesis 5 — "**A** lived **x** number of years, and begat **B**. And the days of **A** after he had begotten **B** were **y** number of years." In the comparison with chapter five, the form has changed in that the structure does not contain the total number of years that a person lived nor the statement "and he died." However, the information about the total number of years that a person lived is given by

Chronology		
Man	At At Birth of Son	Year of Man At His Birth
Adam	130	--
Seth	105	130
Enos	90	235
Cainan	70	325
Mahalaleel	65	395
Jared	162	460
Enoch	65	622
Methuselah	187	687
Lamech	182	874
Noah	500	1056
Shem, Ham, Japheth		1556
Flood in 600 year of Noah		1656

implication, though not expressly stated. Here is the information provided there (Chart 3):

Person	Hebrew Text		LXX		Samaritan		
	Year at Birth	Add. Years	Year at Birth	Add. Years	Year at Birth	Add. Years	Total Years
Shem	100	500	100	500	100	500	600
Arphaxad	35	403	135	430	135	303	438
Cainan			130	330			
Shelah	30	403	130	330	130	303	433
Eber	34	430	134	370	134	270	404
Peleg	30	209	130	209	130	109	239
Reu	32	207	132	207	132	107	239
Serug	30	200	130	200	130	100	230
Nahor	29	119	79	129	79	69	149
Terah	70	135	70	135	70	75	145
No. of years	390		1170		1040		

One will notice that with the inclusion of Cainan, the list in chapter 11 corresponds with that in chapter 5 in that both have ten generations. In both cases the genealogy ends with one who had three sons: Noah (Shem, Ham, and Japheth) and Terah (Abram, Nahor, Haran). In both cases the most important son is listed first (Shem/Abram). The fact that there are ten generations may lead one to think that the generations have omissions in them, that the "ten generations" is a memory device. However, this does not explain the careful detailing of the years a person lived before giving birth to the next generation. There is no purpose in giving those numbers unless the author wishes his readers to understand that they were sequential.

One will notice that the LXX and Samaritan Pentateuch are in agreement against the Massoretic Text on the ages of the various patriarchs at the birth of the designated descendant and that they consistently add 100 years with two exceptions (Nahor [50] and Terah). This significantly extends the years between the Flood and Abram. Scholars generally believe that the Massoretic Text is the superior reading.

Between Arphaxad and Salah, the LXX adds the name of **Cainan**. It adds: "And Arphaxad lived a hundred and thirty-five years and begot Cainan. And Arphaxad lived after he had begotten Cainan, four hundred years, and begot sons and daughters, and died. And Cainan lived a hundred and thirty years and begot Sala; and Cainan lived after he had begotten Sala, three hundred and thirty years, and begot sons and daughters, and died." One might be ready to dismiss the variant reading as a LXX addition. However, in the lineage of Christ given in Luke 3, Cainan is included (3:36), demonstrating the presence of the name in the genealogies of the first century and adding Luke's inspired testimony to its inclusion in the text here. Including Cainan brings the list of names to ten making it correspond to the ten generations in chapter 5. The LXX most probably reflects a variant textual reading that has not been preserved in existing Massoretic texts.

Adding the information gleaned from Genesis 11, we have the following (Chart 4):

Chronological Chart		
Man	**Age at Birth of Son**	**Year of Man at Birth of Son**
Noah	500	1556
Shem	100	1656
Arphaxed	35	1691
Cainan	30*	1721
Shelah	30	1751
Eber	34	1785
Peleg	30	1815
Reu	32	1847
Serug	30	1877
Nahor	29	1906
Terah	70	1976
Abraham was born 1976 years after creation.		

* The LXX has 130 years for Cainan prior to the birth of Shelah. However, the LXX consistently adds 100 years to all of these figures; since I have followed the Hebrew numbers by rejecting the added 100 years in other places, I also have made this adjustment on this number.

Putting this information together, we arrive at an approximate age of the earth. The date for Abraham varied from 2166 B.C. to 1750 B.C. depending upon various items for discussion which are previously mentioned. Rounding 1976 years to 2000, one arrives at an approximate time for the creation of Adam, according to the genealogies found in Scripture at approximately

4166 B.C. to 3750 B.C. One can understand and appreciate Ussher's chronology which dated creation at 4004 B.C. The earth is approximately 6000 years old based on the Bible evidence.

One might speculate about missing generations in the biblical narrative which could add a few thousand years to these figures, but the text of Scripture from Genesis 2 through Revelation simply will not allow room for the spans of time asserted by evolutionary theory. I certainly do not intend to tie the Bible to a specified time when the earth was created, such as Ussher did.

Examination of the Chronologies
Those who believe in an old earth and in the Bible are forced to address the chronological data provided in Scripture. There are a number of different arguments that are made. There are three approaches to the chronological information in Genesis 5

1. The genealogy assumes an unbroken line of descent from the creation to the Flood. This is the assumption underlying the chronology of Archbishop Ussher and others. The twenty generations are twenty literal men. The advantage of this position is that it is the most natural understanding of the text.

2. The genealogy has missing links. The fact that ten generations exist from Adam to the Flood (Gen. 5) and from the Flood to Abraham (Gen. 11) causes some to think that the ten generations is a selective genealogy using ten as a memory device much like that which appears in Matthew 1 which divides the genealogy of Jesus into three sections of 14 names each. W.H. Green's article "Primeval Chronology" (*Bibliotheca Sacra* [1890] 285-303) is generally cited to document that genealogies frequently have missing links. Among the evidences cited by Green are the missing links in Matthew's genealogy of Jesus where three names drop out between Joram and Uzziah (namely Ahaziah, Joash, and Amaziah [Matt. 1:8]) and the omission of Jehoiakim after Josiah (Matt. 1:11). Another example is the omissions in the genealogy of Shebuel, King David's appointee as ruler of his treasures (1 Chron. 26:24), who is described as "the son of Gershom, the son of Moses," which is obviously abridged. Other comparisons of genealogies demonstrate omissions (cf. 1 Chron. 6:3-14 with Ezra 7:1-5). In response to this, one needs to note three things:

a. The fact that some genealogies have omissions is no proof that all of them do. We know that some genealogies have omissions, which omissions are known by other evidences, such as (a) comparison with other texts, (b) the necessity of additional generations known from chronological data drawn from other texts (for example, we know the approximate time from Moses to David; this could not be covered in two generations), (c) the use of a memory device, such as specifically mentioned in Matthew 1:17 ("So all the generations from Abraham to David are fourteen generations; and from David until the carrying away into Babylon are fourteen generations; and from the carrying away into Babylon unto Christ are fourteen generations."), and other indicators. *To assume that every genealogy has omissions is an unwarranted assumption.* To assert that a particular genealogy has omissions without any evidence to sustain the assumption is dangerous exegesis. The burden of proof lies on the person who asserts that there are omissions in the genealogical table in Genesis 5. If there are missing links in Genesis 5 and 11, there is no evidence to prove it (except for Cainan as was discussed above). One can readily admit that some genealogies have omissions and should be alert to that possible problem in any genealogy. However, one is mistaken to assume that, because some genealogies have omissions, all do.

b. A genealogy with gaping holes is no genealogy at all. The genealogy of Jesus would be meaningless if it were made to fit modern evolutionary theory. Let me illustrate what I mean. If the 75 generations of Jesus' genealogy in Luke 3, which traces Jesus' ancestors back to Adam, are to cover a mere ten million years (a low number for the evolutionary model), then each person in that genealogy represents approximately 13,330 years. What meaning does a genealogy have if it is extended that far? This is more drastically shown if the period between Adam and Abraham (twenty generations) covers ten million years. In that case, each person in the genealogical table represents 500,000 years. What meaning does a genealogy have if it is extended that far?

c. One should observe the difference between a genealogy and what appears in Genesis 5. I place the following texts side by side for this comparison:

The book of the generation of Jesus Christ, the son of David, the son of Abraham. Abraham begat Isaac; and Isaac begat Jacob; and Jacob begat Judas and his brethren; And Judas begat Phares and Zara of Thamar; and Phares begat Esrom; and Esrom begat Aram; And Aram begat Aminadab; and Aminadab begat Naasson; and

And Adam lived an hundred and thirty years, and begat a son in his own likeness, after his image; and called his name Seth: And the days of Adam after he had begotten Seth were eight hundred years: and he begat sons and daughters: And all the days that Adam lived were nine hundred and thirty years: and he died. And Seth lived

Naasson begat Salmon; And Salmon begat Booz of Rachab; and Booz begat Obed of Ruth; and Obed begat Jesse; And Jesse begat David the king; and David the king begat Solomon of her that had been the wife of Urias; And Solomon begat Roboam; and Roboam begat Abia; and Abia begat Asa; And Asa begat Josaphat; and Josaphat begat Joram; and Joram begat Ozias; And Ozias begat Joatham; and Joatham begat Achaz; and Achaz begat Ezekias; And Ezekias begat Manasses; and Manasses begat Amon; and Amon begat Josias; And Josias begat Jechonias and his brethren, about the time they were carried away to Babylon: And after they were brought to Babylon, Jechonias begat Salathiel; and Salathiel begat Zorobabel; And Zorobabel begat Abiud; and Abiud begat Eliakim; and Eliakim begat Azor; And Azor begat Sadoc; and Sadoc begat Achim; and Achim begat Eliud; And Eliud begat Eleazar; and Eleazar begat Matthan; and Matthan begat Jacob; And Jacob begat Joseph the husband of Mary, of whom was born Jesus, who is called Christ (Matt. 1:1-16).

an hundred and five years, and begat Enos: And Seth lived after he begat Enos eight hundred and seven years, and begat sons and daughters: And all the days of Seth were nine hundred and twelve years: and he died. And Enos lived ninety years, and begat Cainan: And Enos lived after he begat Cainan eight hundred and fifteen years, and begat sons and daughters: And all the days of Enos were nine hundred and five years: and he died (Gen. 5:3-11).

The difference in the two is noticeable. In a genealogy, the text simply says "*x* begat *y.*" The additional information of how old the person was at the birth of the next person in the genealogical chain, how many years he lived after the birth, and how old he was at death are not part of a bland genealogy. Benjamin B. Warfield admitted that "when brought together in sequence, name after name, these notes assume the appearance of a con-catenated chronological scheme. But this is pure illusion" ("Antiquity and Unity of the Human Race," *Studies in Theology* 243). He asserts that the additional information given about each person is irrelevant parenthetical information that may be compared to a reading such as the following: "Adam was eight cubits in height and begat Seth; and Seth was seven cubits in height and begat Enosh; and Enosh was six cubits in height and begat Kenan" (244). I cannot accept that the information given is parenthetical information that merely gives an illusion of a chronology. The construction of this table consistently cites the age of the father at the birth of the son, which information is meaningless if one is not to understand a chronological sequence and if there are omissions in the list.

One should also recognize that the genealogies of the Bible are not all alike. One must look at the purpose that is served by each genealogy in the context in which it is written. A genealogy designed to show that one is from the seed of David is different from one that is showing the unbroken chain of priests from Aaron to the present. In the former case, omissions would be natural and expected; in the second, omissions would be a serious flaw.

One also needs to call attention to why some men are searching for more time in the genealogical tables. The need for more time is not based on Bible evidence that demands it. Rather, the need for more time is based on geological time tables, archaeological dating sequences, the evolutionary model, and such like presuppositions. The dating systems of such disciplines are far from absolute. One needs to be careful not to lay aside the only inspired and infallible account of man's origins and creation in order to adhere to admittedly fallible dating systems, especially in disciplines of study with flawed presuppositions (such as those affected by the evolutionary hypothesis).

The advantages to the interpretation that postulates omissions in the genealogy are: (a) It explains why ten generations (completeness) are cited; (b) It allows more years for mankind's existence for those who see some need for it.

3. The genealogy refers to dynasties, not individuals. This interpretation explains the narrative as follows: Adam and his successors ruled for 930 years. At the end of 930 years, the dynasty of Seth began. In the 105th year of Seth, the family of Enos came to headship. Seth, after being at the head of the affairs for 912 years was succeeded by the family of Enos in the 1842nd year of man. The totals of the genealogies according to this interpretation is 8,225 years (Davis, *ISBE* I:143). This interpretation has the disadvantage of not using the obvious meaning of the names involved; one most naturally thinks that the names cited are mere men, not dynasties. The advantages to this interpretation are that (a) it explains the longevity of the lives; (b) it asserts no omissions. But even this interpretation will only add 6000 years to the age of the earth, much less than is needed by those who accept the pronouncements of modern science that the earth is 4.5 billion years old.

Summation of the Genealogical Evidence

In conclusion, one must address the biblical material provided in these chronologies. If the earth is 4.5 billion years old, in what sense are Genesis 5 and 11 genealogies? Let's assume that the genealogies cover 100,000,000 years, which is still a mere pittance of time given the evolutionary model. The 100,000,000 years must be divided among the twenty men mentioned in the genealogical tables. Each person represents 5,000,000 years. If there is but one ancestor recorded for every 5,000,000 years, in what sense are Genesis 5 and 11 genealogical tables? Would anyone working on his family's genealogy accept such omissions?

However, let's suppose that there are omissions in the chronological tables provided in Genesis 5 and 11. Let's suppose that there are ten men missing between each entry. Still one is left with a young earth. Abraham was born approximately 2000 years after creation, assuming that there were 20 generations. But, if we insert ten generations of approximately the same proportion of years, we still would have a relatively young earth. The first ten generations occupied 1656 years. We will multiply that by ten to arrive at 16,560 years. The second ten generations occupied 420 years. We multiply that by ten to arrive at 4200 years. Adding 16,560 to 4200 years, we arrive at the figure of 20,760 years old. Compared to the evolutionary model of 4.5 billion years (that is: 4,500,000,000 years), the extremely minor difference of between 6000 years and 20,000 years is minuscule in the light of such enormous figures.

Those who postulate an old earth of 4.5 billion years find themselves in serious contradiction to the biblical evidence. The biblical record simply has no place for eons of time prior to Genesis 1. Those who teach that the earth is 4.5 billion years old cannot fit that amount of time in any place in the Bible after Genesis 1. They are left with one chapter in the Bible to find room for their 4.5 billion years — Genesis 1. If the evidence of a 4.5 billion year old earth is not found in Genesis 1, it cannot be found in the Bible! Those who believe in and teach an old earth are teaching a doctrine that cannot be harmonized with Scripture. To believe in the old earth and that mankind has existed on this earth for millions of years is to deny the historical account of man as related in Scripture.

Belief in an old earth undermines credibility in the biblical account of man: The Old Testament record omits millions of years of man's history, in an account that has the surface appearance of being a straightforward chronological record of man's existence. The truth is, according to those who believe in an old earth, the earth has existed for billions of years; mankind has been on this earth for millions of years. The earth was not created in six-literal days but over millions of years of natural evolution with periodic intrusions by the creative hand of God. If this is a true account of what transpired, the Bible account is untrue. Plainly and simply stated, the old earth theory is an attack on the inspiration of Scripture.

Looking For Years In Genesis 1

In looking at the chronology of the Bible, we have followed the text of Scripture back to Genesis 1. Even giving the most generous interpretation of the genealogies/chronologies of Genesis 5 and 11, there is general agreement that the time from Adam to today is a relatively short period of time. The natural reading of the text approximates 6000 years; a generous insertion of years in the chronology would still leave the world very young (in the tens of thousands of years old). The only other place in the Bible to find the long eons of time necessary for the old earth point of view is Genesis 1. This view states that there are long ages between the creation of the world in Genesis 1:1 and the creation of Adam in Genesis 1:26. A variety of interpretations of Genesis 1 have been introduced in support of this view. These interpretations are not arising from those who are studying the text of Scripture to allow the natural meaning of the text to be elucidated. Rather, these interpretations are arising from those who have allowed scientific pronouncements that the earth is very old to cause them to look for alternative interpretations of the creation account. Such men wish to make Scripture harmonize with the latest scientific pronouncements, in my opinion. Let us look at these alternative interpretations.

The Gap Theory

Genesis 1:1-2 reads as follows: "In the beginning God created the heaven and the earth. And the earth was without form, and void; and darkness was upon the face of the deep. And the Spirit of God moved upon the face of the waters." Some scholars have proposed that there is a long period of time between the time when the universe was initially created and God began to act to make the creation a cosmos. The natural reading of the text does not leave one the impression that there is a long period of time between verses 1 and 2. Scholars generally reject this interpretation of Genesis 1:1-2 on exegetical grounds.

Keil commented about those who wish to find a gap between vv. 1 and 2 as follows, "This suffices to prove that the theosophic speculation of those who make a gap between the two verses, and fill it with a wild horde of evil spirits and their demonical works, is an arbitrary interpolation" (*Genesis* 49).

Thomas Whitelaw addressed the gap theory saying, "Honest exegesis requires that ver. 1 shall be viewed as descriptive of the first of the series of Divine acts detailed in the chapter, and that ver. 2, while admitting of an

interval, shall be held as coming in immediate succession — an interpretation, it may be said, which is fatal to the theory which discovers the geologic
ages between the creative beginning and primeval chaos. . . . There can
scarcely be a doubt, then, that the expression (that the earth was waste and
void as described in v. 2, mw) portrays the condition in which the new-
created earth was, not innumerable ages, but very shortly, after it was summoned into existence" (*The Pulpit Commentary: Genesis* 4-5).

Lange wrote, "Among all the interpretations of Gen. i., the most difficult
as well as the most unsatisfactory is that which regards the first verse as
referring to a period indefinitely remote, and all that follows as comprised in
six solar days. It is barely hinted at by some of the patristic writers, but has
become a favorite with certain modern commentators, as furnishing them
with a method of keeping the ordinary days, and yet avoiding the geological
difficulty, or seeming to avoid it, by throwing all its signs of the earth's
antiquity into this chasm that intervenes between the first and second verses"
(*Lange's Commentary on the Holy Scriptures: Genesis* I:167). He continues to state the motivation prompting this interpretation, "It is evidently
brought in as a possible escape from the difficulties of geology, and would
never have been seriously maintained had it not been for them" (167). Lange
shows how the interpretation violates the principles of grammatical exegesis. He asserts that it changes the usual meaning of the *waw* conjunction
and the structure of the verbs in vv. 1-2 which should be interpreted as
either contemporaneous or in direct continuation (168). Giving the verb
hāyāh (the second "was," mw) a pluperfect sense ("the earth had become waste and void) distorts the grammar. He compares the construction in Genesis 1:1-2 to Job 1:1-2 which says, "There was a man in
the land of Uz, whose name was Job; and that man was perfect and
upright, and one that feared God, and eschewed evil. And there were born
unto him seven sons and three daughters." He then asks, "Who would think of
separating the second *hāyāh* (the second "was," mw) here from the first, or
sundering the evident continuity?" (168). One can just as reasonably insert
a gap of eons between vv. 1 and 2 of Job as he can in Genesis. **Victor P.
Hamilton** (*New International Commentary on the Old Testament: Genesis* I:115-116) and **Kenneth A. Mathews** (*The New American Commentary: Genesis* I:139) reject the gap theory on exegetical grounds.

More recently some have proposed that the gap should be placed between verses 2 and 3 of Genesis 1 rather than between verses 1 and 2.
Verses 1-3 reads as follows:

> In the beginning God created the heaven and the earth. And the earth was
> without form, and void; and darkness was upon the face of the deep. And

the Spirit of God moved upon the face of the waters. And God said, Let there be light: and there was light."

As was stated previously about the proposed gap between verses 1 and 2, the natural reading of the text does not give the impression that there is a long period of time between verses 2 and 3. However, the suggestion is made that during the period between verses 2 and 3, the rocks could cool and the mountains could form through natural means. Consider the following in reply to this suggestion: (a) What evidence is there that the rocks needed to cool? The fact of the matter is the Scripture does not speak about the need for rocks to cool as a result of creation. The very idea that the earth was very hot and needed a long period to cool down stems, not from the statement of Scripture, but from contemporary pronouncements of scientists who posit the "big bang" theory to explain the beginning of the universe. The God who created the world could create the world cool just as easily as he could create it hot and allow billions of years for the natural means to cool down. (b) The Bible evidence says that the world was covered with water when it was created. The statement "darkness was upon the face of the *deep*" states as much. The *deep* is used to describe the primaeval ocean which completely covered the world at creation (BDB 1063). (c) The suggestion has been made that mountains were forming during this time. What Bible evidence is found in verses 1-3 to suggest that this is true? The biblical evidence for the formation of mountains is found in third day of creation when God separated the dry land from the water that covered the earth (Gen. 1:9-10). Again, notice that there is not one scintilla of biblical evidence of a gap between verses 1 and 2 or between verses 2 and 3. One who asserts that there is a gap has the obligation to prove what he asserts.

Though the "gap theory" has been proposed by some brethren (e.g, Robert Milligan, *Scheme of Redemption* 25), it has not been seriously pushed by brethren. Furthermore, the gap theory (aside from its problems for exegesis) is rather harmless. If there was a long period of time between verses 1 and 2, this time provides no help to the evolutionary theory. Neither plants nor animals had yet been created, so having a long period of time between verses 1 and 2 does not explain the fossil record. Since life on earth had not yet been created, billions of years between verses 1 and 2 would not give time for evolution to occur. Furthermore, the condition of the earth as described in verses 1-2 is such that a gap is not useful for geological changes in the earth's surface because the earth is completely covered by water. While the theory is a mistaken interpretation of Genesis 1, it is rather innocuous in its ramifications for evolution so far as I can see. The most serious problem for the gap theory is that it contradicts the statement in Matthew 19:4 which says Adam was created "at the beginning." If billions of years passed before Adam was created, in what sense was he created "at the beginning"?

Through the years, the gap theory has changed in its meaning. One of the most popular meanings of the gap theory has much more serious ramifications for biblical exegesis. This theory is sometimes called the "gap theory" or the "ruin and restoration" theory. According to this theory, between vv. 1 and 2 is a creation of the earth followed by ruin. Here is a description of that theory:

> The widely-held view among Gap theorists today is that the original creation of the world by God, as recorded in Genesis 1:1, took place billions of years ago. The creation was then despoiled because of Satan's disobedience, resulting in his being cast from heaven with his followers. A cataclysm occurred at the time of Satan's rebellion, and is said by proponents of the Gap Theory to have left the earth in darkness ("waste and void") as a divine judgment because of the sin of Satan in rebelling against God. The world as God had created it, with all its inhabitants, was destroyed and left "waste and void," which, it is claimed, accounts for the myriad fossils present in the Earth. Then, God "re-created" (or "restored") the earth in six literal, 24-hour days. Genesis 1, therefore, is the story of an original, perfect creation, a judgment and ruination, and a re-creation. Where there are other minor details that could be included, this represents the essence of the Gap Theory (Bert Thompson, *Creation Compromises* 159).

This understanding of the Gap Theory is a more serious attack against biblical revelation. There is nothing in the biblical text to lead one to the conclusion that the events posited in the Gap Theory ever occurred. They are the invention of man's mind in an effort to explain the old earth interpretation of the geological record without accepting the evolutionary explanation of the fossil record. This explanation is innocuous so far as evolution is concerned, but creates serious textural problems. The ruin and restoration meaning of the gap theory in this explanation is eisegesis, not exegesis. This explanation of the text compromises Matthew 19:4 which states that man was created at the beginning.

The Multiple Gap Theory

Another approach to the Genesis narrative that posits large sections of time in the Genesis account is the view that the days of creation are twenty-four hour days but they are separated by long periods of time. This view asserts that God acts on a given twenty-four day to do what is said to occur on that day. This is followed by long ages to allow the gradual and slow development of nature to occur. For the natural earth, this means that the erosion of water forms the valleys, the natural thrusting of the earth creates the mountains, etc. For the living creatures this means that long periods of time allows the living animals to evolve by micro evolution to develop the various species. This is a hybrid day-gap theory for which there is not one particle of exegetical evidence in the text of Scripture.

This view believes that the six days of creation are twenty-four hour days, but separated by long spans of time. According to this interpretation, God acts in creating something and then allows long periods of time for natural evolution to occur. When evolution reaches an impasse, then God acts again in creating that which is next needed. This is sometimes called *progressive creation* but it is simply *theistic evolution* under a different name. This is a more serious departure from the Genesis text.

Creative Days

A third interpretation of Genesis 1, which has for its purpose accommodating itself to the old earth theory, posits that the days of creation are creative days. The various explanations of the creative days are as follows:

The framework hypothesis. The framework hypothesis states that the days of Genesis 1 are a rhetorical device for the recording the spiritual theme of creation. This view states that the presentation in Genesis 1 is logical, not chronological. This interpretation speaks of the creation account as allegorical, parabolical, or liturgical. The view asserts that Genesis 1 speaks of the fact of creation but not its method.

Day-age theory. This interpretation denies that the days of creation are twenty-four hour days, asserting instead that the days of creation are long eons of time. The primary argument cited from the text of Scripture to support this view is that the Genesis 1 mentions days one through three before the creation of the sun, moon, and stars. The argument affirms that the days cannot be the normal twenty-four hour day, the time necessary for the earth to rotate on its axis, receiving its light from the sun and moon since the sun and moon were not yet created. This view is a rather popular view among Evangelicals who believe in an old earth. To charge that everyone who adopts the day-age theory is an evolutionist would be unfair. No such charge is being made in this series of articles. However, one must insist that there is nothing in the text of Scripture that implies the day-age theory and that acceptance of the old earth chronology is what motivates the interpretation that the days of Genesis 1 are long ages.

The Days of Creation

Much has been written about the "days" of creation inasmuch as some

scholars try to fit Genesis into the modern geological tables of the evolutionary mold. Scholars on both sides of the issue of whether the Genesis account of creation is history or myth are agreed that the effort to make the
days of Genesis 1 eons of time is misguided.

On the liberal side, scholars such as Skinner (*International Critical
Commentary: Genesis*), who holds that the creation narrative is legend or
myth, said, "It is recognised by all recent harmonists that the definition of
'day' as 'geological period' is essential to their theory: *it is exegetically
indefensible*" (5). He continued, "It is therefore shown conclusively, not
only that the modern attempts at reconciliation fail, but (what is more important) that the point at issue is not one of science, but simply of *exegesis*.
The facts of science are not in dispute; the only question is whether the
language of Genesis will bear the construction which the harmonising
scientists find it necessary to put upon it" (5). Similarly, Simpson in *The
Interpreter's Bible* said, "There can be no question but that by **Day** the
author meant just what we mean — the time required for one revolution
of the earth on its axis. Had he meant an aeon he would certainly, in
view of his fondness for great numbers, have stated the number of
millenniums each period embraced. While this might have made his
account of creation less irreconcilable with modern science, it would
have involved a lessening of God's greatness, one sign of which was his
power to do so much in one day" (I:471). Davidson (*The Cambridge
Bible: Genesis*) wrote, "Attempts to make it (*yôm*) still more flexible,
to mean different aeons or stages in the known evolution of the world,
and thus reconcile Genesis I with modern scientific theory, are misguided" (18).

On the conservative side, scholars say the same thing. Keil who defends the historicity of Genesis 1 says, "But if the days of creation are
regulated by the recurring interchange of light and darkness, they must be
regarded not as periods of time of incalculable duration, of years or thousands of years, but as simply earthly days" (I:51). Similarly Leupold (*Barnes
Notes*) commented, "Nothing but the desire to secure harmony with the
contentions of certain physical sciences ever could have induced men to
tamper with this plainest of exegetical results" (69).

What the scholars observe coincides with the evidence in the lexicons.
In their classic work, *Hebrew and Chaldee Lexicon*, Brown, Driver, and
Briggs gives these definitions for *yôm*: (a) day as opposed to night; (b) day
as a division of time (as is used in the phrase "a day's journey"), which is
defined by "evening and morning"; (c) day of the Lord, "chiefly as time
of his coming in judgment"; (d) the plural form occurs with various

meanings (days of his life, in the days of . . . , etc.); (e) the plural days as an indefinite period (some days, a few days), of long time (many days), or days of old; (f) time (time of harvest); (g) today; etc. (398-401). There is no cited use of the singular form of day being used with the meaning of long eons of time.

Moses had an extensive vocabulary at his command. Here are some of the words that Moses used to describe time:

Day = *yôm*
Week = *šāb°a'*
Month = *ḥōdeš*
Year = *šānāh*
Long periods of time = *dōr* — "period, age, generation" (cf. Ps. 90:1)
Eternity or long periods of time = *'ôlām* — "long duration, antiquity, futurity" (cf. Gen. 9:12)

Moses also had the ability to use large figures. He could relate that Adam lived to be 930 years old and that Methuselah lived to be 969 (Gen. 5:9, 27). He could relate that the number of fighting men in Israel's army when they departed Egypt was 603,550 (Num. 2:32). Had Moses wished to express the idea that there were long eons of time represented in the period of creation, he had the vocabulary to express that idea. But to do so, he could not use *yôm*. He would have to use other words to express that idea. But, he chose not to use those words, choosing instead to use the word *yôm*. To be sure that there is no doubt as to the meaning of *yôm*, Moses places in apposition to it the phrase "evening and morning" (Gen. 1). Simply stated, *there is no lexicographical data to support the concept that the six days refer to long periods of time; there is no textual evidence to suggest that long periods of time transpired between the days of creation.*

The position that the days of creation means long periods of time raises other serious questions to be answered. If "days" means long eons of time, what does "years" mean? If "day" means long eons of time, what does the appositional phrase, "it was evening and morning, day . . . ," mean? Does "evening" mean a half eon of total darkness? Does "morning" mean a half eon of total light? Or, is the long eon of time in day three (prior to the creation of the sun, moon, and stars) a long eon of twenty-four hour days consisting of evening and morning? If so, how does one learn that? In what sense does an eon have an evening and a morning?

The idea that the days of creation represent long periods of time creates problems rather than solving them. In the creation account, plant life is created on day three and the sun, moon, and stars on day four. This poses no problem for those who understand Genesis 1 to be referring to six twenty-four hour days. However, for those who believe that the days of Genesis 1 are long eons of time, this is an enormous problem. Those who make science the authority to guide one's interpretation of the Bible need to use their science to explain for us how plant life survived for long eons of time without sunlight? And, how did those plants which depend upon animals to pollinate and reproduce survived for the millions of years between days three and six as is demanded by this theory? The symbiotic relationships so critical for the survival of both plant and animal life demand that the days of Genesis 1 be twenty-four hour days. Those who follow the long day interpretation of the days of Genesis 1 are forced to believe in unrevealed miracles to avoid believing the plain statement that creation occurred in six days.

As one reads those who are presenting the position that the days of creation are long eons of time or twenty-four hour days separated by long eons of time, he is provoked to ask, "Why are these long periods of time necessary?" "What is going on during these long periods of time that is so critical to the beliefs of those who hold this position?" The only answer that makes any sense is this: The long periods of time are necessary to allow time for evolution of animal life, to allow the geological effects that are observed to occur (rivers eroding valleys, the fossil record, etc.), and to explain the great distances for light to travel posited by astronomy. In each of these, the motivating force is to bring the interpretation of Scripture in line with early twenty-first century pronouncements of science.

The text of Genesis 1 gives not an iota of evidence that the days of Genesis 1 refer to long eons of time or that long eons of time separated the six days of creation. There is nothing in Genesis 1 to support the old earth theory.

Furthermore, this interpretation of Genesis 1 contradicts other plain and unambiguous statements of Scripture about creation. Scripture emphasizes that the omnipotent power of God is demonstrated by his creation. The psalmists wrote,

> For he spake, and it was done; he commanded, and it stood fast (33:9).

> Let them praise the name of the Lord: for he commanded, and they were created (148:5).

The instantaneous nature of creation was viewed as proof of God's omnipotent power. Twice the Scriptures state that God created the world in six days:

> For in six days the Lord made heaven and earth, the sea, and all that in
> them is, and rested the seventh day: wherefore the Lord blessed the sab-
> bath day, and hallowed it (Exod. 20:11).

> It is a sign between me and the children of Israel for ever: for in six days the
> Lord made heaven and earth, and on the seventh day he rested, and was
> refreshed (Exod. 31:17).

In both of these texts, the six days of creation followed by the day of God
resting is the explanation for the week, including the day of Sabbath rest. If
the creation account does not explain the division of time into weeks, there
is no explanation for its beginning. The year can be explained by the rotation
around the sun, the month can be explained by the new moon, and the day
can be explained by the earth's rotation on its axis. But, why has the division
of time into a week occurred? The only explanation posited is the days of
creation!

The New Testament statements about the chronology of man are con-
tradicted by the view that God created the material universe billions of
years before he created man. In the model presented by those who believe
in an old earth, the earth was created billions of years before man was
created. Man was created relatively recently, a few million years ago. In
contrast, Jesus said,

> And he answered and said unto them, Have ye not read, that he which
> made them at the *beginning* made them male and female . . . (Matt. 19:4).

In the parallel account in Mark, Jesus said,

> But *from the beginning of the creation* God made them male and female
> (Mark 10:6).

In what sense can these statements that God created man at the beginning
be true if man's creation occurred billions of years after the beginning of
creation and much nearer to the present than the beginning of creation?

The theory that Adam was created billions of years after the earth was
created or that the six days of creation represent long eons of time contradicts the plain statements of Scripture. As such, this theory undermines
confidence in the creation account and, by implication, the inspiration of
Scripture.

Conclusion

How old is the earth? Again, the Bible does not present a specific date, but it does provide a framework that demands belief in a young earth. The contemporary theory that the earth is 4.5 billion years old is not an innocuous doctrine. It is an essential part of a system of unbelief known as naturalism or humanism. Some misguided Bible students whose aim is to harmonize the biblical account of creation with the pronouncements by scientists that the earth is billions of years old unintentionally are undermining the credibility of the Scripture by capitulating to the old earth theory. Once the authority of science is used to govern the exegesis of Scripture, the entire basis for accepting the doctrines of Scripture is undermined. At issue is no less than the inspiration of Scripture. We are reminded, "All scripture is given by inspiration of God, and is profitable for doctrine, for reproof, for correction, for instruction in righteousness: That the man of God may be perfect, throughly furnished unto all good works" (2 Tim. 3:16-17). If God's word cannot be trusted in its account of creation, how can it be trusted in its account of the atonement? If God's account of creation must be reinterpreted to fit the latest pronouncements of geologists, astronomists, and biologists, how can one escape reinterpreting the account of the virgin birth to fit the pronouncements of medical science? The non-literal interpretation of Genesis 1 is not a discussion about how many angels can stand on the head of a pin; it is a serious threat to the inspiration of Scripture.

The "Big Bang" is not the Bible's friend. Those who teach that the "Big Bang" theory harmonizes with Genesis 1 are myopic. There is only one aspect of the "Big Bang" theory that has any resemblance to the creation narrative — namely that the earth had a beginning. Its time for the beginning, its explanation for the beginning, and its explanation for what happened subsequent to the beginning are all grounded in naturalism and naturalistic evolution. Bible believers who tell brethren that the "Big Bang" theory is the Bible's friend are misguided at best and disastrous at worst. Let us be careful not to make the mistake of trying to interpret the Bible to conform to the pronouncements and theories of twenty-first century science. If the Bible is married to twenty-first century science, she will be a widow in the twenty-second century.

The Bible Doctrine of Hell
Mike Willis

The Bible speaks of the eternal punishment of the wicked in such verses as the following:

> But I say unto you, That whosoever is angry with his brother without a cause shall be in danger of the judgment: and whosoever shall say to his brother, Raca, shall be in danger of the council: but whosoever shall say, Thou fool, shall be in danger of hell fire (Matt. 5:22).

> And if thy right eye offend thee, pluck it out, and cast it from thee: for it is profitable for thee that one of thy members should perish, and not that thy whole body should be cast into hell. And if thy right hand offend thee, cut it off, and cast it from thee: for it is profitable for thee that one of thy members should perish, and not that thy whole body should be cast into hell (Matt. 5:29-30).

> And fear not them which kill the body, but are not able to kill the soul: but rather fear him which is able to destroy both soul and body in hell (Matt. 10:28; cf. Luke 12:5).

> And if thine eye offend thee, pluck it out, and cast it from thee: it is better for thee to enter into life with one eye, rather than having two eyes to be cast into hell fire (Matt. 18:9).

> Ye serpents, ye generation of vipers, how can ye escape the damnation of hell? (Matt. 23:33).

> And if thy hand offend thee, cut it off: it is better for thee to enter into life maimed, than having two hands to go into hell, into the fire that never shall be quenched: . . . And if thy foot offend thee, cut it off: it is better for thee to enter halt into life, than having two feet to be cast into hell, into the fire that never shall be quenched: And if thine eye offend thee, pluck it out: it is better for thee to enter into the kingdom of God with one eye, than having two eyes to be cast into hell fire (Mark 9:43, 45, 47).

Harry Buis said, "The fact that the loving and wise Savior has more to say about hell than any other individual in the Bible is certainly thought-provoking" (quoted by Anthony Hoekema, *The Bible and the Future* 266). How ironic that "Christ tells us more about hell, and He is the one we use to assure ourselves that there is no hell" (John H. Gerstner, *Repent or Perish* 15).

The Bible doctrine of hell has generally been ignored. Kenneth S. Kantzer, editor of *Christianity Today*, wrote, "The last sermon on hell I heard, I preached myself. And that was 30 years ago" (February 21, 1986). Martin Marty delivered the 1984 Ingersoll Lecture which was published in 1985 *Harvard Theological Review* (Vol. 78, Nos. 3-4:381-98); it was entitled "Hell Disappeared. No One Noticed." Jurgen Motlmann wrote, "The Church of England has recently done away with 'hell.' Its Commission on Doctrine has substituted 'total nonbeing' for hell" ("In The End, All is God's: Is Belief In Hell Obsolete?", *Sewanee Theological Review* 40:2 [1997]:232-4). Free-man Barton quotes Richard Buckham in "Universalism — A Historical Survey" as saying,

> ... no traditional Christian doctrine has been so widely abandoned as that of eternal punishment. Its advocates among theologians today must be fewer than ever before. The alternative interpretation of hell as annihilation seems to have prevailed even among many of the more conservative theologians ("Evangelicals In Defense of Hell — An Annotated Bibliography With Extended Introduction," *Journal of Religious and Theological Information*, Vol. 2, No. 2 [1996]:73-94; see p. 74).

The Bible doctrine of hell has been under increasing attack in recent years. A Gallup poll conducted through ten European countries showed the following:

> Proportion in percentages of believers in the hereafter compared with the proportion of believers in Hell among ten European countries: 45.6% believe in "Life after death"; 52.7% believe in "Heaven"; 29.3% believe in "Hell." Though belief in hell is always less frequent than belief in the here after, the survey shows that there are more people who profess to believe in heaven than there are who believe in the hereafter. (There is a) lower proportion of believers in hell compared to those who believe in heaven (Pierre Delooz, "Who Believes in the Hereafter?", *Death and Presence* 34).

American statistics are not as bad as the European numbers, but the issue of the nature of eternal punishment is moving to the front burner because of recent assaults against the doctrine. A survey of periodical literature at a good religious library will confirm that this is so. The threat is so great that the Evangelical Alliance Commission on Unity and Truth Among Evangelicals (ACUTE) prepared a report on the *The Nature of Hell* (2000) to address the subject. Apparently, positive teaching is having some success because the June 16, 1997 issue of *Christianity Today* reports that "hell is on a come back." In 1981, 53% of Americans believed in hell; in 1990, 60% believed in hell.

Robert A. Morey affirms that there is a cycle in man's belief after hell. The cycle begins with a long period during which it is acknowledged that the Scriptures clearly teach eternal punishment. This is then followed by the following successive stages:

- *Indifference.* The teaching on hell is ignored and often downplayed while the positive side of God's love is over-emphasized.
- *Ignorance.* Because God's teaching on hell is ignored, men become ignorant of why they should believe what they do about hell.
- *Doubt.* Doubts begin to creep into people's mind. People begin to speak of the doctrine of hell as being "unkind," "unloving," and "negative."
- *Denial.* Cults begin to present universalism or annihilation as the alternative to the biblical doctrine of hell. Because people have not been taught, these doctrines spread.
- *Irritation.* Those who know the Bible doctrine are irritated by the spread of the doctrine, but they "don't have time to deal with this issue right now."
- *Affirmation.* As the issue heats up, the Bible doctrine is re-affirmed.
- *Acknowledgment.* After the Bible doctrine is re-affirmed, another lengthy period of the acknowledgment of the doctrine follows (see *Death and the Afterlife,* "Introduction").

Clearly, the denominations are somewhere in the stages when men have been indifferent toward the doctrine of hell, an ignorance has blossomed, doubt has set in, and the cults' doctrine of annihilation is winning support among Evangelicals. Gerstner commented on the acceptance of annihilation among Protestant churches by observing that the denial of hell was formerly a litmus test of a cult such as Jehovah's Witnesses, Christian Science, Mormonism, Seventh-day Adventists, etc. until recently (*Repent or Perish* 30). However, the views of hell propagated by these cults are now being espoused by mainstream Evangelicals. Already some Evangelicals are in the stage of reaffirming the doctrine of hell, just as brethren are beginning to publish materials that question the doctrine.

Attacks on the Bible Doctrine of Hell
Through the years, there have been a variety of attacks on hell. Here are some of them:

1. Materialism. The doctrine of materialism denies that man has an eternal soul and, with this doctrine, that there is no eternal punishment for man. The philosophical doctrine of materialism is defined as "the doctrine that matter is the only reality and that everything in the world, including thought, will, and feeling, can be explained only in terms of matter." Materialism is the underlying doctrine for atheism or humanism.

2. Universalism. The doctrine of universalism believes in the ultimate salvation of every individual, including the Devil himself. The doctrine is usually defended on the grounds of the universal love of God. It is based on the rather emotional argument, "Could a God of love punish anyone eternally?"

3. Restorationism. This is a name given to the doctrine that ultimately all rational beings will be restored to the fellowship of God. It is sometimes defended on the misinterpretation of Acts 3:21 ("until the times of restitution of all things"). There are very few people who hold to this doctrine.

4. Annihilation. The doctrine of annihilation teaches that God will annihilate the wicked, not eternally punish them. This is the doctrine taught by Jehovah's Witnesses who believe that, when the wicked die, they cease to exist. At the resurrection, only the righteous will be raised to eternal life. Anthony Hoekema described two forms of annihilationism as follows:

> The other main form which the denial of eternal punishment has assumed is found in the doctrine of annihilationism. This doctrine may take either of two forms. According to one form, man was created immortal, but those who continue in sin are deprived of immortality and are simply annihilated — that is reduced to nonexistence. According to the other form, also known as "conditional immortality," man was created mortal. Believers receive immortality as a gift of grace, and therefore continue to exist in a state of blessedness after death. Unbelievers, however, do not receive this gift and hence remain mortal; therefore at death they are annihilated. Both forms of annihilationism teach the annihilation of the wicked, and therefore deny the doctrine of eternal punishment (*The Bible and the Future* 266).

The first form of annihilationism is held by the Jehovah's Witnesses and the second form by the Seventh Day Adventists. Because of its rise to prominence among Evangelicals in recent years, this second form will be treated more extensively.

5. Conditional immortality. As mentioned above, this is but a form of annihilationism. According to this doctrine, at death both soul and body die.

There is no consciously existing soul that survives the death of the body. In contrast to the view of the Jehovah's Witnesses who believe that only the righteous will be raised from the dead, the conditional immortality advocates believe that both the righteous and the wicked will be raised from the dead. During the time between death and the resurrection, the soul is "asleep," that is, the soul does not have separate, conscious existence in contrast to the rotting and decaying body. Both the righteous and the wicked will be raised from the dead, but an immortal body is only given to the righteous. After the resurrection, the wicked will be punished for a time commensurate with each person's wickedness before being completely annihilated. This is the position of the Seventh Day Adventists. Hoekema describes their position as follows:

> Seventh-day Adventists teach that, after Satan's final assault on the "camp of the saints," fire will come down from heaven and will annihilate Satan, his evil angels, and all the wicked. Before this happens, however, those to be annihilated will be subjected to gradations of suffering, depending on the guilt of the persons or demons involved; Satan himself will suffer the longest and will therefore be the last to perish in the flames. At the end of this period of suffering, however, all those who have rebelled against God will be wiped out of existence (*The Four Major Cults* 360).

More relevant than the fact that the Seventh Day Adventists believe in conditional immortality with reference to the influence of this doctrine among Christians is the fact that this is the view advocated by Edward Fudge in his book *The Fire That Consumes*. The significance of brother Fudge's book may have escaped some of our brethren. *The Fire That Consumes* is the most extensive defense of the "conditional immortality" doctrine presently available. The book has been reviewed in many denominational publications and its conclusions accepted by such prominent Evangelicals as John Wenham, John R.W. Stott, and Clark H. Pinnock (see *Two Views of Hell* 12). F.F. Bruce wrote the Foreword to Fudgd's book. The ACUTE report on *The Nature of Hell* said, "In his 1974 study *The Goodness of God*, Wenham had offered careful arguments which gained a respectful hearing and prompted some lively responses. Not least, he inspired the American scholar Edward William Fudge to produce a full-length study of the biblical material which rapidly became the standard reference-work on evangelical conditionalism" (66-7). Fudge has participated in discussions with Evangelicals on the subject (see *Two Views of Hell,* a written debate between brother Fudge and Robert A. Peterson, professor of theology at Covenant Theological Seminary). In replying to Fudge, John Gerstner said, "If Edward Fudge's *The Fire That Consumes* (1982) was not the start of the current conservative attack on hell, it at least has a central role" (*Repent or Perish* 64).

After brother Fudge accepted the tenets of the unity-in-diversity movement in the 1970s, he worked among institutional brethren, holding membership in the Bering Drive church in Houston. Because of his departure from among us, his influence has been felt less than would otherwise have been the case had he stayed. The issue of annihilationism had little impact among brethren, at least so far as we knew. In 1984, brother Curtis Dickinson published *What the Bible Teaches About Immortality and Future Punishment* which takes the conditional immortality position. More significantly, a few weeks ago a notice from Stanley Paher announced the publication of a book by the late brother Homer Hailey which reaches the conclusion that the soul ceases to exist as it is destroyed in hell. With the advent of brother Hailey's new book, the danger of annihilationism, as advocated by Fudge, resurfaces.

In the present day circumstances of the influence of unity-in-diversity, the issue may lead to yet another step down the slippery slopes of liberalism. We have already read brother Ed Harrell's defense of Homer Hailey (as a prelude to his 17-article series that advocated unity-in-diversity) in which he affirmed that churches who decide to invite brother Hailey for meetings, even though he is teaching his erroneous views on divorce and remarriage, are guilty of no sin. We have been told by others that the teaching of a non-literal interpretation of Genesis 1 by Shane Scott and Hill Roberts should not interfere with the fellowship of the saints. Will the next step be as follows? "We cannot know for sure whether hell is eternal punishment or annihilation. Brethren have disagreed on this subject. Therefore, we must tolerate the teaching of different views of the subject among us without it affecting the fellowship of the saints." Probably so, for some of those who worked most closely with brother Hailey while he lived were aware of his material on the subject but did not draw a line of fellowship. I fear that the toleration of annihilationism — the Seventh Day Adventist doctrine of hell — will be but another step down the slippery slope of liberalism. And, of course, the one causing the problem will no doubt be judged by some to be, not the one who teaches annihilationism, but the one who warns that this is a departure from sound doctrine!

The Biblical Definition of Hell

There are many passages which discuss the subject of hell. In this section, the biblical data will be presented so that one can see what the Bible teaches about the subject. John Gerstner defined the issue, "The issue is really eternal versus non-eternal suffering. The conditionalist notion of temporary suffering prior to annihilation is virtually nothing compared with eternal suffering. . ." (*Repent or Perish* 67). Here are some biblical evidences that show that hell is eternal punishment:

• *Matthew 25:41.* In Jesus' parable of the separation of the sheep and the goats at the final judgment, he says to the goats, "Depart from me, ye cursed, into everlasting fire, prepared for the devil and his angels." In this passage the place to which the wicked are sent is the place "prepared for the devil and his angels." The destiny of wicked angels is the destiny of wicked men. In the intervening time between the sin of the wicked angels and their eternal punishment, these angels are reserved in a place of torment described as follows:

> For if God spared not the angels that sinned, but cast them down to hell (*tartarus*), and delivered them into chains of darkness, to be reserved unto judgment (2 Pet. 2:4).

> And the angels which kept not their first estate, but left their own habitation, he hath reserved in everlasting chains under darkness unto the judgment of the great day (Jude 6).

Already the angels who sinned have suffered for thousands of years as they await the final judgment. They are not in a state of unconscious existence but in a place of torment. Wicked men who pass away are placed in this place along with sinful angels. Peter described the wicked dead as "spirits in prison" (1 Pet. 3:19). This picture is remarkably similar to the intermediate state of the wicked dead as described in Luke 16:19-31.

The final end of the Devil is described in Revelation 20. After his thwarted attempt to oppose God's will, the Devil is ultimately defeated and cast into torment. The text says,

> And the devil that deceived them was cast into the lake of fire and brimstone, where the beast and the false prophet are, and shall be tormented day and night for ever and ever (Rev. 20:10).

The devil "shall be tormented." The word "tormented" is from *basanizō* which is defined as "to torture (2 Macc. 7:13); hence **4.** univ. *to vex with grievous pains* (of body and mind), *to torment*" (Thayer 96). The passage Thayer cited in 2 Maccabees 7:13 refers to the torment administered to a man before his final execution: "they *tormented* and mangled the fourth in like manner." It does not describe annihilation, but an endless torment. The passage does not say that they will be destroyed with an irreversible destruction; rather they will be tormented day and night for ever and ever.

What does the Bible teach is the ultimate destiny of the devil and his angels? They will be "cast into the lake of fire and brimstone" and "shall be tormented day and night for ever and ever" (Rev. 20:10). "Day and night" means without intermission (Thayer 278; cf. its use in Luke 2:37; Acts 26:7). Its use in Revelation is particularly important: The phrase is used of the angels ceaselessly praising God around his throne (Rev. 4:8); of the righteous who serve God day and night in heaven (Rev. 7:15); of the uninterrupted accusations that the Devil makes against the saints (Rev. 12:10); and here of the uninterrupted torment given to the devil (20:10).

The uninterrupted ("day and night") torment shall continue "for ever and ever." The phrase is *aiōnas tōn aiōnas*. The word *aiōnas* is a critical word in reference to several verses which will be used in this study, so this is as good a place to study its meaning.

The Meaning of *Aiōn*
Like most other words, the word *aiōn* has several nuances of meaning. It is used in the following ways:

1. Of eternity. The word means "forever." In this use, it means "an indefinite period of time; time without limitation; ever, forever, time without end, eternity" (Moses Stuart, *Future Punishment* 17). In this sense, the word is used of the everlasting God (Rom. 1:25; 9:5; 11:36; 16:27; 2 Cor. 11:31; Gal. 1:5; Eph. 3:21; Phil. 4:20; 1 Tim. 1:17; 2 Tim. 4:18; Heb. 13:21; 1 Pet. 1:25; 4:11; 5:11; 2 Pet. 3:18; Rev. 1:6, 18; 4:9, 10; 7:12; 10:6; 15:7).

The word is used in the sense of an endless future. It is used in this sense in reference to the future happiness of the saints (John 6:51, 58; 8:51, 52; 10:28; 11:26; 2 Cor. 9:9; 1 John 2:17; Rev. 22:5). The word is also used in this sense to "designate a period unlimited and without bounds, i.e. *ever*, and (with a negative) *never* (Matt. 21:19; Mark 11:14; 3:29; Luke 1:33, 55; John 4:14; 8:35; 12:34; 13:8; etc.). All of these uses are with reference to the future.

The word can also be used of eternity in the past. Thus *aiōn* is sometimes used of "an indefinite or long period in time past, ancient days, times of old, long ago, always in time past, generations or ages long since" (Stuart 24). See such passages as Luke 1:70; Acts 15:18; 1 Corinthians 2:7; Ephesians 3:9, 11; Colossians 1:26 which illustrate this use.

The phrase *eis ton aiōna tou aiōnos* is a special use "to emphasize the concept of eternity" (TDNT I:199). The phrase appears 21 times in the Pauline epistles and Revelation as a "distinctive formula" to refer to eternity. Significantly, this is the phrase used in Revelation 20:10 which we are examining!

2. Age, period of time. In this use, the word *aiōn* approaches the meaning of "age" in the sense of dispensation (1 Cor. 10:11; Eph. 2:7; Heb. 6:5; etc.). The phrase is used with this meaning in passages which speak of the present age and the age to come (Matt. 12:32; Mark 10:30; etc.).

3. The world with its cares. The word *aiōn* is sometimes used to denote the world with "all its cares, or business, or temptations, or allurements to sin" (Stuart 28). See Matthew 13:22; Mark 4:19; Luke 16:8; 20:34; Romans 12:2; 1 Corinthians 1:20; 2:6, 8; 2 Corinthians 4:4; Galatians 1:4; 2 Timothy 4:10; Titus 2:12. From this use, the word can be used of the world itself (Matt. 13:40, 49; 24:3; 28:20; Luke 20:35; 1 Cor. 3:18; etc.).

From this brief survey one can get a grasp of the use of this word. (For a more extended treatment of this word, see Moses Stuart, *Future Punishment* 5-47; TDNT I:197-209; Thayer 18-21; Arndt and Gingrich 26-28.)

With this background, one has to ask himself which use of the word best fits the context under consideration. The context is Revelation 20:10 — "And the devil that deceived them was cast into the lake of fire and brimstone, where the beast and the false prophet are, and shall be tormented day and night *for ever and ever*." What does "for ever and ever" mean in this context? Does it mean "the world with its cares"? Obviously not. Does it mean "an age, period of time," such as the meaning when it is used of "this present world" (Matt. 12:32)? Assuming this were so, what is the duration of the "age to come"? Significantly, the duration of the age to come for the righteous is the same duration for the wicked for both are described by the same word (Matt. 25:46, see notes below). Defining the word with the meaning "age" does not shorten the torment of eternity unless it also shortens the duration of "eternal life." The only meaning of *aiōn* which fits the context of Revelation 20:10 is the definition of "eternal" in the sense of an endless future. The devil and his angels "shall be tormented day and night for ever and ever."

Eternal Torment Redefined

Brother Fudge only redefines "eternal" with reference to eternal torment. That is, he wants eternal life to go on forever, but he wants eternal punishment to have an end. So he affirms that "eternal" does not mean "never ending" or "unlimited future," with reference to torment, although it has that meaning when used of "life." Rather, he affirms that "eternal" (*aiōnios*) describes a "quality." Just what "quality" does "eternal" describe? Is it not the duration quality that is so defined? Fudge cites several examples to support his contention that "eternal" means "eternal in its effect," not an ongoing process. He uses the following examples to sustain his point:

"Eternal salvation" (Heb. 5:9)
"Eternal redemption" (Heb. 9:12)
"Eternal sin" (Mark 3:29)
"Eternal judgment" (Heb. 6:2)

He argues that the act of saving did not last forever, only its consequences; the act of redeeming did not last forever, only its consequences; the act of sinning did not last forever, only its consequences; the act of judging does not last forever, only its consequences. If the argument has validity with reference to eternal punishment, it has equal validity with reference to "eternal life." In that case, "eternal" does not describe an eternal living but a resurrection to a life that has eternal consequences but not an eternal duration. Robert A. Morey notes how in each case, Fudge changes the nouns (salvation, redemption, judgment, sin) into verbs (saving, redeeming, judging, sinning) which creates the problem (132). He wrote:

> We fail to see how the annihilationists are correct in their attempt to make "judgment" into a verb, i.e., a work of action. It is a noun, not a verb. Yet, this is exactly how annihilationists argue. They begin their argument by defining "judgment" as "a word of action." They ridicule the idea of an eternal act or process of judging. They then state that the results of judging are eternal but not the process.

> What these annihilationists fail to recognize is that the word "judgment" is in its noun form which means that an endlessly binding verdict is being described. Also, the endlessness of this verdict is part of the superiority of the new covenant (132).

Those who wish for a limited torment recognize the significance of the word *aiōn*. They cannot deny its meaning in the context of Revelation 20:10 of the endless future. Consequently, they explain that the torment is "eternal in its effect" (that is, the wicked are annihilated which annihilation lasts forever — that is, it is eternal in its effect). In this they are mistaken.

Returning now to Matthew 25:41, we see the significance of this verse for our study. Jesus said to the wicked, those on his left hand, "Depart from me, ye cursed, into everlasting fire, prepared for the devil and his angels." The wicked go "into everlasting fire" (*to pur to aiōnion*). The appositional phrase modifying this eternal fire is the fire "prepared for the devil and his angels." The fire prepared for the devil and his angels is referred to in Revelation 20:10 — "And the devil that deceived them was cast into the lake of fire and brimstone, where the beast and the false prophet are, and shall be tormented day and night *for ever and ever*." The torment of the devil and his angels is uninterrupted (day and night) and endless (for ever and ever). Their punishment is not annihilation but "torment." Remember that, if the torment of wicked men ceases, so also does the torment of the Devil.

• *Matthew 25:46.* In the same context as Matthew 25:41, Jesus said, "And these shall go away into *everlasting* punishment: but the righteous into life *eternal.*" The significance of this verse is that the same word, *aiōnion*, is used to describe the duration of punishment and of life. This has not escaped scholars' attention as the following quotations show:

> **Augustine:** Then what fond fancy it is to suppose that eternal punishment means long-continued punishment, while eternal life means life without end, since Christ in the very same passage spoke of both in similar terms in one and the same sentence, "These shall go away into eternal punishment, but the righteous into life eternal!" If both destinies are "eternal," then we must either understand both as long-continued but at last terminating, or both as endless. For they are correlative, — on the one hand, punishment eternal, on the other hand, life eternal. And to say in one and the same sense, life eternal shall be endless, punishment eternal shall come to an end, is the height of absurdity. Wherefore, as the eternal life of the saints shall be endless, so too the eternal punishment of those who are doomed to it shall have no end (*The City of God* 21.23).

> **Moses Stuart:** I take it to be a rule of construing all *antithetic* forms of expression, that where you can perceive the force of one side of the antithesis, you do of course come to a knowledge of the force on the other side. If *life eternal* is promised on one side, and *death eternal* is threatened on the other and opposite one, is it not to be supposed that the word *eternal* which qualifies *death*, is a word of equal force and import with the word *eternal* which qualifies *life*? In no other case could a doubt be raised, with regard to such a principle. I venture to say that the exception here, (if such an one must be made), is without any parallel in the just principles of interpretation (Stuart, *Future Punishment* 56).

If then the words *aiōn* and *aiōnios* are applied 60 times (which is the fact) in the New Testament, to designate the *continuance* of the future happiness of the righteous; and some twelve times to designate the *continuance* of the future misery of the wicked; by what principles of interpreting languages does it become possible for us, to avoid the conclusion that *aiōn* and *aiōnios* have the same sense in both cases?

> ... It does most plainly and indubitably follow, that *if the Scriptures have not asserted the ENDLESS punishment of the wicked, neither have they asserted the ENDLESS happiness of the righteous, nor the ENDLESS glory and existence of the Godhead.* The one is equally certain with the other.

Both are laid in the same balance. They must be tried by the same tests. And if we give up the one, we must, in order to be consistent, give up the other also (Stuart, *Future Punishment* 56, 57).

Anthony Hoekema: If, however, the word *aioonios*, means "without end" when applied to the future blessedness of believers, it must follow, unless clear evidence is given to the contrary, that this word also means "without end" when it is used to describe the future punishment of the lost (*The Four Major Cults* 369).

Charles Hodge: The same word is used in both clauses; the wicked are to go *eis kolasin aiōnion*; and the righteous *eis zōēn aiōnion*; it must have the same sense in both (Matt. xxv. 41, 46) (*Systematic Theology* III:875-6).

Citing such quotations could be extended should one choose to do so. Sound exegesis demands that one understand that "eternal" punishment lasts just as long as "eternal" life.

• *John 3:36.* John writes, "He that believeth on the Son hath everlasting life: and he that believeth not the Son shall not see life; but the wrath of God abideth on him." "Everlasting life" and "the wrath of God abideth on him" are placed in juxtaposition to each other. The word "abideth" is from the present tense — the wrath of God is presently abiding on him and will continue to do so. Dr. Robert A. Morey writes, "When John said that the wrath of God 'abides' on the wicked, he used the word *meno* in the present indicative tense to state that the wrath of God was continually abiding on the wicked as an ongoing process" (*Death and the After Life* 155).

• *Where the worm dieth not and the fire is not quenched.* Several verses are used to describe the eternal nature of the punishment of hell in which these two figures are used.

And they shall go forth, and look upon the carcases of the men that have transgressed against me: for their worm shall not die, neither shall their fire be quenched; and they shall be an abhorring unto all flesh (Isa. 66:24).

Where their worm dieth not, and the fire is not quenched. (Mark 9:44, 46, 48).

The figure of the worm used by Isaiah and Jesus is drawn from worms consuming dead bodies. When an animal dies, worms eat its flesh. When all of the flesh has been consumed, the worm dies. Job used the figure to describe man's death, "Drought and heat consume the snow waters: so doth the grave those which have sinned. The womb shall forget him; *the worm shall feed sweetly on him*; he shall be no more remembered; and wickedness shall be broken as a tree" (Job 24:19-20). The significance of Jesus' expression is that the worm does not die. Worms which eat decaying bodies ultimately consume the body and die. However, in hell the worm never dies because the body is never completely consumed, for the punishment never ends.

A similar comparison is involved in the "unquenchable fire." When something is burned, the burning consumes what it burns. Eventually the fuel is exhausted and the fire dies. Both figures are drawn from what occurs in the city dump. Dead bodies are thrown there for worms to consume and there trash is burned. But this fire is unique in that the burning never ceases. It is unquenchable fire (see Matt. 3:12; Luke 3:17). "Unquenchable" does not mean that it cannot be withstood (which is also true of God's judgment), but that it cannot be extinguished.

• ***Eternal or everlasting fire.*** Though not tied to the figure of the dump, the phrase "eternal fire" or "everlasting fire" is used to describe the punishment of the wicked. In Jude 7, the text says, "Even as Sodom and Gomorrha, and the cities about them in like manner, giving themselves over to fornication, and going after strange flesh, are set forth for an example, suffering the vengeance of eternal fire." The punishment of the cities of the plain by fire is used as an example to show that God will punish the wicked. However, the punishment of Sodom and Gomorrah did not end when the smoke of their temporal destruction ceased. They also will suffer the "vengeance of eternal fire" as Jude states. The lessons drawn from the destruction of Sodom and Gomorrah are that it was overthrown in a moment (Lam. 4:6) and that it was complete (in contrast to cities that were overthrown and later rebuilt, Jer. 50:40; Zeph. 2:9). Undoubtedly that their destruction came by fire typifies the future eternal destruction in hell fire. However, the citizens of Sodom and Gomorrah still must face the punishment that results from the final judgment. Jesus said, "Verily I say unto you, It shall be more tolerable for the land of Sodom and Gomorrha in the day of judgment, than for that city" (Matt. 10:15; 11:23, 24; Mark 6:11; Luke 10:12). This is the "eternal fire" of Sodom's punishment mentioned in Jude 7 that awaits all of the wicked. To argue that eternal fire is a limited punishment because the temporal fire that destroyed the cities did not burn forever misses Jude's point, for verse 7 does not state that "eternal fire" struck Sodom and Gomorrah in Genesis 19 but that the inhabitants of that city who were destroyed by temporal fire still must face the eternal fire of God's judgment.

Elsewhere Jesus speaks of "everlasting fire." "Wherefore if thy hand or thy foot offend thee, cut them off, and cast them from thee: it is better for thee to enter into life halt or maimed, rather than having two hands or two feet to be cast into everlasting fire" (Matt. 18:8). "Then shall he say also unto them on the left hand, Depart from me, ye cursed, into everlasting fire, prepared for the devil and his angels" (Matt. 25:41). The pain and agony that results from burning is easily understood, for most of us have been burned to some degree at one time or another. The significance of this burning is that it is "everlasting," that is never-ending, ceaseless.

It is also called the fire that is not quenched. Jesus said,

> And whosoever shall offend one of these little ones that believe in me, it is better for him that a millstone were hanged about his neck, and he were cast into the sea. And if thy hand offend thee, cut it off: it is better for thee to enter into life maimed, than having two hands to go into hell, into *the fire that never shall be quenched:* Where their worm dieth not, and *the fire is not quenched.* And if thy foot offend thee, cut it off: it is better for thee to enter halt into life, than having two feet to be cast into hell, into *the fire that never shall be quenched:* Where their worm dieth not, and *the fire is not quenched.* And if thine eye offend thee, pluck it out: it is better for thee to enter into the kingdom of God with one eye, than having two eyes to be cast into hell fire: Where their worm dieth not, and *the fire is not quenched* (Mark 9:42-48).

The context of this passage is eternal life and judgment. The point is not to teach self-mutilation but to emphasize that eternal life is worth whatever sacrifices one must make to obtain it and eternal damnation is so horrible that avoiding it is worth whatever sacrifices one must make. The punishment of hell is so bad Jesus said it is better to enter life maimed than to pass into hell with all of one's bodily parts intact. This is true because the fire "never shall be quenched." This is but another way of saying it lasts forever. "Unquenchable fire" does not mean a fire which no one can withstand (which is also a true statement, for no one can prevent God's judgment). Rather, the word *asbestos* means "unquenched (Ovid, *inexstinctus*), unquenchable" (Thayer 79), "inextinguishable" (Arndt and Gingrich 114). If annihilation is true, then the fires of hell eventually will be quenched when the last wicked person shall have suffered the full extent of his torment. However, Jesus said this fire is "never quenched," never extinguished. Therefore, the torment is endless.

• *The smoke of their torment ascendeth up forever and ever.* John wrote, "The same shall drink of the wine of the wrath of God, which is poured out without mixture into the cup of his indignation; and he shall be tormented with fire and brimstone in the presence of the holy angels, and in the presence of the Lamb: And *the smoke of their torment ascendeth up for ever and ever*: and they have no rest day nor night, who worship the beast and his image, and whosoever receiveth the mark of his name" (Rev. 14:10-11). The figure is tied to that burning of unquenchable (inextinguishable) fire. The smoke of the torment goes up "for ever and ever" because the burning never ends. In all earthly fires, the smoke ascends so long as the burning continues. In earthly burnings, what is burning is consumed and the last embers are extinguished, at which time the smoke ceases to rise. However, for the wicked, the smoke never ceases; the smoke of their torment "ascendeth up for ever and ever." "For ever and ever" (*aiōnas aiōnōn*) also appears in Revelation 4:9 — "And when those beasts give glory and honour and thanks to him that sat on the throne, who liveth for ever and ever (*eis tous aiōnas tōn aiōnōn*)" (Rev. 4:9). If "forever and ever" does not describe an endless future, what does it mean when it is used to describe God's eternal nature? One also should notice that what goes up forever and ever is the smoke of their "torment." The word *basanismos* means "torment, torture" and the phrase "smoke of their torment" means "the smoke of the fire by which they are tormented" (Thayer 96).

• ***Until the last penny is paid.*** Jesus said, "That whosoever is angry with his brother without a cause shall be in danger of the judgment: and whosoever shall say to his brother, Raca, shall be in danger of the council: but whosoever shall say, Thou fool, shall be in danger of *hell fire*. Therefore if thou bring thy gift to the altar, and there rememberest that thy brother hath ought against thee; Leave there thy gift before the altar, and go thy way; first be reconciled to thy brother, and then come and offer thy gift. Agree with thine adversary quickly, whiles thou art in the way with him; lest at any time the adversary deliver thee to the judge, and the judge deliver thee to the officer, and thou be cast *into prison*. Verily I say unto thee, Thou shalt by no means come out thence, *till thou hast paid the uttermost farthing*" (Matt. 5:22-26; cf. Luke 12:58-59). Note that "hell fire" is the prison into which one is cast until the last penny is paid. How is the last penny to be paid? John H. Gerstner correctly explained Jesus' words, "That judge was God; that prison was hell; and until you have paid the 'very last cent' meant 'never'" (*Repent or Perish* 2).

• ***Punished with everlasting destruction.*** Paul wrote, "Seeing it is a righteous thing with God to recompense tribulation to them that trouble you; And to you who are troubled rest with us, when the Lord Jesus shall be revealed from heaven with his mighty angels, in flaming fire taking vengeance on them that know not God, and that obey not the gospel of our Lord Jesus Christ: who shall be punished with *everlasting destruction from the presence of the Lord*, and from the glory of his power" (2 Thess. 1:6-9).

Paul's comments are in the context of the final judgment when the righteous receive rest and the wicked are destroyed. The wicked will face the vengeance of the Lord when they "shall be punished with everlasting destruction from the presence of the Lord."

The punishment is "destruction." The word *olethros* means "ruin, destruction, death." That it does not mean annihilation is evident from its use in 1 Corinthians 5:5 where Paul describes the punishment of withdrawal of fellowship from the Corinthian fornicator; he said, "To deliver such an one unto Satan for the *destruction* of the flesh, that the spirit may be saved in the day of the Lord Jesus." The flesh is not annihilated. Thayer defines the word in 2 Thessalonians 1:9 to mean "the loss of a life of blessedness after death, future misery" (443). The destruction is further defined as "from the presence of the Lord." The sense of this is correctly interpreted by Scot McKnight as quoted by Peterson who wrote,

> Eternal separation from God is the essence of God's punishment on the wicked, as eternal fellowship with God is the essence of God's final deliverance of the faithful. But separation from God's presence must be defined as nonfellowship, not annihilation. In other words, it could be argued that since God is omnipresent, then banishment from his presence means extinction. It is more likely, however, that Paul has in mind an irreversible verdict of eternal nonfellowship with God. A person exists but remains excluded from God's good presence (quoted in *Two Views of Hell* 152).

Heaven is described as participating in God's fellowship. Those who enjoy heaven enter the marriage supper of the Lamb, but those who are unprepared are excluded (Matt. 25:1-13). In Jesus' parable, those who do not participate are not annihilated but excluded from participation.

> And while they went to buy, the bridegroom came; and they that were ready went in with him to the marriage: and the door was shut. Afterward came also the other virgins, saying, Lord, Lord, open to us. But he answered and said, Verily I say unto you, I know you not. Watch therefore, for ye know neither the day nor the hour wherein the Son of man cometh (Matt. 25:10-13).

The same figure is used when heaven is compared to eating with Abraham, Isaac, and Jacob, but the wicked are excluded from the banquet and suffering torment; they are not annihilated. Jesus said, "That many shall come from the east and west, and shall sit down with Abraham, and Isaac, and Jacob, in the kingdom of heaven. But the children of the kingdom shall be cast out into outer darkness: there shall be weeping and gnashing of teeth"

(Matt. 8:11-12). Note that those separated from God are gnashing their teeth. The final separation from God is endless. The sense is not that the wicked are annihilated, but that they continue to exist but are forever separated from the beneficence of God, resulting in so much pain that they are gnashing their teeth.

• ***The blackness of darkness forever.*** In describing the punishment of the false teachers who were wreaking havoc on the church, Jude writes, "These are spots in your feasts of charity, when they feast with you, feeding themselves without fear: clouds they are without water, carried about of winds; trees whose fruit withereth, without fruit, twice dead, plucked up by the roots; raging waves of the sea, foaming out their own shame; wandering stars, *to whom is reserved the blackness of darkness for ever*" (Jude 12-13). Peter's statement is very similar, "These are wells without water, clouds that are carried with a tempest; *to whom the mist of darkness is reserved for ever*" (2 Pet. 2:17). The blackness of darkness reminds one of Jesus' words "outer darkness."

> But the children of the kingdom shall be cast out into *outer darkness*: there shall be weeping and gnashing of teeth (Matt. 8:12).

> Then said the king to the servants, Bind him hand and foot, and take him away, and cast him into *outer darkness*; there shall be weeping and gnashing of teeth (Matt. 22:13).

> And cast ye the unprofitable servant into *outer darkness*: there shall be weeping and gnashing of teeth (Matt. 25:30).

The significant statement is that this darkness (this separation from God, who is the source of the light which illumines heaven, Rev. 21:23) lasts "for ever" (*aiōna*). The blackness of darkness is not a place of unconscious existence or annihilation but a place where "weeping and gnashing of teeth" occur.

• ***Destruction and perdition.*** Paul wrote, "But they that will be rich fall into temptation and a snare, and into many foolish and hurtful lusts, which drown men *in destruction and perdition*" (1 Tim. 6:9). The interesting note about this verse is that perdition follows destruction. Thayer says that perdition means "with the included idea of misery" (70-71). Those who argue that the punishment of hell is destruction define destruction as annihilation, cessation of existence. In what sense can perdition follow destruction? If perdition follows destruction then destruction cannot mean "annihilation." To fit brother Fudge's model, this passage should say perdition (first) and then destruction.

• *Matthew 26:24.* Jesus said about Judas, "The Son of man goeth as it is written of him: but woe unto that man by whom the Son of man is betrayed! It had been good for that man if he had not been born" (Matt. 26:24). This passage is devastating for those who hold the position that annihilation is the end of man's existence. I.M. Haldeman replied to Charles Taze Russell as follows:

> If death means the extinction of being, why should life be worse for him (Judas) than any other wicked traitor? No matter how great his guilt, death would end it all. . . .
>
> Never to have been born means never to have come into existence.
>
> If death means going out of existence, then never to have been born and to die are equivalent conditions; they mean the same thing — non-existence.
>
> Why, then, did the Lord say it would have been good not to come into existence? Why did he not say (seeing the man was born and there was no use in wasting regrets over his birth) — why did he not say, "It will be good for that man when he dies, for when he dies he will then be just as if he had never been born — non-existent"?
>
> If death means non-existence, this is what he *ought* to have said.
>
> To say anything else — if death means non-existence — was utterly meaningless.
>
> But if death does not mean the end of existence; if death means an eternity of condition; if in this conditioned eternity of being Judas is to suffer for his deed of betrayal, then it is comprehensible why the Son of God should say it would have been good for that man if he had never been born — if he had never come into existence.
>
> On no other basis is the "Woe to that man" of any intelligent force (quoted in *The Four Major Cults* 371).

Additional evidence is available to show that the Bible describes hell in terms of eternal punishment, not annihilation. However, this evidence is conclusive. The doctrine that man is annihilated, whether taught by the Jehovah's Witnesses, the Seventh Day Adventists, Edward Fudge, or Homer Hailey, is contrary to God's revelation that everlasting torment awaits the wicked.

The Meaning of Everlasting Torment
Any discussion of heaven and hell must ultimately face the fact that the

Bible uses non-literal speech to describe heaven's bliss and hell's torment. One does not ultimately look to a place with literal streets of gold, gates made out of pearl, and walls made of precious stones. These are figures of speech to describe the consummate city as man's eternal home. In the same way, the figures that are used to describe hell deserve one's consideration. Do we expect literal fire, literal darkness, etc.? Indeed, some of the metaphors of hell seem to conflict with each other (fire/darkness). Let's examine what these figures are conveying to man.

• *The second death.* Hell is described as the second death in contrast to physical death as the first death. Such statements appear in these passages in Revelation:

> He that hath an ear, let him hear what the Spirit saith unto the churches; He that overcometh shall not be hurt of the second death (2:11).

> Blessed and holy is he that hath part in the first resurrection: on such the second death hath no power, but they shall be priests of God and of Christ, and shall reign with him a thousand years (20:6).

> And death and hell were cast into the lake of fire. This is the second death (20:14).

> But the fearful, and unbelieving, and the abominable, and murderers, and whoremongers, and sorcerers, and idolaters, and all liars, shall have their part in the lake which burneth with fire and brimstone: which is the second death (21:8).

James Orr wrote about the concept of life and death saying, "Life is not, in the Scripture usage, simple existence; death is not simply non-existence, but separation from true and complete life. This theory itself being witness, the soul survives in the state of natural death. It passes into the intermediate condition, and there awaits judgment. Life, in short, is, in the Scripture sense, a word with a moral and spiritual connotation; a person may not possess it, and yet continue to exist" (*The Christian View of God and the World* 342). Writing along the same lines with reference to eternal death, Joseph Stump wrote,

> Eternal death is the eternal continuance of the spiritual death incurred by sin. It becomes the lot or fate of all those persons in whom grace in this world does not succeed in replacing spiritual death with spiritual life. It involves eternal persistence in enmity and antagonism against God, and hence eternal separation and exclusion; namely, an eternal abiding in that condition and place in which there is an utter absence of light and love

and a constant presence of indescribable darkness, hatred, raging passions, unutterable woe, and endless despair (*The Christian Faith* 413).

• *Gehenna.* The picture of hell as gehenna is drawn from a valley on the southwest side of Jerusalem. The location drew its name "from the cries of the little children who were thrown into the fiery arms of Moloch, i.e. an idol having the form of a bull. The Jews so abhorred the place after these horrible sacrifices had been abolished by king Josiah (2 K. xxiii.10), that they cast into it not only all manner of refuse, but even the dead bodies of animals and of unburied criminals who had been executed. And since fires were always needed to consume the dead bodies, that the air might not become tainted by the putrefaction, it came to pass that the place was called *geenna tou puros.* . . . and then this name was transferred to that place in Hades where the wicked after death will suffer punishment" (Thayer 111). One sees the appropriateness of the metaphors of "where the worm dieth not" and the "fire is not quenched" from a reflection on the use of the word Gehenna to describe hell.

• *A place where both body and soul are tormented.* The torment of hell is a place where both body and soul suffer. Jesus said, "And fear not them which kill the body, but are not able to kill the soul: but rather fear him which is able to destroy both soul and body in hell" (Matt. 10:28). The word "destroy" is not used in the sense of annihilation but in the sense of the loss of well-being. *Apollumi* means "to destroy, i.e. to put out of the way entirely, abolish, put an end to, ruin." The word is used in Matthew 10:28 with the sense of "to devote or give over to eternal misery" (Thayer 64). The word is used to describe the lost coin and lost sheep, which were not annihilated, but were simply lost (Luke 15:6, 9). The word is used in Matthew 9:17 to describe the burst wineskins and in Matthew 26:8 for the *waste* of pouring the expensive ointment over Jesus' head. An interesting passage is Luke 9:24 — "For whosoever will save his life shall lose (*apollumi*) it: but whosoever will lose (*apollumi*) his life for my sake, the same shall save it." In the first instance, "lose" refers to the torment of hell, which those who affirm conditional immortality must say means "annihilation." However, the second half of the verse has one losing his life for Christ's sake. Has his life been annihilated? If so, in what sense is it saved? Obviously, the idea of annihilation does not inhere in the meaning of the word.

Understanding that the word "destroy" does not mean annihilate, one should consider the significance of both soul and body being destroyed in hell. Hell involves the loss of well-being for both body and soul. In this respect, hell and hades differ. The hadean torment in which the wicked are held between one's death and the resurrection is a place where the souls of men are tormented while the body rots in the earth (Luke 16:19-31). At the resurrection, the body of man is raised from the dead with immortal quality (fitted to its eternal habitation, see 1 Cor. 15:42-44) and reunited with his spirit. Those who are alive at the second coming will experience a change in the nature of their bodies (1 Cor. 15:51-54). This body will be fitted for eternal habitation, whether that be in torment or heaven. The torment of hell will, therefore, involve the torment of both body and soul. Hell is not limited to the torment of the soul (mental anguish).

Annihilation is Not Punishment

Annihilation is not punishment. According to the doctrine of conditional immortality, at the resurrection both the wicked and righteous will be raised. The wicked will be raised to judgment. When they are sentenced, they will be punished with a punishment commensurate with their crimes. When that punishment is over, they will be annihilated. Even this statement distinguishes between the punishment for sin and the annihilation that follows.

One notices then that annihilation is not punishment (Gerstner, *Repent or Perish* 81). Quite the contrary, annihilation is relief from punishment. When Job was suffering the debilities of his illness, he asked to be relieved of his suffering, wishing that he had never been born (Job 3-4). He thought that annihilation would bring him relief from his suffering. It was not suffering. Gertsner wrote,

> I must keep repeating that annihilation is an alternative to or substitute for pain, not a form of it. People in misery beg for annihilation as the cessation of pain. Fudge himself recognizes this, which is the reason he avoids the usual annihilationist doctrine (*Repent or Perish* 91).

Understanding that annihilation is not punishment and that the Bible promises to punish the wicked, Fudge asserts that each person will be punished with a punishment commensurate with his sins prior to being annihilated. This raises the question, "What is adequate punishment for sin against an infinite and holy God?" Gerstner observed, ". . . Fudge thinks adequate punishment for a life of sin against an infinite God is some finite time period while the orthodox see guilt against an infinite being itself infinite. Punishment must, therefore, go on forever" (113). "Extinction is no punishment at all, because it leaves no one to suffer any punishment" (153). Limiting the punishment for sin minimizes the seriousness of sin.

The idea of resurrection to annihilation was addressed by Tertullian. He wrote, "Else it would be most absurd if the flesh should be raised up and destined to 'the killing in hell,' in order to be put an end to, when it might suffer such an annihilation (more directly) if not raised again at all. A pretty paradox, to be sure, that an essence must be refitted with life, in order that it may receive the annihilation which has already in fact accrued to it" (*Ante-Nicene Fathers* III:571).

Immortality of the Soul

Bible doctrine is a seamless garment. When one looses one thread of that garment, it ultimately unravels the whole garment. Such is true with reference to the doctrine of conditional immortality, as espoused by brother Fudge. Fudge's denial of the eternal punishment of hell stems from his denial of the immortality of the soul. Let me define immortality of the soul. I do not mean to imply that man's soul has "essential immortality" in the same sense as God is immortal (1 Tim. 6:16). Only God exists from eternity to eternity (Ps. 90:1-2). Man's soul has a beginning and comes into existence through the creation of God. Whatever man's existence is, it is dependent upon God and does not autonomously exist. The soul of man is not immortal in the sense of the eastern religions which teach reincarnation, that man's soul exists before it enters a body (of whatever sort it may be) and continues through a cycle of incarnations. Rather, what the Bible describes as the nature of man's soul is that it does not cease to exist when the physical body dies, but continues to have conscious existence in the intermediate time between death and the resurrection. At the resurrection that soul is reunited with the resurrected body for eternal existence in heaven or hell.

> ### Scare Tactics
>
> Men belittle "hell fire and brimstone" preaching because it tends to scare people into obeying the gospel. Yet, Paul wrote, "Knowing therefore the terror of the Lord, we persuade men; but we are made manifest unto God; and I trust also are made manifest in your consciences" (2 Cor. 5:11). The truth is that men are not opposed to "scare tactics" as a means of motivation. They scare children away from fire, from electric sockets, from poisonous drinks or pills, from snakes, from certain toys, from anything that threatens them. Why should one be ashamed to scare people about the dangers of hell?
>
> One cannot be scared into heaven, but he may be so afraid of hell that he turns to Christ as the means of escape from this torment. Very few people who will go to heaven ever obey the gospel to be saved unless they first realize their lost condition outside of Christ and recognize that being lost means going to everlasting hell.

Brother Fudge acknowledges that, fundamental to his concept, is the rejection of the idea that man has an immortal soul. He wrote,

> The writers of the Bible never speak of the "immortality of the soul."
> Rather, Paul says that only God has inherent immortality (1 Tim. 6:16) and
> that in the resurrection he will give bodily immortality to those who are
> saved (Rom. 2:6-7; 1 Cor. 15:53-54). . . . The pagan theory of the immortality
> of the soul says that every human being has an invisible, immaterial part
> called the *psyche* or "soul," which can never die but will live forever. The
> traditionalists notion of everlasting torture in hell springs directly from
> that nonbiblical teaching (*Two Views of Hell* 185).

Thomas Gray wrote, "Annihilationism is thus virtually a corollary of conditional immortality, for if immortality were inherent, then it follows that
annihilation will not be a satisfactory explanation of hell" ("Destroyed For
Ever: An Examination of the Debates Concerning Annihilation and Conditional Immortality," *Themelios* 21 [Jan. 1996]:14-18).

To adequately answer brother Fudge, one must reassert the Bible doctrine of the soul of man (for a good study of this subject, one should read
Handbook on Materialism by Roy J. Hearn). The Bible affirms that the
soul continues to exist following the death of the body:

• **2 Corinthians 4:16-18.** "For which cause we faint not; but though
our outward man perish, yet the inward man is renewed day by day. For
our light affliction, which is but for a moment, worketh for us a far more
exceeding and eternal weight of glory; while we look not at the things
which are seen, but at the things which are not seen: for the things
which are seen are temporal; but the things which are not seen are eternal." This passage speaks of man's "outward" and "inward" part. The
inward man is "renewed day by day" and will receive an "eternal" weight
of glory.

• **2 Corinthians 5:1-10.** The theme of the preceding chapter is continued in this text which speaks of man's earthly house in which he tabernacles (the body) being dissolved, but he is being clothed with "an house not
made with hands, eternal in the heavens" (5:1). When death occurs, man
does not cease to exist, but is in that condition of being "absent from the
body" and "present with the Lord" (5:8). For Fudge there is no time when a
person is "absent from the body" but present with Lord.

• **Philippians 1:21-23.** Paul said, "For to me to live is Christ, and to die
is gain. But if I live in the flesh, this is the fruit of my labour: yet what I shall
choose I wot not. For I am in a strait betwixt two, having a desire to depart,
and to be with Christ; which is far better." Notice that at death, Paul would
depart to be with Christ, not cease to exist.

• **1 Peter 3:18-19.** Peter wrote, "For Christ also hath once suffered for sins, the just for the unjust, that he might bring us to God, being put to death in the flesh, but quickened by the Spirit: by which also he went and preached unto the spirits in prison." The wicked are described as "spirits in prison." Their existence continued after the death of this body; they were not annihilated.

• **2 Peter 2:4-9.** In this text, Peter assures men that God can preserve the righteous from destruction and keep the wicked in reserve for eternal punishment.

• **Luke 23:43.** Jesus said to the penitent thief on the cross, "To day shalt thou be with me in paradise."

• **Matthew 17:1-9.** The Transfiguration of Jesus occurred when Elijah and Moses appeared with him on the mountain. Both men had been dead for years and yet they were yet existing and living.

• **Matthew 23:23-33.** In Jesus' response to the Sadducees' question about the resurrection, he stated that God is not the God of the dead, but of the living, implying that those whose bodies are dead are still living.

• **Luke 16:19-31.** The story of the rich man and Lazarus is the most extended text that speaks of man's intermediate state. Like the Jehovah's Witnesses, brother Fudge dismisses this text as a parable built on first century folklore (*The Fire That Consumes* 203-08). He states that the basic plot of the "parable" (203) was "well-known folklore" (204). He says, "The two-fold circumstances after death are a vehicle for the story, and they involve language familiar to Jesus' hearers — language drawn, not from the divine revelation of the Old Testament, but from intertestamental and first-century folklore" (208). The word "folklore" attacks the inspiration of the Bible. What else in the Bible is folklore — the account of creation, the flood, the fish swallowing Jonah, etc.? Fudge also calls attention to the fact that the "parable" describes the condition "before the final judgment while others are still living on the earth." However, if it is a true picture, then his doctrine on immortality is wrong! Those whose bodies have died are still alive and conscious, either suffering in torment or in peace in Abraham's bosom.

These passages show that the Bible teaches that man's soul does not cease to exist when the body dies. The Scriptures show that it has conscious existence between the time of the body's death and the resurrection.

Jesus' Death

Since brother Fudge does not believe that man's soul survives the death of his body, this raises serious problems for him in interpreting many texts as mentioned above, but none is more serious than what it does for the death of Jesus. Fudge wrote about Jesus' death, "What the cross shows us is a picture of total destruction and death from which God alone can deliver." This statement was footnoted with the following comment, "In some sense consistent with his deity, Jesus was totally dependent on God to raise him from the dead (Mk. 14:36; Lk. 23:46; Heb. 5:7; 1 Pet. 2:23)" (*Two Views of Hell* 55).

Let sink in what brother Fudge has just said. When Jesus died on the cross, he died just like all men die. But brother Fudge believes that when men die, they die both body and soul; there is no spirit or soul that survives the death of the body, for he rejects as pagan the belief in the immortality of the soul. Therefore when Jesus died, there was no part of him which survived the death of the body. Where the thief on the cross joined Jesus on that day, in a place that could be properly described as paradise, is anyone's guess (Luke 23:43). Fudge says that Jesus was totally dependent upon the Father to raise him from the dead, just as other men are. How this is to be harmonized with the following statements in John is not explained:

> Jesus answered and said unto them, Destroy this temple, and in three days *I* will raise it up (John 2:19).

> No man taketh it from me, but I lay it down of myself. I have power to lay it down, and *I have power to take it again.* This commandment have I received of my Father (John 10:18).

These passages state that Jesus had power both to lay down his life and to take it up again. But, according to brother Fudge, there was no spirit to survive the death of the body, no divine spirit with power to resurrect his own body as he raised Jairus' daughter, the son of the widow of Nain, and Lazarus. The death of Jesus poses serious problems for brother Fudge.

The spirit in Jesus was the divine Spirit. This is reflected in the statement in Hebrews 10:4-5, "For it is not possible that the blood of bulls and of goats should take away sins. Wherefore when he cometh into the world, he saith, Sacrifice and offering thou wouldest not, but *a body hast thou prepared me.*" The "me" who inhabited the body which the Father prepared was God the Son. What became of this Spirit at the death of Jesus on the cross? Did the Spirit of Jesus die, as he believes the human spirit dies at the point of death? If so, that spirit did not possess immortality. Yet, Paul wrote, "Who only hath immortality, dwelling in the light which no man can approach unto; whom no man hath seen, nor can see: to whom be honour and power everlasting" (1 Tim. 6:16). Hebrews 13:8 says, "Jesus Christ the same yesterday, and to day, and for ever (Heb. 13:8). If Jesus ceased to exist, even for three days, he was not the same yesterday, today, and forever.

Another alternative for brother Fudge is to believe that there were two spirits in Jesus — a human spirit and a divine spirit. (If Jesus had two spirits, he is not like other men.) In that case, he could affirm that the two spirits were separated at the point of death and that only the human spirit ceased to exist. This is a position that brother Fudge is not willing to affirm. Consequently, he simply replies that this is a mystery beyond human comprehension (*Two Views of Hell* 204-06). This is a fine way to resolve a logical conclusion from one's position which he cannot answer.

What Is Motivating the Redefining of Hell

The ACUTE report on *The Nature of Hell* recognizes the tie between the modern feel-goodism and the redefining of hell. It said, "There may be some truth in Fernando's assertion that the growth of conditionalist thought in recent times reflects the increasingly 'feel good', self-esteem-based culture of the contemporary West" (117).

Conclusion

As we bring to a close this study of hell, we are reassured that the Bible teaches that the wicked will suffer eternal torment. The doctrine that men will be annihilated, while comforting to the wicked, is not consistent with divine revelation. One could wish that no one would be eternally lost in hell, but that would not be consistent with divine revelation and would reflect one's own weaknesses in that he has not brought his own will into harmony with God's divine revelation. No one should wish another in hell (see Rom. 9:3-5), but he should preach the fullness of the gospel, including its promise of salvation to the righteous and its threat of eternal torment to the wicked. One cannot be faithful to Christ in preaching his divine revelation while preaching anything less.

The Church Growth Movement

Andy Alexander

The apostle John wrote, "They are of the world. Therefore they speak as of the world, and the world hears them. We are of God. He who knows God hears us; he who is not of God does not hear us. By this we know the spirit of truth and the spirit of error" (1 John 4:5-6). God's word teaches that not everyone will accept his word. It is not a popular message in the world. Gospel preachers would like for all to come and hear the gospel. Having this desire is good, but we must be careful not to fall into the devil's trap by changing the message or watering down the message in the hopes that more will come and hear the gospel.

It is obedience to the truth that makes men free, not something less than the truth (1 Pet. 1:22-23; John 8:32). Much of what is being passed off in the world today as Bible teaching is nothing more than lessons designed to please the ears of worldly men. Modern mega-churches craft their message to be appealing to those in the world. Repentance and purity of life are left out of these modern pulpits as well as many other vital lessons from God's word. The message and command of Jesus, John the Baptist, the apostles, and all God's faithful preachers from the beginning of time has been "Repent!" (Matt. 3:2; 4:17; Acts 2:38; 17:30-31). This is not a popular message in a sinful, stubborn world and it will not attract large crowds (Matt. 11:20-24). Jesus had a large following for various reasons and when he informed them that following him would lead to difficulties in this life, "many of His disciples went back and walked with Him no more" (John 6:66).

Over the past few decades a new type of church has been developing and having an impact on religion in the United States. It is called the community church, or we could refer to it as the mega-church operation. In this article we want to examine some of the reasons for the emergence of the mega-church movement, what propels it, their tactics for church growth, and what effect, if any, it has on those of us in the non-institutional churches of Christ.

These mega-churches have sprung up in almost every area of the country and many of them are growing exceedingly fast. Some barely finish a new edifice before they have to begin making plans for another even larger one. This phenomenal growth has attracted the attention of many people including both local and national media. Newspaper articles and segments on news shows have been devoted to these mega-churches. The Willow Creek Community Church in the Chicago area, the Saddleback Church in Mission Viejo, California, and the Southeast Christian Church in Louisville, Kentucky are examples of such mega-churches.

Factors Leading to the Emergence of Mega-Churches

A combination of factors has led to the formation and growth of these community churches. Many of the members and leaders in these churches are baby boomers who were influenced by the radicals of the sixties. These radicals rejected the establishment and anything they associated with the establishment. Mainstream denominational churches were seen as part of the establishment so they were affected by the rebellious, anti-war protesters of the day. We are not saying that the people who are a part of these mega-churches were the actual protesters, but their views and ideas were probably influenced by the general rebellious attitude of that era.

A general decline in membership among traditional mainstream denominations was one of the results of this anti-traditionalist attitude. Young people began to question and reject the religion of their parents. Many quit attending services altogether. In an effort to counteract this decline in membership mainstream denominations experimented with many different programs or ministries designed to attract their disenchanted members back to their folds.

As these baby-boomers began to grow and have children, they recognized a need for God in their lives. Some turned back to their roots, others turned to more unconventional charismatic or Pentecostal-like churches. Still others searched for something else. These people grew up in churches that taught by precept and example that there are many different roads to heaven; therefore, they searched for another road that suited their lifestyles and their anti-traditionalist youth better. The community church was created to fulfill this desire. Rick Warren, founder of the Saddleback Community Church, stated in a letter written to people of the Saddleback Valley area, "At Last! A new church for those who've given up on traditional church services" (Rick Warren, *The Purpose Driven Church* 41). These churches openly proclaim their desire to reach the "unchurched," a term used by Rick Warren throughout his book on church growth, *The Purpose Driven Church*. This goal of reaching the "unchurched" betrays their belief that those already in other churches are saved. They view their community churches as just another one of the many roads that lead to heaven.

Another reason for the emergence and growth of the mega-church movement is the downward moral spiral of mainstream denominational churches. As these denominations declined in membership, they grasped at almost anything to solve their dilemma. Many extended fellowship to practicing homosexuals and lesbians and some have even opened their pulpits to them as a means to stop their decline in membership. Abortion is also being condoned by some of these same groups. One suggestion made by a committee of the Presbyterian Church was to "re-evaluate its definition of sin to reflect the changing mores of society." They also went on to say that the church should sound "a call for widening the circle of the faithful — not with children, but with non-reproductive gays, lesbians, and heterosexual singles who practice 'safe sex.' We feel that marriage is not what legitimates sexual gratification" ("Roll Over John Calvin," *Time Magazine* [May 6, 1991], 59). Many of the so-called "unchurched" will not accept the depth of depravity these denominations have gone to in order to sustain their numbers. So these community churches with no apparent denominational tie and a somewhat stronger moral message seem to be the answer to this problem that some of the unchurched may have with the mainstream denominations.

Characteristics of the Mega-Church Movement

A strong dynamic leader is a characteristic of these mega-churches. The Saddleback Community Church revolves around Rick Warren; the Willow Creek Community Church is lead by Bill Hybels, and the main figure of the Southeast Christian Church is Bob Russell. A parallel can be seen in the beginning of the mainstream denominational churches years ago. Martin Luther (Lutheran Church), John Calvin (Presbyterian Church), Charles Wesley (Methodist Church), Joseph Smith (Mormon Church), Charles T. Russell (Jehovah Witnesses), and Mary Baker Eddy (Church of Christ Scientists) were all strong personalities who helped create denominational churches that still exist today. People follow these personalities as if they could do no wrong. "What saith our earthly leader?" is more important than, "What saith the Scripture?"

These mega-churches utilize various means and methods to promote and sustain their growth. One thing many of them do to distance themselves from their denominational brothers is to adopt a neutral, non-denominational name. Many of the so-called community churches are actually denominational churches operating under an assumed name. One such example is the Saddleback Community Church. It is actually a part of the Southern Baptist Association. We have a local example here in Shepherdsville, Kentucky; the Little Flock Ministry Center was formerly the Little Flock Baptist Church. They built a new multi-purpose facility and underwent a name change in order to appeal to more people in the community. A little research into most of these community churches will reveal their denominational roots.

Another tactic used by these mega-churches is to use "Attraction Evangelism" as a means of building large memberships. This concept grew out of the ball teams, pizza suppers, and chicken dinners sponsored by denominational churches in times past. The attractions now used are much grander and more professional in appearance than their predecessors. Rick Warren defended the practice of "attraction evangelism" at the Saddleback Church by appealing to Jesus' example of inviting people to "come." He referred to Luke 14 "where Jesus compared the kingdom of God to a great banquet, the Master's servants are to go out and invite the hungry to come in and eat, 'so that my house may be full'" (Rick Warren, *A Purpose Driven Church* 235). This is offered as his scriptural authority to use attraction evangelism.

Bill Hybels and the Willow Creek Church offer "seeker-sensitive" services for the unbelievers in their community. They emphasize "large outreach events . . . contemporary Christian concerts, creative presentations that utilize drama, multimedia, and the arts . . . men's breakfasts, women's luncheons, leader's dinners" and so on to introduce the church to unbelievers (Bill Hybels, *Becoming A Contagious Christian* 207-208). Creative thinking, innovative ideas, taking risks, and non-traditional thinking are integral to maximizing their impact and attracting unbelievers to their services.

Another important aspect of their appeal to the unchurched or unbeliever is to make the services as non-threatening as possible. Do not condemn or make the unbeliever feel guilty. Rick Warren states it like this, "Don't hit them over the head with everything they're doing wrong. A lot of their sins will be dealt with *after* they come to Christ" (Rick Warren, *A Purpose Driven Church* 216). He uses an illustration of a couple of new converts who had been living together and came to him to be married after their conversion. He writes about this incident, "Sanctification comes *after* salvation" (*Ibid.* 218). This illustrates the idea that you don't address people with their sin lest you offend them. What if this couple had not come and asked to be married? How many other couples are living together and members of the Saddleback Community Church?

Bill Hybels and the Willow Creek Church use what they call amnesty to attract believers who have fallen away. This is also designed so as not to make sinners, even believers, feel condemned. He stated it to a waitress one time like this, "No matter what you've done or why you left, you can come back, no questions asked" (Bill Hybels, *Becoming A Contagious Christian* 49). On pages 55 and 168 he uses some extreme examples to illustrate the lack of compassion shown by some Christians who address sin directly, thus making the sinner feel guilty and condemned. He then states this about what he calls authentic Christians, "Christians favor love over law-keeping, truth over trivialities, and faith over frenetic religious activity" (*Ibid.* 168). Also, Hybels twice warns about the negative effect of discussing internal problems. He writes that some churches have no real vision for reaching the lost because they are "too busy debating internal policies and dealing with all kinds of in-house strife" (*Ibid.* 200). Rick Warren also warns about legalists that "erect theological walls to defend personal preferences" (236). Evidently, there are no doctrines worth debating to these church growth specialists. Also, the apostles must have had no real vision for reaching the lost, because they dealt with many internal problems like circumcision and keeping the old law, abuses of the Lord's Supper, the resurrection, errors on the gifts of the Holy spirit, and other issues that are discussed in the epistles (Acts 15; 1 Cor. 11:17-34; 15:1-58; 12, 13, 14).

These mega-churches also utilize a myriad of ministries. These ministries are designed to keep their members busy while at the same time offering to the unchurched a vast number of activities and services, one or more of which will surely appeal to them. A couple of examples will suffice. One could go to their web sites or the books mentioned to obtain an entire list of their ministries. Saddleback has a "High Touch" ministry where members enrolled in this ministry touch other people on the shoulder or arm as a gesture of concern. A survey that was used by Saddleback indicated that large numbers of their members were interested in obtaining help with "potty training" so "the church held a 'Parenting Preschoolers' conference which, among other things, taught this vital skill" (Rick Warren, *A Purpose Driven Church* 221). He goes on to state about their many ministries, "When it comes to using felt needs as an open door for evangelism, the possibilities are limitless. Saddleback has over seventy targeted ministries to the crowd and community, each built around a specific need" (*Ibid.* 222). Among their many ministries is one entitled "Hula Dance to worship, praise, witness, bless." **Description from the website:** "Our purpose: To worship & share God with others through Christian lyrics songs (Shout To The Lord; Reach One More For Jesus) & Hawaiian style dancing" (Website: *www. saddleback.com*).

Worship takes a back seat in the services of these mega-churches as well. They give lip service to the need for the gospel message and that we should not compromise the gospel, but obviously the gospel is the last thing appealed to in these churches. About worship Bill Hybels states, "Even going to church and worshiping God — important as these are — sometimes leave us feeling that something is missing. After all, we'll worship God for eternity in heaven; we don't have to be here to do that" (Bill Hybels, *Becoming A Contagious Christian* 23). Emphasizing the need for storytelling over Bible instruction Rick Warren writes, "Stories stir our emotions. They impact us in ways that precepts and propositions never do. If you want to change lives, you must craft your message for impact, not information" (Rick Warren, *A Purpose Driven Church* 232). He criticizes "pastors" who proudly say, "We're not here to entertain." He states further down the same page, "I believe it is a *sin* to bore people with the Bible" (*Ibid.* 231). The statements are made supporting his use of entertainment in the ministry. He, of course, claims to teach the Bible, but uses music, drama, and professional presentations to do so in an entertaining way. With this attitude toward Bible instruction, we might wonder who Mr. Warren might think was at fault in Troas when Eutychus fell to his death after falling asleep during a sermon the apostle Paul was preaching (Acts 20:7-9).

These are some of the means and methods used by the community churches to attract large crowds. We can easily see that their methods are working for they have large crowds and huge complexes to show for their success. They offer any and every thing in the name of Christ. In reality they are nothing more than glorified country clubs with a little Scripture sprinkled in to give them a spiritual flavor. They are also ecumenical. That is they would accept or have fellowship with almost every other church in town. They condemn almost no one, so it is hard for the denominational brothers to condemn them.

The Influence of the Church Growth Movement on Churches of Christ

The danger these mega-churches pose, besides the number of souls that will be led astray by their error, is in the influence they have over the Lord's church. Do they affect us? In what ways might they affect us? What are some danger signs that some churches of Christ may already be mesmerized by their success?

Looking to denominational churches has always been a problem. We have witnessed their success in the past at being able to attract large numbers and some churches have been led astray as a result of their infatuation with denominational ways. The sponsoring church, the fellowship hall, church ball teams, and orphan homes have all had their roots in denominational churches, not in the word of God.

What is taking place among the conservative churches of Christ today that may have roots in these mega-church concepts? Consider these things:

- Vacation Bible schools geared toward fun instead of Bible instruction.
- Secular activities planned after every VBS service — zoo trips, outings to the park, trips to pizza parlors, etc.
- Emphasis placed on fun during the educational portion of the school.
- Plays worked on and acted out for audiences.
- Playing limbo in the auditorium.
- Tents and basketball goals in the parking lot.
- Drama videos played during youth lectures.
- Youth lectures advertisements that advertise the secular with spiritual.
- Churches changing their name to non-offending names.
- Changes in preaching:
  - Non-controversial message: don't call names; don't offend.
  - Not make hearers feel guilty.
  - Positive Projection from the Pulpit: cover controversial and negative issues in classes.
  - Less Scripture and almost no application.
  - Over-emphasis on personal stories, humor.
  - No plan of salvation given when offering the invitation.
  - Seminars with no prayers, no Bible allowed, no reference to God by name.
  - More emphasis on presentation than content; feelings than truth.
  - Change services to accommodate secular activities — Super Bowl, Basketball games, high school games, etc.
  - Willingness to fellowship false teachers, especially if they are popular and attract a crowd.
  - Refusal to publicly discuss current issues and questions among us.
  - Tolerant toward error and those who teach it; intolerant of those who expose the error and those who teach it.

These are some of the things happening among us today. Where did these ideas come from? Did they come from the Bible, the inspired word of God, or did they originate in the mind of man?

Conclusion
The Bible is a complete guide for the man of God (2 Tim. 3:16-17; Ps. 119:105). Sectarian books written by men who are interested in large crowds,

big budgets, and large compounds are not proper guides for real church growth. Many centuries ago Israel rejected God's leadership and desired to have an earthly king rule over them. They rejected the Perfect Ruler for an imperfect one because of the influence of their neighbors (1 Sam. 8:5).

Jeroboam instituted a new religion to solidify his throne and please the people. When defending his new religion he appealed to the convenience of his new religion, not the Law of Moses (1 Kings 12:8-14). His goal was not to please God and help his fellow Israelites get to heaven. He was interested in promoting self and "his" new kingdom and, if it cost the souls of all Israel to do it, then so be it. These modern day Jeroboam's are not interested in pleasing God. It is evident by how far removed they are from the Scriptures. They promote themselves and their own little kingdoms at the cost of men's souls.

There is no light in the teaching of these men. Isaiah warns, "To the law and to the testimony! If they do not speak according to this word, it is because there is no light in them" (Isa. 8:20). These men do not appeal to God's word for support of their practices. When they do refer to a Scripture, they twist it out of its context. For instance, on page 224 of *The Purpose Driven Church*, Rick Warren uses Luke 4:18-19 when Jesus preached in Nazareth, to support the idea of a soft, non-threatening approach to preaching the gospel to the lost and meeting their felt needs. Mr. Warren failed to relate the rest of the passage that tells of the crowd being so angry with Jesus that they took him to the edge of the city in order to thrust him over the hill to his death. We must suppose that Jesus failed to teach his audience about anger management or the proper way to handle stress.

Isaiah also knew the audience of some of these modern-day mega-church leaders. He writes about the people of his day, "That this is a rebellious people, Lying children, Children who will not hear the law of the Lord; Who say to the seers, 'Do not see,' And to the prophets, 'Do not prophesy to us right things; Speak to us smooth things, prophesy deceits'" (Isa. 30:9-10). These people found prophets who would scratch their itch. "An astonishing and horrible thing has been committed in the land: The prophets prophesy falsely, And the priests rule by their own power; And My people love to have it so. But what will you do in the end?" (Jer. 5:30-31). Jeremiah warned the people and pleaded with them to return to the old paths.

> Because from the least of them even to the greatest of them, Everyone is given to covetousness; And from the prophet even to the priest, Everyone deals falsely. They have also healed the hurt of My people slightly, Saying, "Peace, peace!" When there is no peace. Were they ashamed

when they had committed abomination? No! They were not at all ashamed; Nor did they know how to blush. Therefore they shall fall among those who fall; At the time I punish them, They shall be cast down, says the Lord. Thus says the Lord: "Stand in the ways and see, And ask for the old paths, where the good way is, And walk in it; Then you will find rest for your souls." But they said, "We will not walk in it" (Jer. 6:13-16).

Paul warned Timothy of a time when men would not endure sound doctrine (2 Tim. 4:3-4). His solution was for Timothy to "Preach the word! Be ready in season and out of season. Convince, rebuke, exhort, with all longsuffering and teaching" (2 Tim. 4:2). We must determine to preach like the apostle Paul who said, "But as we have been approved by God to be entrusted with the gospel, even so we speak, not as pleasing men, but God who tests our hearts" (1 Thess. 2:4). This type of preaching is not what the world will want to hear, but it is what they need to hear (1 John 4:5-6). Let us resolve to preach the whole counsel of God, to preach it in season and out of season, and to preach it in love for the souls of men and for God who revealed it (Acts 20:27; 2 Tim. 4:2; Eph. 4:15). Let us never be "ashamed of the gospel of Christ, for it is the power of God to salvation for everyone who believes, for the Jew first and also for the Greek" (Rom. 1:16).

The Influence of F. LaGard Smith Among Non-Institutional Brethren

Johnny Stringer

Introduction

F. LaGard Smith is an attorney who served for a number of years as a law professor at Pepperdine University. Currently, he is "Scholar in Residence for Christian Studies" at David Lipscomb University. Smith is well-known as the author of a number of books, and through these he exerts considerable influence among brethren.

LaGard Smith's influence among non-institutional brethren is enhanced by the conservative stance he has taken on certain issues. He has forthrightly condemned homosexuality. He has taken Max Lucado to task with regard to Lucado's teaching on baptism. He is strongly critical of the "youth ministries" and "youth ministers" of which our liberal brethren are so fond. And he defends the need for the restoration of New Testament Christianity. Such conservative positions may lead non-institutional brethren to place their confidence in Smith, thus making them susceptible to his erroneous teachings.

I want to direct our attention particularly to his two latest books, the teachings of which I view as a serious threat to non-institutional brethren. The first of these is *Who Is My Brother?* which sets forth the author's views on fellowship, and the second is *Radical Restoration*.

Fellowship

In the book, *Who Is My Brother?* Smith denies that the unbaptized are in God's family. He would not extend "Christian fellowship" to them. Yet, in his discussion of five levels of fellowship, he affirms that we have fellowship, in varying degrees, with all people.

Smith's View of Unbaptized Believers

His discussion of "faith fellowship" yields some revealing — and sometimes shocking — insights into LaGard Smith's thinking. He says we share with them a level of fellowship called "faith fellowship." Unbaptized believers, he says, are not family, but they are "like family." Explaining this description, he writes, "In virtually every way they think and act as those in the family would think and act" (106). Really? Do they *think* and *act* as those in the family? Their *thinking* utterly rejects what Jesus said to do to be saved as well as the need for scriptural authority in religion, and their *actions* in worship and service to God are not governed by his word. They do not think and act as those in the family should. They are not "like family."

Smith emphasizes the need to appreciate and value unbaptized believers, stressing that we may benefit from the accomplishments of those in religious error. In this discussion we find the following astounding comment: "Globally, it is hard to overestimate the good that has been done by Anglican and Roman Catholic missionaries in civilizing pagan cultures. (Their notorious errors and excesses pale when compared to the good done.)" (109). Just think about that! These false religious systems teach errors that lead souls away from Christ and into the eternal agonies of hell. Does that horrible fact pale when compared to the material good they have done? Is the fact that they lead souls to eternal damnation outweighed by the fact that they have civilized some cultures?

Smith extols the spirituality and commitment of certain unbaptized believers and writes of the edification he receives from his fellowship with them. Remember that our brother is talking about people who profess faith in Christ but reject his conditions for salvation, teach others to reject those conditions, and engage in human religious practices rather than those that are divinely revealed. I do not share with them a common faith and I do not consider myself to be in fellowship with them. I commend them for their zeal, but they and I are going in different directions. When people renounce fundamental truths of the gospel and vigorously oppose faithful saints who teach those truths, I do not consider them to be "like family." Paul's question of 2 Corinthians 6:14 seems appropriate: "What fellowship hath righteousness with unrighteousness: and what communion hath light with darkness?"

Fellowship and Doctrinal Differences Among Brethren

We are particularly interested in Smith's teaching regarding fellowship among brethren. What about fellowship with brethren with whom we have doctrinal differences? Smith correctly points out the need to make allowances for differences of conscience in our personal lives. He acknowledges that we are not free to tolerate practices that are clearly sinful, citing as examples homosexual marriages and "also heterosexual re-marriages that violate Jesus' clear teaching" (143). In this vein, he denies that Romans 14 teaches that sin is to be tolerated in the name of fellowship. Sounds good. Having said that, however, our brother warns of the danger of confusing sin with doctrinal differences. Seemingly, he believes that if someone's doctrinal belief leads him to believe that a remarriage is not adulterous, then allowance should be made for this view. The matter is then in the category of a doctrinal difference rather than sin. He charges that we may be guilty of "accusing others of tolerating adultery without acknowledging that, if the other person is right about the remarriage not being adulterous, then there is no sin at all being tolerated" (146). He evidently believes that, if a person's doctrinal belief leads him to think the remarriage is okay, then we must tolerate his remarriage in case he may be right. Why would this reasoning not apply to those whose doctrinal stance justifies their homosexual unions? The truth is, if the Bible clearly condemns a practice, the fact that some brethren do not accept that teaching does not make the practice any less sinful or any worthier of acceptance.

Fellowship and Congregational Practices

Smith's view of fellowship allows him to participate in congregational practices he believes to be wrong. In chapter 6 he tells of attending a church in England and singing with an instrument despite his opposition to the use of instrumental music in worship. He explains, "As for the instruments, I tried to content myself with the thought that while everyone else was singing *with* the instruments, I was singing *without* them!" He acknowledges that the instruments marred the worship for him. Nevertheless, his conscience was flexible enough to allow him to continue the practice.

Moreover, our brother knows that the institutional churches are wrong; yet, he continues to worship with them. If you doubt that he understands the truth about institutionalism, note his own words about the institutional controversy: "Deeper down, the fight was really about the principle of congregational autonomy — a fight which the 'non-institutional' brothers were warranted in waging. Had they not raised a hue and cry, who knows what organizational superstructure might now exist among the churches of Christ?" If non-institutional brethren were warranted in waging the battle, and if their efforts prevented an undesirable organizational superstructure, then they must have been right. Yet, LaGard Smith worships with institutional congregations. His view of fellowship allows that.

Is there ever a situation, according to LaGard Smith, when one would need to leave a congregation because of its practices? Yes, and he sets forth six questions to consider when one is determining whether he should remain with a congregation. They are: (1) "Is my discontent a matter of

conscience or *comfort zone?*" (2) "What efforts have I made to effectu-
ate change?" (3) "What endorsement am I lending by my continued presence?" (4) "What good influence might I have by staying?" (5) "What are
my alternatives?" (6) "Is my discomfort worth the cost of broken fellowship?" These are legitimate questions worthy of sober consideration. However, regardless of how good the questions are, one who is seeking to justify
a particular course of action can answer them so as to justify that course.
The author says, "Having struggled with these complex questions for many
years now, I have somehow managed to maintain a continuing, if rocky,
fellowship among brothers and sisters with whom I sometimes disagree
almost as much as I love" (165). He somehow manages to participate with
them even though he believes them to be in error.

Smith believes that his remaining in the congregation despite his strong
disagreements with its practices has enabled him to be a part of vital evangelistic work in his community. He writes, "It's easy to be so consumed
with the problems of family fellowship that we forget our far greater responsibility to bring others into the family" (165). One must consider, however, into what are we bringing these converts? When we baptize people,
we should teach them to observe all our Lord's commandments (Matt.
28:18-20), not lead them into a congregation teaching or practicing error.

In his discussion of congregational fellowship, Smith acknowledges that
doctrinal differences may require two groups within the congregation "to go
their separate ways." In discussing our attitude toward congregations engaging in practices contrary to our conscience, Smith says that "we must
nevertheless honor the collective conscience of each and every other congregation" (172) and that we have no biblical right to ostracize them (173). Yet,
he says that we should seek to teach them what we believe to be the truth.

In considering our attitude toward such congregations, we must remember this: When a congregation is engaging in unscriptural activities, it is not
just one individual practicing his personal conscience. The leadership is leading
the whole congregation to believe and practice error. In addition, it is binding those unscriptural practices on everyone who would become a part of
that congregation. The congregation's message is, if you do not join with us
in these practices, you may not be a part of us. Far more than individual
conscience is involved. Even though we love these brethren, we cannot be
tolerant of their propagation of error and their efforts to involve others in
error.

How do we apply Smith's teaching in our relations with such congregations? He says we are to respect their collective conscience and we are not

to ostracize them. Does this mean that we must announce their activities, such as gospel meetings and Vacation Bible Schools. If we fail to do so, are we not ostracizing them? Or if one of the elders or the preacher of such a congregation were an excellent song leader, would we ask him to lead singing in our gospel meeting? To have a practice of not doing so would be ostracizing them, would it not? But to use these men to lead in our public worship would surely give the impression that we regard them as faithful. It would constitute an endorsement of them and their teaching, and we may not do that.

Who Is a False Teacher?

In chapter 11 of *Who Is My Brother?* Smith discusses what makes one a false teacher. He contends that the teaching of false doctrine does not make one a false teacher. He states, "Common to both false prophets and false teachers are not just their false doctrine but also their ungodly character" (204). With reference to 2 Peter 2:1-19, where Peter described certain false teachers of his day, our brother says, "How much clearer could it be? Being a 'false teacher' is not simply about *doctrine* but about *character* as well."

The fact is, false doctrine destroys souls regardless of the character of the one who is presenting it. Error does not make one free from sin no matter how sincere and morally upright the one who teaches it may be (John 8:32). The belief of error results in condemnation (2 Thess. 2:10). Make no mistake about it: *Error's destructive power lies not in the character of the teacher but in the character of the teaching.* If an individual is led by false teaching to engage in sinful behavior, and therefore loses his soul, does it matter whether or not the one who deceived him was sincere and morally upright? If a teacher defends homosexuality as an acceptable practice, do we have to know the character of that teacher before we can determine whether or not he is a false teacher?

Smith gives particular attention to the case of our beloved brother Homer Hailey. He opines that brethren have been guilty of libel, slander, and character assassination in their opposition to brother Hailey's teaching regarding divorce and remarriage. Describing his perception of brethren's treatment of Brother Hailey, Smith writes: "No credit for years of faithful service. No brotherly kindness. No love" (208). These are the terms Smith uses to characterize the opposition to brother Hailey's doctrine. I submit to you it is F. LaGard Smith who is guilty of libel, slander, and character assassination, by his characterization of faithful brethren who have, with deeply felt sadness, taken on the heart-rending task of exposing a beloved brother's false teaching. In Smith's view, brother Hailey's character precluded his being regarded a false teacher. If a couple are deceived into remaining in an adulterous relationship and thus losing their souls, does the character of the one who deceived them really matter?

Those who hold to Smith's view with regard to false teachers often argue that if teaching anything false makes one a false teacher, then if one is wrong about *anything* he is a false teacher. For example, if one is mistaken about what constitutes the gift of the Holy Spirit in Acts 2:38, then he is a false teacher. This argument is wrong. If one's teaching about the gift of the Holy Spirit leads one to sin or is contrary to plain Bible teaching, then that person is indeed a false teacher. This is the case of those who teach Pentecostalism, for example. However, there are a number of interpretations of Acts 2:38 that do not lead to sin and that are in harmony with all other biblical teaching. If a brother disagrees with me on the interpretation of a verse, I do not regard him as a false teacher so long as his interpretation does not conflict with plain biblical truth. One is a false teacher not because of an incorrect interpretation of a particular verse, but because his doctrine conflicts with clear biblical teaching.

Radical Restoration
Smith's "Dawning of Disillusionment"

Now let us turn our attention to Smith's latest book, *Radical Restoration*. The author contends that our efforts at restoration have fallen miserably short. He says that when he was a teenager he began to question the differences between what the Scriptures teach and what he saw being practiced in "the Church of Christ of the 1950s and '60s." The "first dawning of disillusionment" came during a study of Roy Cogdill's book, *The New Testament Church*, in the chapter on "Church Finances." That lesson cites 1 Corinthians 16:1-2 as authority for the church to raise funds through a contribution each Lord's day. Smith explains that he had heard that text cited for as long as he could remember, but this time he looked more closely at it. He discovered that this was "only Paul's practical instructions about how to handle a special contribution." From that time on he was "on high alert" and was repeatedly troubled by apparent "variances between the first-century church and what we claimed was *fully-restored* primitive Christianity."

Our brother was wrong in the conclusion he reached with regard to our use of 1 Corinthians 16:1-2, and he is wrong about other similar conclusions. It is true that Paul's instructions in 1 Corinthians 16 related to a specific collection for a particular work: aiding the needy saints in Jerusalem. However, there are other works that local churches are to engage in, and there is an ongoing need to raise funds to do those works. The New Testament includes letters that inspired men wrote to various churches and individuals, dealing with their problems and needs, and giving them instructions pertaining to their responsibilities. In God's wisdom, as he dealt with their particular problems and needs and gave them instruction, he set forth the principles that would provide the teaching needed for all Christians through the ages. Hence, when the church in Corinth needed to raise funds to do a work, God used that occasion to set forth the means by which he wanted churches to obtain the money to do their work. It was right for the observance of that teaching to be restored.

Thinking that efforts at restoration up to this point have failed, Smith proposes that what we need is *radical restoration*. Many non-institutional brethren who reject his teachings on fellowship, may be susceptible to his views on radical restoration because of their desire to practice pure, New Testament Christianity — and that is what LaGard Smith claims to be advocating. There is a special danger here for sincere young people. I believe that one danger for non-institutional brethren is that some will conclude that we have no right to criticize others for failing to follow the New Testament, for, according to Smith, we are not following it ourselves. They will conclude that we are no better than brethren involved in institutionalism or the social gospel and therefore have no business criticizing those brethren. Let us consider some areas in which Smith says we have fallen short.

The Lord's Supper

Smith argues that the proper observance of the Lord's supper has not been restored. In fact, we do not even come close to approximating what the first-century Christians did. Radical change is needed. Smith affirms that the Lord's supper "was observed in conjunction with a fellowship meal. That is, a normal, ordinary meal with the usual variety of food. However, unlike normal, ordinary meals, this combined table fellowship and memorial was shared among the disciples for the special purpose of strengthening, not just their physical bodies, but their common bond in the spiritual body of Christ. Hence, Jude's reference to their 'love feasts' (v. 12)" (128-9). He describes the Lord's supper as a "memorial within a meal." After describing the wonderful Thanksgiving meal that he and his relatives enjoyed in his Nashville home, Smith says, "Apparently, their love feasts were a mirror image of our own Thanksgiving celebrations" (146). His idea is that brethren gather each first day of the week for a big meal, and sometime during the festivities, take time to observe the Lord's supper.

Smith refers to the occasion on which Jesus instituted the Lord's supper, stating that "the memorial was part of an actual meal being shared" (129). It is true that Jesus and his apostles were sharing a meal when he delivered his teaching pertaining to the Lord's supper. We should note, however, that when he gave them the bread and the fruit of the vine, explaining the meaning of those emblems, he and the apostles were not then observing the memorial. The *memorial* of his death could not be observed *before his death occurred.* This was not an observance of the Lord's supper. Jesus was simply teaching the apostles the means by which he wanted his disciples in the future to have his death brought to their remembrance. A meal was a convenient time to give these instructions because of the presence of the bread and fruit of the vine, so Jesus used the occasion to give the instructions. Jesus may have given instructions on various subjects while eating with his apostles, but the fact that instructions are given at a meal does not mean that they must be carried out at a meal.

Our brother gives an interesting treatment of Paul's discussion of the Lord's supper in 1 Corinthians 11. He says that the large consumption of wine (some were drunk) "underscores the significant point that, for early Christians, gathering around the Lord's table was not the token ritual with which we are familiar, but an actual food-and-drink meal." Note our brother's unwarranted inference. He says, "for early Christians," thus drawing an inference about early Christians in general. Yet, this passage is not about the early Christians in general; it is about the Corinthian Christians only. And they were being rebuked!

I'm sure that most of you are thinking of Paul's question, "What? Have ye not houses to eat and to drink in?" (v. 22) and his command, "And if any man hunger, let him eat at home" (v. 34). You are probably thinking that these verses condemn eating a common meal in connection with the Lord's supper. Well, Smith warns us that we must be careful not to be thrown off track by those remarks. He explains, "Far from prohibiting a fellowship meal in conjunction with the Lord's Supper, it is clear that Paul is saying (in current vernacular): If the reason you are participating in the fellowship meal is to feed your stomach, then you'd do better to stay home and pig out!" This is a good attempt to harmonize the teaching of verses 22 and 34 with the concept of a common meal in connection with the Lord's supper. The problem is, Smith has not produced any scriptural justification for such a meal. Hence, there is no need to try to harmonize the teaching of these verses with the concept of a common meal.

It has been said that the command to "tarry one for another" (v. 33) fits in well with the practice of gathering to eat a common meal together. What is needed, however, is not a command that fits in with the practice. What is needed is a passage that teaches us to engage in the practice. There is *no direct command or statement* to that effect. There is no passage that *nec-*

essarily implies that the Lord's supper is to be eaten in connection with a common meal. And there is *no divinely approved example* of Christians eating the Lord's supper in connection with a common meal. The only example of such is that of the Corinthians, and their actions were condemned. There is no indication that God approved anything they did in connection with the Lord's supper. As for the command to tarry for one another, the reference is to waiting until all in the assembly were present to eat the Lord's supper together.

A few words need to be said about the "love feasts." There is no indication that they were meals eaten in connection with the Lord's supper or that they were provided for from the treasury of the local church. If God desired the church to sponsor such a feast, the Scriptures would so indicate, but Jude 12 gives no hint of it. If these were feasts that we were required to have, the Scripture would give us the information we need to have them. As it is, we must remain uncertain about them. Perhaps they were meals provided by prosperous brethren to aid the poor.

The Nature of Assemblies

Smith contends that we have not restored the kind of assemblies the first-century Christians had. He believes that the early Christians assembled in private homes and in small groups. The worship in these small assemblies, he says, was far more informal and spontaneous than ours is. Describing his perception of our worship, our brother paints a picture of a stilted, formal procedure in which most Christians are spectators rather than participants. His concept of the first-century assemblies is of a small group in a home, informally talking about spiritual matters, praying, and singing. Their activities were informal and spontaneous, not at planned times under the direction of designated leaders.

In the first place, our brother does not prove that all assemblies were in private homes. As he discusses the disciples' coming together in Troas to eat the Lord's supper, Smith assumes that the upper room in which they assembled was in a private home. In reality, he does not know whether or not it was. He speculates that there were many house churches in Jerusalem, but indications are that there was only one congregation in Jerusalem, and this congregation consisted of a multitude. Consider, for example, references to that church in Acts 6:1-6 and Acts 15. This church could not have met in one private home. It is quite possible that these Christians utilized the courts of the temple. Jesus indicated that the place of worship is of no significance; the important thing is whether worship is in spirit and in truth (John 4:20-24).

In the second place, I do not know where Smith got his information about the informal, spontaneous nature of the first-century assemblies. He simply assumes that this was they way they were. He cites Paul's reference to the Corinthians' assembly in which various ones had songs, teachings, etc. (1 Cor. 14:26). Two points need to be made: First, this was an assembly in which spiritual gifts were being exercised, and these were brethren who were speaking under the influence of the Holy Spirit. Second, as Smith admits, Paul commanded that, as they exercised these gifts, they were do so in an orderly fashion. "Let all things be done decently and in order" (v. 40). Smith opines we have taken the command for orderliness to an extreme, but this is nothing more than his opinion.

In the third place, Smith is presuming to judge the hearts of worshipers when he describes them as spectators rather than active participants. I'm sure that too many are mere spectators, but many are not. Whether or not one is a mere spectator has nothing to do with how orderly the assembly is. In the most orderly of assemblies, one can sing wholeheartedly, contemplating the meaning of the words of the song. Such a one is not a mere spectator. He is an active participant. In the most orderly of assemblies, one who is eating the Lord's supper can meditate deeply on the death of our Savior. Such a one is not a mere spectator. During the prayer, even in the most orderly of assemblies, one can listen to the leader, and as he expresses to God his "amen," he can do so fervently. Such a one is not a mere spectator. In the most orderly of assemblies, one can listen intently as the word of God is being proclaimed and derive all the benefit that the word provides. Such a one is not a mere spectator; he is participating.

Our brother strongly criticizes our assemblies, but the truth is this: When we gather and sing, pray, listen to the proclamation of God's word, and on the Lord's day, eat the Lord's supper and contribute a portion of our prosperity to the work of the church, we are doing what the Bible teaches us to do. Whether or not an individual is participating wholeheartedly in these activities depends on his attitude.

Church Organization

Smith's concept of house churches affects his view of church organization. All passages pertaining to elders must be understood in the light of Acts 14:23, which teaches that each local church had its own elders. Hence, when Paul said that elders were to be appointed in every city in Crete (Tit. 1:5), we interpret his words in the light of Acts 14:23. Thus, we conclude that either (1) there was only one church in each city in Crete, or (2) elders were to be appointed in each church within every city. Smith's speculations, however, include many possibilities. He wonders if perhaps all the house churches of a city composed a larger congregation. Or perhaps elders in individual house churches came together "as a group of city-wide elders to discuss matters of importance to the entire community of believers" (178). He opines that this "may well have been the case in Jerusalem. Regarding the reference in Acts 15 to Jerusalem's elders, Smith says, ". . . nothing necessarily precludes 'Jerusalem's elders' from being gathered from among elders in a multiplicity of house churches" (178).

God did not leave us to speculate about the organization of the church. He taught the principle of "elders in every church" and that is what we are to practice. If God intended us to have citywide elders to deal with things pertaining to all the local churches in a city, he would have revealed it. We must be governed by what God revealed, not by what LaGard Smith has conjectured or what he thinks perhaps may have been the case.

Preachers
Finally, I want to make brief mention of Smith's view regarding preachers. He believes that elders should not utilize a preacher to occupy the pulpit during the assemblies of the church. By doing so, we are not practicing first-century Christianity, and a radical change needs to be made. Elders, he says, are to teach the congregation and build it up, while evangelists are to teach the lost. He believes that preaching in an assembly of Christians is not evangelism. In fact, Paul defined the work of an evangelist as he gave instructions to Timothy. He instructed Timothy to "do the work of an evangelist" (2 Tim. 4:5). In the context of that command, Paul gave the specifics of that work: "Preach the word; be instant in season, out of season; reprove, rebuke, exhort with all longsuffering and doctrine" (2 Tim. 4:2). When one proclaims the word of God, whether in the assembly or not, he is doing the work of an evangelist. We recognize of course, that the evangelist should seek opportunities to teach the lost outside the assembly, proclaiming the word in whatever setting is available.

It is true that elders are to teach and build up the congregation. They are shepherds whose responsibility it is to tend the flock, and this includes teaching. In fulfilling their responsibility to tend the flock, however, they may also utilize the abilities of one who has devoted himself to learning God's word and developing the skill to present it effectively. In Ephesians 4:11-12, Paul lists certain functionaries as gifts Christ gave for the building up of the church. These include apostles, prophets, evangelists, pastors, and teachers. These are for the perfecting (that is, "equipping") of the saints so that the saints can do the work of ministry (service), and as the perfected saints serve, the body is edified. Note that evangelists are listed along with pastors (elders) as functionaries God has given for the perfecting (or equipping) of the saints. It is clear that the evangelist's work includes helping saints to develop. For preachers to perform this work in the assemblies of the saints is eminently scriptural.

Conclusion

LaGard Smith's views on fellowship are appealing to some non-institutional brethren, but some who would reject those views may be susceptible to his views on "radical restoration." In the preface to his book, *Radical Restoration*, Smith stated that he had sequestered himself and read the New Testament afresh, as though he had never read it before, to let its teachings alone guide him. I am unable to understand how this process resulted in a book consisting mostly of the author's own conjectures and assumptions rather than New Testament teachings.

Fight the Good Fight of Faith
Harry Osborne

To say that our culture has been given to an ever-growing pattern of tolerance in moral, doctrinal, and ethical areas is an understatement. If any trait became the defining characteristic of our society in the 1990s, "tolerance" was the word most often used to describe it. A scarlet "A" was emblazoned on our national garb from the White House on down — and the sad fact is that it became a fashion statement rather than a source of shame. Like Israel of old, we could no longer blush. We were not ashamed. So, we were urged not to fight it, but to passively accept a higher cultural evolution by being "open" and "tolerant" of unspeakable immorality.

When people rose to fight this manifestation of moral depravity, they were denounced as "right-wing bigots," "fanatics," "conservative nuts," "extremists," "watchdogs of morality" and similar epithets designed to demonize the objectors. The very people who could have helped to avert the disaster brought on our society were so vilified that their warnings went unheeded.

But the saddest evidence of a growing tolerance for immorality and evil was not found in the Oval Office, or the "Gay Pride" marches, or the abortion rights rallies, or a pornography retailer, or the increasing filth on television, or the alarming sensuality of popular music across the spectrum, or the skimpy fashions of the world. The saddest evidence of a growing tolerance was found when brethren across our land began to mirror the world around them by justifying and popularizing a renewed plea for "unity-in-diversity" which "tolerates contradictory teaching and practice on important moral and doctrinal questions" (Ed Harrell, *Christianity Magazine*, series beginning November 1988 ending May 1990; quotation from May 1990, 6). With that principle, the salt rapidly started to lose its savor and brethren began to "tolerate" an ever growing number in their on-going and continuous fellowship despite sinful practices and doctrinal errors.

It started with a justification for receiving brother Homer Hailey while he taught doctrinal error on divorce and remarriage. Those who would fight the good fight of faith were accused of "unheroic attacks." They were portrayed as "watch-dogs" and "snarling curs" having no other purpose than to "bite and devour one another." Widely known preachers like Paul Earnhart and Bob Owen joined Ed Harrell in so vilifying faithful brethren in print and in meetings across this country. Others soon joined the chorus. With faithful brethren portrayed as vicious dogs, many brethren got the not-so-subtle message that these savage creatures were to be excluded. Consequently, a new form of quarantine was put in place with meetings canceled and communications severed. It seemed the only one our "more tolerant" brethren could not tolerate and fellowship was a brother who militantly proclaimed the truth — him they would attack with militance. When it came time to fight the good fight of faith concerning the Bible doctrine on fellowship, modesty, the use of intoxicating drink, and even the creation account, those who fought for truth were characterized in similar terms by a growing number.

Where has the effect of such tolerance led us? The spring, summer, and sporting fashions of many brothers and sisters showing a vastly increased level of exposure has accompanied this greater "tolerance." A growing number of congregations now receive those in unlawful marriages. We now have "non-institutional" brethren who decry even debating against denominationalism and its doctrines in honorable controversy which was integral to the spread of the gospel in the first century and in past efforts by brethren in this country. These brethren claim to walk the way of truth, but they actually travel a far different road. They deny the need to fight the good fight, telling us the fighters are the real problem. One can almost hear the familiar refrain from their lips, "Just preach the gospel and leave everyone else alone." They are more comfortable with rank error than with those who fight against it.

As brethren in previous generations came to understand the errors of denominationalism that enslaved the souls of men, they fought against such. Many truths understood by each of us today were given clear form in the crucible of honorable controversy. Reading the debates and heavily polemic writings of brethren in past centuries not only helps readers today to understand the fallacy of error, but to more fully grasp the clarity of truth. The expansion of the kingdom of God within the hearts of men will always demand the use of the sword alongside the tools for construction (cf. Neh. 4:17-18).

Alexander Campbell spoke on the need for righteous conflict in these words:

> If there was no error in principle or practice, then controversy, which is only another name for opposition to error, real or supposed, would be

unnecessary. If it were lawful, or if it were benevolent, to make a truce with error, then opposition to it would be both unjust and unkind. If error were innocent and harmless, then we might permit it to find its own quietus, or to immortalize itself. But so long as it is confessed that error is more or less injurious to the welfare of society, individually and collectively considered, then no man can be considered benevolent who does not set his face against it. In proportion as a person is intelligent and benevolent, he will be controversial, if error exists around him. Hence the Prince of Peace never sheathed the sword of the Spirit while he lived. He drew it on the banks of the Jordan and threw the scabbard away (Alexander Campbell, *Millennial Harbinger,* Vol. I, No. 1, [4 Jan. 1830], 41).

But Alexander Campbell is not the only one to recognize that need, nor does he establish our pattern for action. The inspired word of God establishes our pattern for faith and practice in all things (2 Tim. 3:16-17; 1:13). The divine mandate for us to be militant and fight the good fight of faith could not be clearer. Let us notice a few passages plainly declaring the divine directive to fight in the spiritual battle for truth and righteousness.

Fight the good fight of the faith, lay hold on the life eternal, whereunto thou wast called, and didst confess the good confession in the sight of many witnesses (1 Tim. 6:12).

This charge I commit unto thee, my child Timothy, according to the prophecies which led the way to thee, that by them thou mayest war the good warfare; holding faith and a good conscience; which some having thrust from them made shipwreck concerning the faith: of whom is Hymenaeus and Alexander; whom I delivered unto Satan, that they might be taught not to blaspheme (1 Tim. 1:18-20).

The prophecies of Scripture were to lead Timothy so that he might engage in proper warfare. The same is true today. When we by faith hold to the faith, having a good conscience confirming our effort as consistent with our knowledge of the truth, we are both prepared to fight and vigilant to the need for fighting. Faithful saints who take to heart the direction found from God's truth do not look lightly upon error which will lead souls to destruction. They have seen the devastating effects of soul-damning error upon the lives of those led astray. They recall the names and faces of brothers and sisters whose souls have been dashed on the rocky shores of various false doctrines. To them, the effect of false teaching is not merely theoretical — it is real and it is deadly! They will not stand idly by while the teachers of false doctrine beckon others to be torn asunder on the hidden reefs of destructive error. Faithful Christians who let the word abide in and direct their hearts will fight to deliver the errorist to Satan and save the souls in peril.

> I charge thee in the sight of God, and of Christ Jesus, who shall judge the living and the dead, and by his appearing and his kingdom: preach the word; be urgent in season, out of season; reprove, rebuke, exhort, with all longsuffering and teaching. For the time will come when they will not endure the sound doctrine; but, having itching ears, will heap to themselves teachers after their own lusts; and will turn away their ears from the truth, and turn aside unto fables. But be thou sober in all things, suffer hardship, do the work of an evangelist, fulfil thy ministry. For I am already being offered, and the time of my departure is come. I have fought the good fight, I have finished the course, I have kept the faith: henceforth there is laid up for me the crown of righteousness, which the Lord, the righteous judge, shall give to me at that day; and not to me only, but also to all them that have loved his appearing (2 Tim. 4:1-8).

Paul's parting charge to Timothy again made the connection between fighting the good fight and receiving the incomparable reward. The apostle's life demonstrated the degree to which that fight encompassed every part of his life and focused him on the single goal of eternal life (Gal. 2:20; Phil. 1:21; 3:13-14). The fight required self-control and self-denial (1 Cor. 9:27). It involved opposition to people of repute (Gal. 2:11-14). It was often contrary to popular will (1 Cor. 4:13). At times, it demanded that he stand alone to face the opposition (2 Tim. 4:16). The fight often left him battered, bruised, and bloodied literally and figuratively from perils of every kind (2 Cor. 11:23-28). Paul yearned for the rest beyond more earnestly because his daily fight for the faith was an agonizing struggle. Could it be that we fail to long for heaven as Paul did because we have not invested the effort to fight as he did? No mere spectator has the intense yearning for peace that is in the very soul of the man who has paid the price of battle. Brethren, the world and its ways have not changed in character since Bible times (1 John 2:15-17). If we find ourselves more tolerant of that world and less militant than Paul was, it should tell us that we have not fought the good fight as he did. If we refuse to fight, we cannot expect to receive the victory crown in reward as Paul did.

Good Fight of Faith vs. Needless Disputes of Words (Opinion)
The same apostle Paul who emphasized the necessity of fighting distinguished between essential battles for truth and needless disputes over mere words and opinions. We must understand that same distinction if we are to fulfill our responsibility to fight for truth rather than quarrel over matters of judgment. Differentiating between a good fight and a needless dispute is sometimes difficult, but the difference can be seen when we reduce the conflict to investigating the origin of its fundamental point. In his two letters to Timothy, Paul stated the principles involved in this effort. Notice those principles affirmed in these two passages:

If any man teacheth a different doctrine, and consenteth not to sound words, even the words of our Lord Jesus Christ, and to the doctrine which is according to godliness; he is puffed up, knowing nothing, but doting about questionings and disputes of words, whereof cometh envy, strife, railings, evil surmisings, wranglings of men corrupted in mind and bereft of the truth (1 Tim. 6:3-5).

Of these things put them in remembrance, charging them in the sight of the Lord, that they strive not about words, to no profit, to the subverting of them that hear. Give diligence to present thyself approved unto God, a workman that needeth not to be ashamed, handling aright the word of truth. But shun profane babblings: for they will proceed further in ungodliness, and their word will eat as doth a gangrene: of whom is Hymenaeus and Philetus; men who concerning the truth have erred, saying that the resurrection is past already, and overthrow the faith of some (2 Tim. 2:14-18).

Good Fight of Faith	Needless Disputes
Sound Words	Words to No Profit
Words of Jesus Christ	Disputes of Words
Doctrine	Opinion
According to Godliness	Subverting Hearers
Words of Truth	Wranglings of Men
Approved of God	Envy, Strife, Railing, Evil Surmising

At the core of some conflicts, we see a fight based upon "sound words, even the words of our Lord Jesus Christ," while other conflicts are disputes over "words to no profit." Some issues involve doctrinal principles which affect godliness, but some issues are based upon the opinions or judgments which only subvert hearers, if the opinions are bound on them. While God approves the teaching and practice of "words of truth" found in divine revelation, he abhors "envy, strife, railings, evil surmisings, wranglings of men corrupted in mind and bereft of the truth." Let us be sure of the nature of the fight before we engage in it. One who decries all efforts to defend and fight for the truth in honorable controversy has surely replaced the banner of the cross with a white flag of surrender. In so doing, he stands condemned. However, equally condemned is the one who elevates his opinions and hobbies as the rallying point for needless battle aimed at faithful brethren who do not submit to his efforts to impose his judgments as binding. He sees every difference as a call to battle. The extremes of viewing either *no cause* or *every cause* as worthy of conflict are both wrong.

What principles help us to distinguish between good fights of the faith and needless disputes over opinions? Clearly, if we immediately and correctly recognized every issue as involving doctrine or opinion, we would have no problem in discerning when to fight. While issues do not come with "dog tags" denoting the category to which they belong, there are some principles from Scripture that will help us correctly distinguish where they belong. Let us examine a few cases from God's word.

Differences Over Eating of Meats. First century Christians had differing practices regarding the eating of meats (Rom. 14; 1 Cor. 8, 10). Not all of these differences were a result of eating meat from types of animals forbidden as unclean under the Mosaic law. Prohibitions against eating blood and meat from things strangled had been binding before the law of Moses and continued to be binding under the gospel of Christ (Gen. 9:4; Acts 15:19-21). Many of the Jewish traditions dealt with details of how the slain animal must be bled and how the meat must be washed so as not to eat the blood. Those who sought to serve God could all agree that drinking a cup of blood straight from the animal would have been wrong. They could also agree that this prohibition did not mean it was sinful for one to consume one molecule of blood while eating meat, for that would have made it impossible to eat any meat.

The doctrine prohibiting the eating of blood was an absolute necessity for all to obey, but that doctrine did not specify certain details which were involved in obeying the doctrine (i.e., exactly what amount of time was permitted between the animal being slain and it being bled, how long the animal was to be bled, how much should the meat be washed, etc.). At that level, there was a *generic* principle rather than a specific one. To keep the doctrine, one must make *unspecified judgments* in making application of the doctrine. Those applications or judgments may vary with different people depending on conscience and other factors while all accepted one another as obedient to the doctrine. Hence, there is no call for battle over differences of this type.

The same could be noted for those who sought to obey the doctrinal injunction to "flee from idolatry" (1 Cor. 10:14). All could agree that eating meat in stated deference to an idol was sinful. Yet, Paul examined a few cases in which one might lawfully eat meat that others might have offered to an idol (1 Cor. 8, 10). Were there other situations which may have been faced that were not specified by Paul? Yes. How were the brethren to decide what to do in each one of those cases? They had to apply the principles of "sound words" in good conscience, though no specific statement was made to detail the necessary action in that exact situation. Though brethren may have differed in a particular case as to what should be done, they could be united in doctrine as they continued in forbearance of one another in a given application not specified by divine law. Again, fighting in this realm would have been a needless dispute.

Differences Over Keeping of Days. The requirement to give thanks to God for our physical blessings, such as our food, was a necessity under Mosaic law just as it is under the gospel (Deut. 8:10; 1 Tim. 4:4; 1 Thess. 5:18). Jewish Christians in the first century may have lawfully kept the Feast of Tabernacles which was a thanksgiving for the harvest. In fact, they may have felt the conscientious necessity to do so in order to keep the doctrinal requirement of being thankful to God. But could they bind that expression of thanksgiving on all? Romans 14 shows that they could not do so. Though the doctrine was binding and all could unite in that doctrine, Christians of Jewish and Greek backgrounds could differ in their specific expressions of that doctrine. Why? Because those differing expressions were *not specified by law, but left in the generic realm.* No battle was needed here.

The above differences took place between brethren with strong convictions on the matters involved. They did not agree in every detail for reasons of conscience as they strove to maintain proper hearts before God (Rom. 14:23; etc.). Yet, they were to receive one another and not engage in conflict over these differences because they were abiding in the same doctrine. This is the very point Ed Harrell, Bob Owen, and other teachers of error regarding Romans 14 have denied. Such men have blurred the distinction by labeling differences in matters of conscience as "doctrinal differences." We are not inconsistent to *oppose* the use of Romans 14 to include doctrinal error and sinful practices while *advocating* the inclusion of varying judgments in applying unspecified details concerning a commonly held doctrine. Having debated the legitimate use of Romans 14, this writer is teaching the same thing now that I affirmed in debate and writing for the past twelve years since *Christianity Magazine* advanced the error on Romans 14 and a broader fellowship.

The above differences in judgments were clearly distinguished from differences over doctrinal error and sinful practices. Doctrinal error and sinful practices have an inherently corrupting nature. They are based upon the misuse and abuse of God's word, twisting it into destructive errors (2 Pet. 3:16; Gal. 1:6-9). They are like a gangrene (2 Tim. 2:17). They wax worse and worse (2 Tim. 3:13). They corrupt the hearer (Matt. 16:11-12). They corrupt the church (1 Cor. 5; 15:33). They give license to ever more sin (Rev. 2). By their very nature, they do not stand still. They are progressive in their increasing perversion of Scripture and the growing number of sinful manifestations. This progressive nature of corruption is inevitable because doctrinal error and sinful practices inherently involve a different mind-set than the way of truth. Hence, we may objectively observe those who advocate a teaching or practice, and see whether it truly manifests that different mind-set which inherently accompanies doctrinal error and sinful practices (Matt. 7:15-20). This will help us distinguish between a necessary battle and a needless dispute.

A quick look at the history of various doctrinal errors and sinful practices in the religious world can illustrate this point. The doctrinal error of Gnosticism during New Testament times had a corrupting influence on other doctrinal truths and the daily lives of its adherents. The apostasy into Roman Catholicism carried with it a growing perversion of doctrine and morality which confirmed its evil nature. The same can be noted about Calvinism. Among brethren of a past century, we can notice the progressive degeneration borne of those who introduced innovations such as the missionary society and instrumental music in worship. The resulting Disciples of Christ/ Christian Church with its vast changes in doctrine and practice made clear the nature of the differences involved. The same can be seen with institutional brethren whose basic premise has been followed to its ultimate, consistent end in the "New Hermeneutics" movement which has swept liberal brethren into a growing flood of progressive apostasy.

In New Testament times, brethren who upheld the same doctrine, but differed in unspecified judgments, did not manifest the same progressive degeneration. There was no inherent, corrupting effect of those following different applications about eating meat or keeping days. Why? The differences were not of a doctrinal nature. When brethren hold to the doctrine of Christ, but differ concerning judgments over unspecified details, let us not decimate the ranks of the faithful by turning the battle inward. In cases of this nature, we must apply the apostolic admonition: "If it be possible, as much as in you lieth, be at peace with all men" (Rom. 12:18).

Goodness and the Fight of Faith

Another qualifying statement about the fight required of us has to do with its goodness of character. The injunction to engage in the fight of faith is inherently tied to goodness. Why? The fight is first good by design because God authorized it as noted earlier. Being good can only come from following the good doctrine of Christ (1 Tim. 4:6). Our fight is also good in that its focus is on the cause of good and right, not upon self or selfish desires.

When one denies self in the battle between flesh and Spirit, part of the consequent fruit of the Spirit is goodness (Gal. 5:16-24; Eph. 5:7-10).

One who fights the good fight of faith will not use the carnal tactics of the devil because he has been filled with the goodness found in the truth and shows that goodness forth in his character. Though the forces of Satan will falsely accuse him of evil, objective evaluation will show the soldier of Christ has engaged in "good works" (1 Pet. 2:11-12).

We live in an age where some in halls of academia and even in halls of Congress blur the distinction between terrorists and honorable soldiers who uphold the law and principles of right. They see the use of force on the part of both soldier and terrorist as analogous. They fail to see the honorable soldier fighting to maintain justice as different from the terrorist murdering in disregard for justice. They fail to distinguish between the honorable soldier who fights to restore lawful order and the terrorist who fights to overthrow that lawful order and impose one of his own liking. In short, their failure to distinguish between the two is a failure to distinguish between the nature of goodness and evil. Those who cannot understand the differences between honorable soldiers and terrorists do more to expose their own lack of discernment than to discredit lawful use of force.

Sadly, we have a growing number in churches across the land who cannot see the difference between fighting the good fight of faith and "spiritual terrorism." Their attempts to label honorable debate and controversy as "spiritual terrorism" do not change the charge of God to engage in such, but such charges do manifest their utter lack of biblical understanding. When one looks at all fighting for truth as "bad," "evil" or "terrorism," his evaluation clearly differs from God's.

We MUST Fight

After being certain of the necessity and character of the fight, the divine mandate to "fight the good fight of faith" still remains our obligation. Accusing others of bad attitudes when they engage in the fight does not excuse us from the obligation to join the fight with a proper attitude. Suggestions that others are desirous of "killing a giant" in an attempt to "make a name for themselves" do not excuse us from the obligation to do battle with worthy motives. Efforts to label those who contend for the faith as "watchdogs," "snarling curs," "extremists" or similar epithets do not change the fact that we must fight the good fight of faith no matter what opponents of truth may call us. Dear brother, if you do not like the way others are handling the sword of the Spirit, pick it up yourself and show them how to do it correctly. If you merely object to the way others do it, while refusing to soil your hands in the fight, do not be surprised when you are taken no more seriously than a French diplomat giving instructions on proper warfare. Some folks have never met an enemy of truth they could not appease or ignore. Jesus and the apostles never met an enemy of truth they could not defeat with Scripture.

As we prepare for the warfare commanded, let us always remember that we have been given all of the equipment necessary for battle. Let us remember these inspired words of admonition and assurance:

> Finally, be strong in the Lord, and in the strength of his might. Put on the whole armor of God, that ye may be able to stand against the wiles of the devil. For our wrestling is not against flesh and blood, but against the principalities, against the powers, against the world-rulers of this darkness, against the spiritual hosts of wickedness in the heavenly places. Wherefore take up the whole armor of God, that ye may be able to withstand in the evil day, and, having done all, to stand. Stand therefore, having girded your loins with truth, and having put on the breastplate of righteousness, and having shod your feet with the preparation of the gospel of peace; withal taking up the shield of faith, wherewith ye shall be able to quench all the fiery darts of the evil one. And take the helmet of salvation, and the sword of the Spirit, which is the word of God (Eph. 6:10-17).

Soldiers in battle array are not stationed far from the fray. They are on the front-lines of the war. So it is in the army of God. Our equipment is given for us to use in the spiritual battles surrounding us daily. Our battle armor is strong enough to meet the task and bring us to the victory promised by Christ, even as the apostle said,

> For though we walk in the flesh, we do not war according to the flesh (for the weapons of our warfare are not of the flesh, but mighty before God to the casting down of strongholds), casting down imaginations, and every high thing that is exalted against the knowledge of God, and bringing every thought into captivity to the obedience of Christ; and being in readiness to avenge all disobedience, when your obedience shall be made full (2 Cor. 10:3-6).

The fight against this mighty foe is not a fight of containment, but until *every* evil way and *every* evil thought is vanquished and obedience to Christ reigns triumphant. There is no armistice to be offered to sin and error. Only the unconditional surrender of the soul stained by sin and error is sufficient to cause the change of heart and action necessary for salvation. Yes, it takes courage to undertake such a fight. To that end, the apostle urged,

> Only let your manner of life be worthy of the gospel of Christ: that, whether I come and see you or be absent, I may hear of your state, that ye stand

fast in one spirit, with one soul striving for the faith of the gospel; and in nothing affrighted by the adversaries: which is for them an evident token of perdition, but of your salvation, and that from God; because to you it hath been granted in the behalf of Christ, not only to believe on him, but also to suffer in his behalf: having the same conflict which ye saw in me, and now hear to be in me (Phil. 1:27-30).

Throughout his life in defense of the gospel, we never found Paul cowering in the corner for fear of the adversaries of truth. His boldness was evident. His determination was resolute. His charge was ever forward — never retreat. The confidence did not come from an innate bravado, but from an absolute confidence in the Lord who gave him the charge to fight and the certainty of the cause. Those at Philippi were exhorted to form a united front and follow his example in "striving for the faith of the gospel." Only in that way were they using the life God had given them in a way "worthy of the gospel of Christ." There has always been a priority and urgency to the battle against error and evil. Making it clear that he diverted his original intent in writing to meet the pressing demand to "contend earnestly for the faith," Jude said,

Beloved, while I was giving all diligence to write unto you of our common salvation, I was constrained to write unto you exhorting you to contend earnestly for the faith which was once for all delivered unto the saints (Jude 3).

The word translated "contend" is *epagonidzomia*, a compound of two Greek words. The prefix of the word (*epi*) serves to strengthen or intensify the root verb (*agonidzomai*). From the latter word, we get our word "agony." What is the point? We must put agonizing effort and sacrifice into the fight against the adversaries of truth. It requires, not just contending for the faith, but earnestly or strenuously contending for the truth revealed by God. The good fight of faith . . .

Is not evil	*Is righteous*
Is not enjoyable	*Is tiring*
Is not easy	*Is difficult*
Is not self-serving	*Is self-sacrificing*
Is not popular	*Is hated*
Is not optional	*Is mandatory*

Let us not plant the sword of the Spirit in the dust and replace it with a bouquet of daisies for the enemies of the truth. Let us never be ashamed of the crimson banner of the cross or the truth ratified by the blood of our Savior. Let it never be lowered to raise in its place a white flag of surrender in compromise with carnality.

Let us remember who it is that opposes the truth — they are enemies of the cross of Christ. When we begin to look with greater favor on those who teach error than on brethren teaching truth, albeit with a different approach, we have our priorities badly out of order. Already we are seeing brethren who join together in associations and "ministry" efforts with those in denominationalism. Hill Roberts and his affiliation with Hugh Ross and other evangelicals is a case in point. How can we fight the fight of faith while making a pact of cooperation with the enemies of the cross? Let us again set our goal upon "*casting down imaginations, and every high thing that is exalted against the knowledge of God, and bringing every thought into captivity to the obedience of Christ.*"

Conclusion

While in the Philippine Islands in December of 2002, Ron Halbrook and I were able to visit the memorial honoring General Douglas MacArthur's return to Filipino soil in World War II. On October 20, 1944, General MacArthur landed at Red Beach on the island of Leyte near Tacloban. Among the things included in the memorial on that site is a monument inscribed with the following words from MacArthur's radio address to the Filipino people on that day:

> By the grace of Almighty God our forces stand again on Philippine soil — soil consecrated in the blood of our two peoples. We have come, dedicated and committed, to the task of destroying every vestige of enemy control over your daily lives, and of restoring, upon a foundation of indestructible strength the liberties of your people. . . . The hour of your redemption is here. Your patriots have demonstrated an unswerving and resolute devotion to the principles of freedom. . . . Let the indomitable spirit of Bataan and Corregidor lead on. As the lines of battle roll forward to bring you within the zone of operations, rise and strike. Strike at every favorable opportunity. For your homes and hearths, strike! For future generations of your sons and daughters, strike! In the name of your sacred dead, strike! Let no heart be faint. Let every arm be steeled. The guidance of divine God points the way. Follow in His Name to the Holy Grail of righteous victory!"

Brother Halbrook and I discussed the striking similarities that exist between that struggle in the physical realm and the struggle enjoined upon us in the spiritual realm. The Japanese occupation of the Philippine Islands brought tyranny, slavery, misery, and death to untold multitudes. With every liberty denied and every atrocity committed, the Filipino people were further humiliated and degraded to an unspeakable horror. MacArthur's stirring words called upon Filipinos to contrast their present circumstances with the bright promise of a freedom within their grasp if only they would rise with courage and meet their responsibility to fight. The Filipino people met the challenge with a dogged determination that still ranks among the most courageous exhibitions in modern history of a people yearning for freedom. Should we not be stirred to greater fervency in our calling to a more noble spiritual battle?

Let us remember the slavery and tyranny of sin and error is the most sordid horror of all — for it enforces its evil cruelty, not just upon this earth, but throughout eternity. Thus, our fight is not a war of containment, but a fight to slay evil and reach the glorious freedom and victory promised by our Lord. The examples of faithful saints of old, who suffered and died in terrible ways in service to the Lord, cry out for us to continue the fight and press on to the victory in Christ (Heb. 11:32-12:4). The sacred blood of our Savior calls for us to rise and strike!

Can we summon in our hearts no compassion for the souls of men that would compel us to needful conflict to bring freedom to spirits in jeopardy of eternal torment? Can we not be lifted in spirit and stirred in mind to a call for spiritual battle which aims to defeat the tyranny of sin? Have we grown so complacent in our ease that we can sit by in silence while the truth of God is pilloried by an ever-increasing number of errors from every quarter? Brethren, there is something worse than a growling and gruesome fight — it is a dishonorable peace with unrighteousness and error.

May the attitude of true soldiers again animate the people of God to arise for a battle with sin and evil too long ignored and too dimly viewed. Let us be steeled with the heart of righteous warriors and strike!

Gospel Preaching, Gospel Preachers, Gospel Papers:

The Heritage of *Truth Magazine*
Ron Halbrook

God ordained the gospel message and the role or work of gospel preachers in spreading that message (1 Cor. 1:18, 21; 2:2, 13; 15:1-4; Eph. 4:11; 2 Tim. 2:2). Preachers utilize the avenues, forums, and methods available to them for spreading the gospel. Since the advent of the printing press, the medium of the printed page has been used to spread all kinds of messages, good and bad, true and false. Gospel preachers have used gospel papers to spread the gospel message.

Gospel papers are as strong or as weak as the men who write in them. Whether any particular paper is a blessing or a danger at a given time depends on the message taught in its pages. If the men and message change for good or ill, the paper changes for good or ill. *Truth Magazine* represents the highest tradition of gospel preachers spreading the gospel message through gospel papers. The paper is seen as one more avenue through which to "preach the word," to declare "all the counsel of God," to "use great plainness of speech," to "earnestly contend for the faith which was once delivered unto the saints," in short, to proclaim "the gospel of Christ" as "the power of God unto salvation" (2 Tim. 4:2; Acts 20:27; 2 Cor. 3:12; Jude 3; Rom. 1:16). This magazine takes its place in history as a medium to be used by sound and faithful men in passing the torch of truth from one generation to another. Those who share in this tradition of gospel journals understand well that the paper is not in any sense a source of religious authority but is simply a medium for men to preach God's Word as the only source of authority in religion (2 Tim. 3:16-17).

The outline below helps to tell the story of gospel journals published by men who insist that the gospel be preached not in a spirit of fear, timidity, or compromise but in the spirit "of power, and of love, and of a sound mind" (2 Tim. 1:7).

Heritage and History

1. *The Christian Baptist* (1823-30) was edited by Alexander Campbell with emphasis on "A Restoration of the Ancient Order of Things." Campbell's *Millennial Harbinger* (1830-70) continued this emphasis but moderated to promote the missionary society and similar organizations unauthorized by the ancient order of things.

2. *The Gospel Advocate* (1855-61, 1865-present) has been edited by Tolbert Fanning, William Lipscomb, David Lipscomb, E.G. Sewell, F.D. Srygley, J.C. McQuiddy, A.B. Lipscomb, H. Leo Boles, James A. Allen, Foy E. Wallace, Jr., John T. Hinds, B.C. Goodpasture, J. Roy Vaughn, Ira North and Guy N. Woods jointly, F. Furman Kearley, and Neil W. Anderson. In the early years, the *Gospel Advocate* was a stalwart in defending the Bible pattern against the onslaught of instrumental music and missionary societies. F.B. Srygley said of "the second generation of writers for the *Advocate*," "Soft preaching was not characteristic of the preaching of any of them" (*Gospel Advocate*, 2 Mar. 1939, 193). Under Goodpasture (1939-77), the *Gospel Advocate* began to moderate and drift. The *Gospel Advocate* became an advocate of many things not found in the gospel such as institutionalism and related practices.

3. *The American Christian Review* (1856-87), edited by Benjamin Franklin, helped to hold the line against instrumental music and missionary societies in the north and mid-west.

4. *Lard's Quarterly* (1863-68), edited by Moses E. Lard, carried many strong articles and protested any departure from the truth but tried to accommodate the missionary society.

5. The *Octograph* (1883-87), *Octographic Review* (1887-1913), *Apostolic Way* (1914-40), and *Apostolic Review* (1920-40) were edited by Daniel Sommer, who was influenced greatly by Benjamin Franklin.

6. The *Firm Foundation* (1884-present) has been edited by Austin McGary, G.H.P. Showalter, Reuel Lemmons, William S. Cline, and H.A. Dobbs. In its early years, it helped hold the line against instrumental music and missionary societies west of the Mississippi River. Lemmons led the *Firm Foundation* away from the firm foundation of truth on institutionalism and related practices.

7. The *Gospel Guardian* (1935-36) was edited by Foy E. Wallace, Jr., and the *Bible Banner* (1938-49) by Foy E., Jr. and Cled E. Wallace jointly, with much help from Roy E. Cogdill beginning in March of 1946. Both were

strong papers during the battles over premillennialism and the rising tide of pseudo-unity movements. The *Bible Banner* openly opposed and restrained the move to get colleges in church budgets.

8. The *Gospel Guardian* (1949-80) began with Foy E. Wallace, Jr.'s blessings and was edited by Yater Tant, William Wallace, Eugene Britnell, and James W. Adams. Roy E. Cogdill was owner and publisher of the *Gospel Guardian* during 1949-62, and wrote often in its pages. It focused on defending the Bible pattern against the onslaught of institutionalism and related issues. After the last copy of the *Gospel Guardian* appeared in December of 1980, it merged with *Truth Magazine* to form the *Guardian of Truth.*

9. *Truth Magazine* (1956-80) has been edited by Bryan Vinson, Jr., Cecil Willis, and Mike Willis. Roy E. Cogdill was close to Cecil Willis and had a significant influence on *Truth Magazine* until his death in 1985. At first, *Truth Magazine* focused on modernism in the Chicagoland area, where seventeen preachers had been lost in seventeen years. Then, the paper faced the onslaught of institutionalism, and fought back a false unity movement in the 1970s-80s. Under the name *Guardian of Truth*, it continued to provide a forum for preaching the gospel and defending sound doctrine in the face of current dangerous trends during the years 1981-97. In 1998 the paper reverted to its original name. The purpose and posture of *Truth Magazine* remain the same today as in its beginning.

10. *Searching the Scriptures* (1960-92) was first edited by H.E. Phillips and James P. Miller jointly, then by Connie W. Adams. *Searching the Scriptures* was a strong voice for the truth first in Florida, then in the southeast, and finally nationwide. After the last copy appeared in December 1992, it merged with *Guardian of Truth.*

Thus, it can be seen that *Truth Magazine* represents the militant spirit of New Testament Christianity in upholding the truth of the gospel and in opposing every departure from it. This spirit was ignited in a large measure by such papers as the *Christian Baptist* and the *Gospel Advocate* in the 1800s and has been sustained by similar journals in the 1900s. *Truth Magazine* represents strong, sound concepts of gospel preaching which can be traced directly back to Foy E. Wallace, Jr., Roy E. Cogdill, and H.E. Phillips. Men who share their faith have followed in their footsteps.

In short, *Truth Magazine* is a gospel paper used by gospel preachers for gospel preaching. It is nothing more or less than a medium for proclaiming the message of truth. It will be as strong or as weak as the men who write for it. May God help us to faithfully pass the torch of truth to lost souls everywhere, and to a new generation who will teach it to others, whether through this medium or some other. Papers come and go, and we must not be wedded to them, but the truth shall stand forever, and we must be wedded to it (2 Tim. 2:2).

Reflecting on the Past, Present, and Future

If the biblical roots and heritage of *Truth Magazine* as a medium of truth are to be nurtured and sustained, we must be keenly aware of trends which lead us away from true biblical faith. The history and heritage of *Truth Magazine* include the efforts of the *Gospel Guardian* and *Searching the Scriptures* to sustain true biblical faith during the years of the institutional digression, primarily the 1950-60s. We have reached a stage of history where we can reflect on the validity and the necessity of that past battle.

One occasion for such reflection is an article published in the Winter 1994 *Discipliana* on "The Churches of Christ: Accommodation to Modernity and the Challenges of Post-Modernity" by Cathy J. Pulley (a professor in the Department of Religious Studies at Southwest Missouri State University, Springfield, Missouri). This article written by a historian in the institutional movement shows what was at stake in the battles of the 1950s-60s and why such battles must be fought if we are to maintain our fidelity to the Lord. As we reflect on the history of the spirit of liberalism with the aid of the Pulley article, we will realize that such a digressive spirit is arising again and already new battle lines are gradually forming. One of the things we learn from both biblical and subsequent history is that God's faithful remnant will be called upon again and again to fight such battles until the Lord returns. Will each of us continue to "fight the good fight of faith," or will we falter? Will *Truth Magazine* continue its heritage as a medium through which men may "fight the good fight of faith," or will it falter?

Pulley's article discusses the emergence of liberal institutional churches and their gradual accommodation into the mainstream of American denominationalism. The sermons and tracts of conservative churches "stress that those in the Church of Christ are representatives of the true and only church, that the Bible is the infallible Word of God, and that there is one true plan of salvation." That message has been absent since at least the 1970s among churches of a more liberal spirit which "no longer speak of the hell that awaits all those who are not members of the true church. Nor do they speak much about any doctrinal matters. The themes today are compatible with those in the pulpits of at least a dozen North American Evangelical groups" which emphasize such topics as the family, interfaith, a right relationship with Jesus, and a "smattering of socio-political rhetoric."

There are clearly "two different types of churches" today among typical churches of Christ. Churches which appeal to "reason and rational thinking" (i.e., definite claims to revealed truth) are doctrinally conservative, exclusive in terms of fellowship with other groups, and exist "in high tension with the world." Churches with a more modern view have "a higher degree of tolerance for the world" and "toward other religious bodies." The more these latter churches accommodate "cultural pluralism," the more they must grope for a new identity and theology to replace their past exclusive truth claims. Pulley gave statistics tracking accommodation to liberalization on a wide range of moral issues (abortion, extramarital sex, premarital sex, homosexuality, easier divorce, marijuana use). These statistics show that the trend toward accommodation among liberal churches of Christ fits "the changing social profile of American church life" in general. While those figures are not high yet for either group, they show that tolerance for new moral trends among these churches of Christ matches the trends among mainstream American churches.

A More Polished, Positive Message

Absorption into the mainstream of the American religious life can also be seen in the effort to present a message which is softer, more polished, and much more positive, according to Pulley. After quoting a denominational historian on the "softening and polishing of the more hard line and barbed elements of the orthodox Protestant world view," Pulley observes that "this 'civilizing' of the Evangelical doctrinal message also would seem to be true of Churches of Christ. . . . Theirs is a 'kinder, gentler' message. Instead of trying to evangelize in order to free others from their fear of the fires of hell, evangelistic efforts seem to be framed much more positively." In keeping with recent history among mainstream bodies, churches of Christ "tend to present an upbeat and positive image about their lives — a characteristic that Peter Berger has referred to as the 'Protestant smile.'"

Pulley points out that Evangelical denominations and many churches of Christ "have accommodated to cultural pluralism in regard to their exclusive doctrinal truth claims." There is less and less appeal to absolute scriptural truth, i.e. less appeal to book, chapter, and verse, and more appeal to subjects which make people feel happier, healthier, and more at peace with themselves. "If the message of old that 'we are the one true church' (consequently the only ones going to heaven), is still spoken in the city church, it is only in whispers." The new emphasis is toward feeling good about one's private life and relationships, mental health, counseling, family life, and psychology. This trend is causing church members to read more literature from other religious groups, another indication that "the walls of exclusivism between the 'true church of Christ' versus all others are crumbling."

The shift away from hard line or exclusive truth claims is gradually replaced by subjective and mystical truth claims. The Restoration Principle must be reinterpreted in a more open and pluralistic way as church members search for security while also searching for a new theological direction, a new identity, a new hermeneutics, a new mission, and a new worship. For such church members, sitting in a worship service and "listening to a somewhat lengthy sermon" based on infallible doctrine and exclusive truth seems more and more irrelevant to their lives in a post-modern world, Pulley observed.

If the battles of the 1950s and 60s had not been fought, partly through journals like *Truth Magazine*, God's people in this country as a whole would have been swept into apostasy to be absorbed into the mainstream of American denominationalism. But who can read Pulley's description of the process of accommodation to American culture without realizing that even among more conservative brethren the process of accommodation is beginning again? F.B. Srygley recognized the early beginning of such dangerous trends in 1939 and encouraged men of faith to resist them at that time. He said,

> I am about all, if not all, left of the second generation of writers who wrote for the *Advocate*. The friends of my youth, so far as the writers of the *Advocate* are concerned, are on the other side of the rim. I feel lonesome without them, and yet I am glad there are young men who have never bowed their knees to Baal. They will carry on and will contend earnestly for the New Testament teaching. I think the church is now in perilous times, but I have not lost confidence in the truth of the New Testament. Let us be able to say with Paul: "I have fought a good fight. I have finished my course, I have kept the faith," and "am now ready to be offered."
>
> . . . In these troublesome times, when compromise of truth is the fashion, the *Advocate* cannot afford to weaken its opposition to error. The tendency, as it appears to me, is now to soft-pedal the opposition to error.
>
> . . . I came in with J.C. McQuiddy, F.W. Smith, M.C. Kurfees, E.A. Elam, and F.D. Srygley. While they differed among themselves, there was no disposition to compromise the truth . . . These men above mentioned, like the rest of us, had their faults, but they stood together for the truth, and their personal differences did not weaken their stand for the pure gospel of Christ or their opposition to error. Soft preaching was not characteristic of the preaching of any of them (F.B. Srygley, "What I Know of the *Advocate*," *Gospel Advocate*, 2 March 1939, 1).

Within 15-20 years of Srygley's 1939 warning, the fruit of softer preaching and compromise was seen in an apostasy which spread all around the country. The *Gospel Advocate* itself became a prime promoter of that apostasy!

As the desire for a softer, more sophisticated, more positive message grows, we will hear that there has been too much preaching about baptism and the church and too much controversy about doctrine. Cecil Willis once observed,

> Some brethren say they get tired of controversy. So do I!!! But the only alternative is capitulation, and the consequence of that is damnation . . . .The wisdom from above will be invoked that all the good within our power may be done, and that no harm at all to any righteous cause will result (*Truth Magazine*, 1 Nov. 1973, 3-5).

In "*Truth Magazine* and Controversy," Connie W. Adams summarized the spirit of the paper from its inception when he said,

> Yes, this is a militant paper. We mean to keep it so. The devil has not called off the battle yet. There are still surging issues which need to be discussed. Brotherly reserve and restraint ought to be employed. But no quarter should be asked or given in the conflict between truth and error. If we are found in error, then let brethren get out their typewriters and point it out. We can take it (*Truth Magazine*, 23 Nov. 1973, 60-61).

The spirit and stamina of *Truth Magazine* will be severely tested in the days which lie ahead. Those who write articles or read them in this paper, or any other paper, should view it as simply a medium for teaching the truth, nothing more or less. *Truth* Magazine has no ambitions or pretensions to control churches, preachers, or anything else, but it will be charged with such unworthy motives by those who feel the pressure of truth and fear the exposure of error. Papers, like individuals, face the challenge of maintaining their fidelity to truth into the third and fourth generations. Those who publish and write for this paper are subject to all of the same strong cultural influences as anyone else in this country, and we ourselves will be tempted at times to accommodate ourselves to the demand for a softer, more polished, more positive posture, and thus to wear the "Protestant smile." If we begin to give in to that demand, may God confuse and confound our purposes, and cause this paper to die forever. If *Truth Magazine* continues in its heritage of boldly proclaiming the gospel of Christ without compromise, may God bless its efforts and extend its usefulness. If the magazine and its writers take any other course or posture, may God raise up faithful men and faithful papers which will renew the heritage of faithful preaching.

(This article originally appeared under the title "Gospel Preaching, Gospel Preachers, Gospel Papers: The Heritage of the *Guardian of Truth*" in the *Guardian of Truth* [XXXIX:14 (20 July 1995): 433-436]. Both the title and some of the content have been slightly edited here in order to update the article. R.H.)

www.ingramcontent.com/pod-product-compliance
Lightning Source LLC
Chambersburg PA
CBHW052042090426
42739CB00010B/2012